Thomas Scott's Body

AND OTHER ESSAYS ON EARLY MANITOBA HISTORY

J. M. BUMSTED

UNIVERSITY
OF MANITOBA
P·R·E·S·S

© J.M. Bumsted 2000

The University of Manitoba Press
Winnipeg, Manitoba R3T 2N2
www.umanitoba.ca/uofmpress

Printed in Canada

Printed on partially recycled, acid-free paper.

Front cover illustration: Winnipeg c. 1870
Design: Steven Rosenberg/Doowah Design

All photographs are reproduced courtesy of the Provincial Archives of Manitoba.

Canadian Cataloguing-in-Publication Data

Bumstead, J.M., 1938-
Thomas Scott's body : essays on early Manitoba history
Includes bibliographical references.
ISBN 0-88755-645-0

1. Manitoba--History--19th century. 2. Red River Settlment
I. Title.
FC3372.B85   2000   971.27C00-920206-4
F1063.B85   2000

The University of Manitoba Press gratefully acknowledges the financial support for its publication program provided by the Government of Canada through the Book Publishing Industry Development Program (BPIDP); the Manitoba Arts Council; and the Manitoba Department of Culture, Heritage and Tourism.

To the memory of Lovell Clark—scholar, teacher, gentleman.

CONTENTS

PREFACE

For more than twenty years I have been researching and writing on various aspects of the Red River Settlement. The fruits of my labour have been a series of books dealing with the writings of Lord Selkirk, with the Red River Resistance, and with the fur-trade wars of the early years of the nineteenth century. In the course of the research, I have come across a number of fascinating questions about Red River that had to be investigated but which did not find a place in the books. Some of these subjects have resulted in published journal articles over the years, but many have remained buried in my notes in various stages of completion. This collection of essays is an attempt to put all this material together and make it available to readers interested in the history of the Red River Settlement.

Most of these essays are in one way or another exercises in revisionism of a somewhat old-fashioned variety. I will admit to being profoundly suspicious of history that does not tell a story, especially because such non-narrative history encourages a level of analytical abstractionism that in effect minimizes chronology and the necessary respect for the historical documentation. One of the first things I learned as a neophyte historian was the importance of chronological sequence. Getting chronology wrong is a disaster if there is to be any cause and effect in the process of history. I have also always had a healthy scepticism about political correctness and current fashion in historical interpretation. It has always seemed to me that it is extremely dangerous to join any academic bandwagon, whether it be quantification or trendy social history or postmodernism. Perhaps the biggest problem with most modern bandwagons is that they tend to emphasize interpretation over a serious respect for the documentary record. Historians may no longer be regarded as objective, but they still have to get their evidence right. I hope that at least some of these essays will provide a useful corrective to some of the excesses of historical writing about Red River by calling attention to the problem of evidence.

If I am resolutely old-fashioned about chronology and documentation, I am equally old-fashioned about the necessary symbiotic relationship between the historian and the reading public. The historian must write for a larger audience than the handful of other academic specialists in his field. If there is a crisis in Canadian history, part of it revolves around the growing gulf between the historian and the larger audience. In my experience, most people are genuinely interested in the historical past, so long as it is presented to them in a form with which they can deal. This brings us back to stories, the telling of which constitute the bulk of the writing in this collection. I hope readers enjoy them.

St. John's College
March 2000

RED RIVER CHRONOLOGY

1811 Selkirk awarded grant of Assiniboia by HBC; first contingent of settlers dispatched to Hudson Bay.

1812 First settlers arrive at the Forks.

1813 Kildonan settlers recruited in Sutherlandshire.

1814 Pemmican Proclamation issued; Kildonan settlers arrive at the Forks.

1815 Settlement dispersed and re-established.

1816 Battle of Seven Oaks.

1817 Selkirk re-establishes control, settles de Meurons, and makes treaty with Saulteaux.

1818 First appearance of grasshoppers; arrival of first missionaries.

1819 Second appearance of grasshoppers.

1820 Death of Selkirk; arrival of John West and George Simpson.

1821 Amalgamation of HBC and NWC; recruitment of more settlers in Switzerland.

1822 Establishment of the Buffalo Wool Company; consecration of J.N. Provencher as Catholic bishop.

1825 Arrival of cattle from United States; visitation of mice.

1826 The Great Flood devastates settlement.

1835 Sale of settlement to HBC; establishment of Legislative Council and court system.

1837 William Dickson filibuster expedition to Red River.

1838 Establishment of Experimental Farm run by Capt. G. Marcus Cary.

1839 Appointment of Adam Thom as Recorder.

1840 Death of Thomas Simpson.

1841 Mixed-blood party under James Sinclair organizes for departure to Oregon.

1843 American Fur Company establishes post at Pembina.

1844 Severe epidemic of scarlet fever and whooping cough.

1845 Council of Assiniboia regulates trade in settlement.

1846 Petitions to Colonial Office by Red River traders; arrival of British regulars of 6th Royal Regiment of Foot.

1848 Arrival of Chelsea pensioners.

1849 The Sayer Trial; David Anderson appointed as first Anglican bishop.

1850 Foss-Pelly Trial.

1851	First Presbyterian church established.
1852	Flooding of Red River.
1853	A.-A. Taché becomes Catholic bishop.
1856	Publication of Alexander Ross's *The Red River Settlement*.
1857	Investigation of HBC charter by Select Committee of House of Commons, which recommends that Red River eventually become part of Canada; Royal Canadian Rifles arrive at Red River.
1857–8	Return of grasshoppers.
1859	First steamboat, the *Anson Northup*, arrives; first newspaper, the *Nor'-Wester*, is established; first recognized postal system begins.
1861	Flooding of Red River; John Schultz arrives in the settlement.
1862	Counter-petitions to Colonial Office about colonial status.
1863	Trial of G. O. Corbett.
1864	Foundation of first lodge of Freemasons in Red River.
1866	St. John's College is re-established.
1868	Schultz gaol break; grasshoppers and famine.
1869	Transfer of Red River and Indian Territories to Canada negotiated in London; Métis oppose transfer; provisional government organized.
1870	Thomas Scott executed; Manitoba Act passed; Wolseley expedition ravels to Manitoba.

Thomas Scott's Body

Thomas Scott's Body

T HE young Irishman, Thomas Scott, was executed by a Métis firing squad on 4 March 1870. Even before his execution, Scott's fate had begun to be shrouded in mystery and mythology. Scott was already well on his way to becoming the "Martyr of Red River," a process encouraged by Canada First and the Orange Order in Ontario. I have written elsewhere about the reputation of Thomas Scott.[1] Here I want to deal specifically with the question of the disposition of his body.

Eyewitnesses disagreed over almost every aspect of Scott's execution, from his last words and last actions, to the exact manner of his death. Over 100 bystanders, apparently drawn by rapidly spreading rumours throughout the village of Winnipeg about his execution, were in place when Scott and the firing squad emerged from within the walls of Upper Fort Garry. These witnesses could agree on little more than that Scott was led out of the east-side gate at Upper Fort Garry and shot against the wall there. Beyond these elementary facts, however, accounts varied.[2]

Some reports had Scott emerging already blindfolded, others claimed he was blindfolded while standing against the wall. Scott apparently prayed continually while in the open air. According to the Reverend George Young, who ministered to him in his last hours, Scott had said on his way from his cell, "This is horrible! This is cold-blooded murder. Be sure to make a true statement." Outside the walls, Scott asked Reverend Young whether he should stand or kneel. He then knelt in the snow and prayed. Young asked, "Can you now trust in Christ for salvation?" Scott answered, "I think I can."[3] Six men, according to most accounts intoxicated, then shot him with ordinary hunting weapons. The guns were presumably muskets, which were what the Métis usually used for hunting. Reports of the number of shots fired varied. Several narratives, including Young's, agreed that the young man did not die instantly after the initial volley. A number of witnesses said that he was dispatched on the spot by one of the firing squad who shot a revolver bullet into Scott's head. No medical authority pronounced him dead at the time, however. His body was then put into a hastily carpentered box, described by one witness as "a large box made of rough boards," which was nailed shut, and carried inside the fort.[4]

Reverend Young attempted at the time to retrieve the body for proper burial. In 1874 he testified that Riel initially consented to releasing the body, but later demurred. Young continued:

> I met Goulet, and he said I had better get a sleigh; I said I should be glad to do so if I should be allowed; at that time the body was in the rough box or coffin; Nault said he objected; I then came to town and tried to use some parties' influence to get the body delivered up to them; I was told that if I would get the Bishop of Rupert's Land to guarantee that it would be buried quietly and without any demonstration, we should have it; accordingly, next morning the Bishop and myself waited on Riel for that purpose; he told us he was very sorry to disappoint us, but the Adjutant-General [Lépine], who was responsible for this case, had instructed it to be interred in the walls of the Fort, as he had a right to dispose of the body; after the Bishop had left I importuned Mr. Riel to give me the body, as I wished to write to Scott's mother that day and inform her of the interment of her son's body, as it would be some little comfort for her to know that her son's body received Christian interment; the answer was as before, he could not interfere with the case; he seemed to be very much displeased with the remark that he had a mother left to mourn over him.[5]

We do not know why Lépine refused to release the body, since he did not testify in the 1874 trial. It is possible that Lépine had already realized the potential problems with the Scott execution. The location of the body could well become the centre for a martyr's shrine, and to make a martyr out of Thomas Scott was the last thing the provisional government wanted. When Young organized a party to disinter the supposed grave in October of 1870, they uncovered a box, but not a body.[6]

One local newspaper complained that Lieutenant-Governor Archibald had only permitted a handful of Scott's former fellow prisoners to participate in the disinterment, "pretending to be afraid of them as a turbulent set of fellows."[7] In addition to Young, Archibald, John Black, Rev. Fletcher, Dr. Codd, John Christian Schultz, Dr. Lynch, J. McTavish of the Hudson's Bay Company, and two members of the Toronto press corps were present on 13 October 1870 when the grave was disinterred. The digging was done "a few paces in front of the north end of the store." According to one eyewitness recalling the event many years later, the top of a box was found about six feet from the surface with its cover partly off. "The silence was most painful. For a full minute we all stood uncovered, when Mr. Young said, 'Boys, off with that cover and end once for all this horrible suspense.' No quicker said than done, only to find the box full of earth and shavings of some kind. It was carefully lifted out and proved to be a fruit tree box about 5 feet 8 inches long."[8] If Mr. Dingman's measurements were accurate, the box found was unlikely to have held a stretched-out Thomas Scott, who was more than six feet tall. In any case, no body was found that day.

All this leaves unanswered the question of when Scott actually died. Several of the bystanders were convinced that Scott was still alive when he was placed in the crude coffin, and others among the Métis guards repeated the same story. According to Reverend Young in 1897, he was told on the evening of Scott's death by Major Henry M. Robinson (editor of the *New Nation*) that Scott was still alive five hours after the firing squad's volley and was eventually killed by Riel and one of the guards. Robinson repeated this story to a reporter who subsequently published it in the pages of the *St. Paul Press*. After the execution, said the *Press*:

> ... Major Robinson stated that he could not credit that the deed of blood had been actually perpetrated, and expressed his incredulity. Seeing this, President Riel asked him to come with him, and led the way into the court and to one of the sheds which lined the interior of the walls, where there was a sentry. Riel and his companion approached, and the former threw open the door, exposing the fatal box, from which blood dripped into the snow. Hardly had he realized this grim fact, when Major Robinson was horrified to hear a voice, proceeding from the box, or coffin, in anguished but distinct tones exclaim: "Oh, let me out of this! My God! How I suffer!" With blood curdling in his veins, he [Robinson] retreated from the spot. Riel called the sentry, and the two entered the shed and closed the door. A moment later there was the sound of a shot within, and the murdered man was probably released from his torture. Riel returned with the major to the fort, where he dismissed him with a significant warning to secrecy. To comprehend the

full horror of this tragedy it must be remembered that this last incident of Scott's life occurred five hours after he had been shot and confined, and with the thermometer many degrees below zero.[9]

On the other hand, it must also be remembered that Riel subsequently fired Robinson as editor of the *New Nation* on 19 March 1870. The American, therefore, had no reason to feel well-disposed toward Riel. This story made Riel out to be a particularly brutal monster, of course.

Most accounts of what happened within the fort immediately after the execution were given under oath at the trial of Ambroise Lépine for Scott's murder in 1874. To some extent they substantiate Major Robinson's story. Modeste Legemonière[10] testified that he was one of the two men who helped carry the box inside the fort. He heard nothing himself, but saw one man stop by the box and kneel to listen at its side. As the man passed Legemonière, he said, "That man is not dead, he still speaks."[11] Atalance Hupe, the man Legemonière saw kneel by the box, testified that he had heard a voice within exclaim, "I say, I say." It was easy to hear because the boards of the box were not well joined. John Bruce insisted that Elzéar Goulet (a member of the firing squad who was killed by a Canadian mob later in 1870) told him that Scott was found to be alive inside his box. Scott said, "For God's sake take me out of here or kill me." He was killed on the spot, testified Bruce, probably with a knife.[12] Others also heard voices from the box. According to Francis Charette, a guard at the fort, after he entered the fort from the scene of execution he heard a voice from the box, saying "O Lord, O Lord." Charette saw the box put into a grave dug between the south gate and Dr. Cowan's house after the execution, but never actually saw the body.[13] Pierre Gladu heard some groaning and talk within the bastion after the execution, apparently from the box, which he testified had been nailed shut outside the walls and carried through the gate by four men. He also heard some words in English he did not really understand, but he thought they were "My God, My God."[14] Baptiste Charette swore that he had heard "hammering like nailing" after Scott's body had been placed in the box. He also saw the hole dug near the HBC store, but never saw the box or the body put in the hole.[15]

Collectively, the witnesses provided evidence that after Scott had been shot—once by firing squad, then with a revolver in the head—his body— which had not been examined by a medical authority—had been placed in the wooden box, which was then nailed shut and carried by a number of men within the gates of the fort. A hole was dug in the ground near the HBC store, and the box, still apparently nailed shut, was placed in the hole

The execution of Thomas Scott, as painted by R.P. Meade.

on or about 6 March 1870. Obviously no single witness stood watch over the box from its arrival inside the walls to its burial in the hole. So nobody could really testify that the body had not been subsequently removed from the box. It is quite conceivable, indeed, given the testimony, quite likely, that Scott's execution was botched not once but twice, and the poor man had to be put out of his misery after noises within the box provided evidence that he was still alive, however barely. The drunken condition of the firing squad, combined with their distance from the prisoner and the sort of weapons they were using, make the possibility of less than immediate death quite likely. Even the revolver shot to the head might well have failed to complete the job.

According to some accounts, the burial outside the HBC store did not really settle the problem of the disposition of the body. John Bruce's evidence on this point, hearsay from Goulet, was heard over the objections of the defence counsel. Bruce had been writing letters to local newspapers about this business for years.[16] In 1874 he said:

Goulet told him that the body had been thrown a quarter of a mile from the mouth of the River La Seine—or German Creek; did not say when; was done by three men; did not tell me who the three were, or who was one; it was conveyed in a light cutter belonging to Dr Schultz; witness had seen Schultz's cutter; witness does not know whether the cutter was taken from Dr. Schultz by the insurgents; saw the cutter at the Fort after the capture of the parties; Goulet told me how the body was sunk; it was sunk by heavy chains; they cut a hole in the ice; it was done about a week after the execution.[17]

The Bruce/Goulet story found some substantiation in other testimony at the Lépine trial. Pierre Gladu reported that when he was on guard at the gate facing St Boniface on the weekend after the Scott execution:

. . . on Sunday morning about two o'clock I saw a horse and cutter coming out of the gate near the Company's store—the east gate— driven by I do not know whom as it was very dark, but I saw three persons in the cutter, it was a large cutter drawn by only one horse; the men in the cutter had hoods over their heads; from the noise he heard he thought [t]he[y] were taking the road leading to the Assiniboine River; immediately after they were out of hearing, I came in the house; was in the [house] about 10 minutes, then returned but did not see the cutter again; returned to the gate and resumed guard; in the course [of] the day I was not on guard and did not see cutter returned; cutters as a general thing were not kept inside the Fort, they were generally kept outside the stable; I opened the gate; went to meet them; heard a voice, it commanded him to open the gate; knew the voice belonged to a man in the cutter, that is reason I opened the gate; the cutter was about six paces from the gate when I heard the voice commanding it to stop; no other words were uttered; the cutter drove out of the gate quickly; saw Goulet the next day; cannot say how he got back to the Fort; cannot say how the cutter came back; the horses were not kept inside; went on guard about 12 o'clock that night; all that witness notices was that those in the cutter commanding him abruptly; their passing out quickly sur- prised him; went close to the cutter and did not see anything except the men they had hoods on; had no time to see anything else; as soon as I opened the gate they dashed out hastily; it was the only time I ever saw a cutter going out while I was on guard.[18]

On cross-examination by the defence, Gladu insisted that the voice he heard was that of Elzéar Goulet.

The defence did its best in 1874 to use all this evidence to cast doubt on whether Thomas Scott was actually dead at all. Defence counsel Joseph Royal insisted to the jury in his summation:

> one of the best authorities states that while there is presumptive evidence, if the body has not been found, there can be no conviction. Facts have been told of men being found guilty by a jury, of murder, and the person said to be murdered turning up living after many years. I might recite three or four examples where innocent persons have been sent to the gallows for crimes that were never committed. You will see as well as others that the greatest care is required and that the most attentive examination is necessary to prove that the man is dead. The Crown has never proved that Scott is dead from the trading guns of the firing party by drunken men at a distance of sixty or seventy feet.[19]

Senior defence counsel Joseph-Adolphe Chapleau told the jury that "no one has stated that he has seen Scott dead and no one has stated what has become of the body."[20] Judge Wood, in his charge to the jury, saw no contradiction in the evidence presented. Wood observed that Scott's body had not been found in 1870. He pointed out that many saw Scott shot, but no one had testified the body was in the box when it was put into the ground. From 4 March to the present, "poor Scott has never been heard of." Wood seemed to prefer the story that the body had been thrown into the river, but insisted that its physical presence was not important. "The body dead was within the power and disposition of the prisoner and those acting with him. They have given no account of it."[21] The jury did not seem bothered by the absence of the body. They convicted Lépine after only a few hours of deliberation.

The 1874 trial did not put an end to the stories circulating about Scott's body. In his book *The Romance of Western Canada*, George MacBeth reported that Scott's body had been dumped in the river, weighted down with chains, "as I learned in later years from one who was there when it was done."[22] But there were other possibilities for explaining what had happened. W.M. Joyce reported another local story which had Scott released by the Métis at the last minute, and paid to disappear into the United States. The execution was then faked.[23] This story may well have its origins in the Métis treatment of another Anglophone troublemaker, William Gaddie, who had been led to one of the bastions of the fort to be executed by Lépine and Elzéar Goulet, but was allowed to escape.[24] Yet another tale was told by A.G. Morice in 1935, who wrote that he had been told by André Nault, who claimed to be one of those who had helped Riel remove Scott's body from the fort, that it had been buried in an unmarked spot in St. John's Protestant cemetery.[25] According to Nault, Riel had been assisted by himself, Elzéar Lagimodière, and Damase Harrison. The body was moved on a sleigh which, according to Morice, had belonged to Dr. Schultz. Morice added, "Riel swore before God and his companions that, to his last hour, he would not reveal what they were going to do with it, an oath which was then repeated by each one of the others, and they left for unknown parts."[26]

Whether or not oaths were sworn in 1870, Louis Riel did indeed die without disclosing the final whereabouts of Thomas Scott's body. This was part of one of his last conversations with Father André, his confessor, before his execution. Riel admitted that Scott's death was a political mistake. He added, "I think I made a mistake, but before God and my conscience I did not commit a crime. Sir John A. Macdonald is now committing me to death for the same reason I committed Scott, because it is necessary for the country's good." When asked about Scott's place of burial he answered, "That's not my secret. I have been pardoned once for his death, but am now going to die for it." [27] It is interesting that Riel himself perceived at the time of his execution that his real crime had been committed not in the North-West Territories in 1885, but in Red River in 1870. In any event, unlike John Brown's body, that of Thomas Scott did not "lie a-mouldering in its grave."

Trying to Describe the Buffalo: An Historiographic Essay on the Red River Settlement

ESPITE its great isolation and relatively small population, the settlement at Red River has always drawn a surprising amount of historical interest. Some of Canada's best and most innovative nineteenth-century historical work was written about Red River, and the settlement continues to draw students. A large part of the modern attraction, of course, revolves around the multi-racial character of the place, although there are a variety of other interesting questions to explore as well. The historiography of Red River has always been characterized by a fundamental paradox. On the one hand, the settlement is sufficiently small and compact to permit close and detailed microcosmic analysis, enabling the historian to feel really in control of the material, however much there are limitations to the documentary evidence.[1] On the other hand, the settlement's line of development from its beginnings in 1811 through its entrance into Canadian Confederation as the province of Manitoba is quite labyrinthian. Moreover, although there is a plethora of writing and scholarship, there are precious few detailed overviews or syntheses. Arguably still the best overall history of the settlement, taking the story only to the late 1840s, was written by a contemporary participant resident, Alexander Ross. A thorough, scholarly, book-length account of the entire history of the settlement has never been undertaken. Most studies of Red River—old or new—are frozen snapshots or at best videos of the development of only one aspect of the colony. Even Frits Pannekoek, who among recent scholars has provided the most depth and breadth, has not really attempted to write the entire history of the colony.[2]

Some implicit themes do wander in and out of the literature, although seldom in any coherent fashion. Periodization has been a perennial problem, and there is no real agreement on what constitute the important dates. Pannekoek has argued that the common ones are 1817 (Lord Selkirk's visit), 1827 (rebuilding after the great flood), 1849 (the triumph of free trade), and 1869 (the insurgency).[3] W.L. Morton in his history of the province agrees on 1817, but then moves to 1856 (an arbitrary, artificial date a few years after free trade), and finally to 1869.[4] James Jackson uses 1812 (the first settlers), 1821 (the merger of the trading companies), 1835 (the transfer from the Selkirk family to the HBC), and 1857 (the parliamentary investigation), before concluding with 1869-70.[5] John Perry Pritchett employs 1821, 1849, and 1869-70.[6] The anonymous author of "The History of the Red River Settlement" published serially in the *Nor'-Wester* in 1861, saw the 1830s as crucial, because of the development of a court system.[7] The editor and authors of the recent *Manitoba 125—A History* use 1812, 1840, and 1865.[8] Obviously much depends on where the historian chooses to focus the analysis. An emphasis on legal/political development produces some different periodization than economic or social concentrations. Too often, however, no really good reason is assigned for the periodization.

The question of internal dynamic versus external pressures has also been an important one. The settlement was obviously driven to some extent by its own dynamic, which is not very well understood, but the relationship between this dynamic and external factors has somehow to be taken into account. Among the externalities which need to be factored into the account are the fur trade, Manifest Destinies (both American and Canadian), British Imperialism, the development of industrial capitalism (which among other things produced rapid changes in transportation facilities and in technology in the Red River Valley beginning in the 1850s), and geographical determinism (including the importance of the frontier).

Even given the absence of coherent overviews, it is possible to distinguish a number of different interpretive traditions in the voluminous literature on Red River. These interpretive traditions are not mutually exclusive and are not always clearly separated from one another in the history. Historians have often employed more than one approach at different points in their analysis. Perhaps four can nevertheless be isolated for discussion. These are: (1) the progressive colony to Canadian province tradition. This interpretation has been sometimes labelled the "expansionist" view, although there are some differences between expansionism as seen in eastern Canada and expansionism from the perspective of Manitoba itself; (2) the victim/subordination tradition, which sees a small isolated community caught first in a great fur-trade war, or dominated by the HBC, and finally subjected to the conflicting Manifest Destinies of the Americans and the Canadians. The American Manifest Destiny has geographical coherence on its side, but the Canadian version has other advantages of its own. One major subset here sees the settlement as little more than an appendage of the fur trade, which is the major institution to be studied; (3) the establishment of a multi-racial society tradition, usually focussing on the Métis and mixed-bloods. There is considerable recent disagreement here over whether the multi-racial society, and especially the Métis presence, was solidifying or diffusing over the course of the second half of the nineteenth century; (4) the internal dynamic tradition. This divides into two contradictory streams. On the one hand, the settlement can be interpreted as an oasis in the wilderness, a view which transmutes after 1870 into a "garden of Eden" interpretation. On the other hand, the settlement has also been seen as a hotbed of underlying socio-racial tensions and conflicts, political and otherwise. Let us turn to examine each of these traditions in more detail.

The Progressive Colony to Province Tradition

The expansionist view of the history of Red River has been explained in some detail by Doug Owram in a chapter entitled "The West as Part: The Foundations of Western History," in his 1980 study *Promise of Eden: The Canadian Expansionist Movement and the Idea of the West, 1856-1900.*[9] The eastern expansionists, chiefly from Ontario, saw Red River's historical development in terms of Canada's legitimate and inevitable right to the West. The Hudson's Bay Company was a feudal obstacle that had to be overtaken by progress and civilization. In terms of the Selkirk settlement period, which saw the great fur-trade war between the North West Company and the Hudson's Bay Company, the expansionists opted for the Nor'Westers. They viewed Selkirk as a tool of the HBC and interpreted the North West Company as the first statement of Canadian involvement in the region. The merger of the two great fur-trading companies produced a period of reactionary darkness which could only be overcome by the introduction of Canadian settlement, law, and representative government.

The line of hostility to the medieval HBC was argued for some years by the settlement's only newspaper, the *Nor'-Wester*, which was begun in 1859 by journalists who had previously worked for George Brown's expansionist *Globe*. As Owram points out, the larger sweep of this interpretation ran afoul of two fundamental realities of the settlement's early history. First, Lord Selkirk and the HBC represented the first thrust of outside settlement of the region, opposed by the Nor'Westers and their mixed-blood allies, partly in the name of the rights of the indigenous people. Secondly, the further development of the mixed-bloods after 1821 culminated in the 1869-70 resistance against Canadian annexation of the region, again partly in the name of the rights of the indigenous residents. It is hard to see the resistance of 1869-70 as progressive, or to relate it positively to the subsequent influx of immigration into the province. Given these contradictions, it was not surprising that most history of the region after 1870 written by eastern Canadians—including work dealing with the progress of the nation—preferred to say as little as possible about the early development of Red River. The tendency of the expansionists to think in terms of the future rather than the past also made Red River's early development somewhat irrelevant.

Many western-based historians of the post-Confederation province shared in the eastern Canadian desire to present the development of the province in progressive, upward and onward fashion. Not all necessarily saw the need to side with the North West Company in the great fur-trade war. Indeed, a number of these historians lionized the early Selkirk settlers as the "Pilgrim Fathers" of the province.[10] It was possible, as was the case with Donald Gunn in his detailed account of the early history of the settlement published in 1880, to distinguish Lord Selkirk from the settlers.[11] Gunn was highly critical of Selkirk as a tool of the HBC, while simultaneously documenting the heroic suffering of the early Scots settlers. Gunn stopped his account in the 1830s, before the Métis had become a serious political force in the settlement. But especially beginning with George Bryce in 1882, Selkirk and the settlers were placed on a pedestal together.[12] For many of the early progressive historians of Manitoba, not the Selkirk settlers but the Métis were the awkward problem in their version of the past, to be dealt with as expeditiously as possible. In an extremely revealing effort, Robert B. Hill in his *Manitoba: History of Its Early Settlement, Development and Resources* (1890) shifted from the Selkirk Settlement to the arrival of the first Canadian settlers in 1862 without skipping a beat, affording the Métis no more than a brief casual glance in the process.[13] For Hill, the resistance to Canada led by Riel culminated in the creation of Manitoba, not in any victory of Métis rights. The main demographic line of descent was from John McLean, who arrived in Red River aboard the steamer *International* and settled in the Portage la Prairie area, through to the Ontario settlers of the 1870s, whose photographic portraits are presented many-to-the-page, scattered throughout the book. Not surprisingly, the inhabitant of Red River to whom Hill devoted the most attention and space was John McLean, treating him as emblematic of the new forces.

R. H. Schofield's *The Story of Manitoba* relied more heavily on original documentation than any of its predecessors. He was sympathetic to the Selkirk settlers and the settlement, and while he did not use the term "massacre" to refer to Seven Oaks, he talked of a post-victory Métis orgy and added that "their poet, an ignorant versifier named Pierre Falcon, composed for them a song of triumph which has been preserved."[14] Subsequent chapters dealing with the 1820s and 1830s were entitled "Progress and Reverses" (chapter xix) and "Progress in Organization" (chapter xx). Schofield did not devote much attention to the Métis in the settlement; his chapter on "The Social Life of the Settlers" distinguished Francophone and Anglophone "half-breeds," noting that "the French half-breeds were inclined to follow the roving lives of their mothers' people; but the English-speaking half-breeds have generally shown a disposition to follow the occupations and adopt the customs of the whites. For this reason they became an important part of the settled population of the country from an early period in its history."[15] Schofield had great difficulty with the insurgency and the creation of the province, and was obviously much happier when he could get past the early 1870s.

Like Schofield, Margaret McWilliams extolled the virtues of the Selkirk settlers.[16] She saw the period from the 1826 flood to 1860 as one of insular tranquility, quoting an American observer of 1856 to the effect that despite its total isolation, "there is more than one good library there, and several good cellars; a man may dine there according to Soyer, drive a two-forty in a dashing cariole over the crisp snow, dance the latest Cellarius polka redowa with ladies of any shade of colour from the pure bronze to the mere white, discuss the principles of human society and the theory of popular governments as learnedly as the thing could be done at Washington or Cincinnati."[17] Both before and after 1860, the settlement made "steady progress," however. The Métis are mentioned but are not prominent players in the story until the insurgency, which does not make much sense in this progressive picture.

As the subsequent provincial histories by W. L. Morton and James Jackson well demonstrate, fitting the early period into some sort of progressive story was never easy. The upward and onward line was particularly difficult for Morton, who had already written extensively about the Métis period and the Métis resistance to the Canadian takeover in 1869-70. Instead of a simple progression, Morton constructed a set of complex dialectical oppositions, which resulted in an unstable synthesis that could not possibly hold. In his *Manitoba: A History* (1957), Morton saw the union of the two fur-trading companies in 1821 as the triumph of the Bay over the St. Lawrence, as well as the "integration of the maritime slope, the fur forest of the Shield, the great swampy tract, and the southern plains, an integration of the fur trade of the north and the provisions trade of the south."[18] His subsequent chapter on the period of HBC dominance advanced another dialectic labelled "The River Lot and Buffalo Hunt, 1821-1856."[19] By the 1850s, he wrote, the synthesis of this opposition, Red River, was ready to move from isolation into the mainstream. "The compromise of river lot and buffalo hunt, of the sedentary life and the nomadic, which was Red River, was beginning to crumble."[20] It would become increasingly challenged, even before 1869, by the first harbingers of the agricultural frontier from the East. The resistance of 1869-70 became in Morton's hands in 1957 a sort of last desperate effort of a traditional society to save itself in the face of the future.

"The *métis,*" summarized Morton of his discussion of the period 1869-70, "as the militant element of the native population of the old Northwest, had won a victory for their land rights, language, and faith. This victory had been consolidated in the Manitoba Act. They had not, however, won a victory for their mode of life. The old order by which they had lived was disintegrating before the inflow of Ontario settlers and the rise of a new society founded on agriculture, the railway, and the complex commerce of the nineteenth century."[21] Whether his narrative was intended to produce a prose epic in a strategy which Lyle Dick has described as "the deployment of an antiquated literary form to advance the historical role of his ethnic group, class, and profession" is perhaps open to question.[22] My own sense is that Morton was far more sympathetic to the uneasy synthesis that was Red River than Dick's analysis would allow, although he did view the Métis as a static force, unable or unwilling to adjust to changing circumstances. His creation of the dialectical opposites reflected the ambiguities of his own sympathies, which were more positively engaged by the Métis than Dick would see. Certainly one problem with the dialectical approach was that it posited antithetical opposites and total syntheses rather than continuums and constant change. By whatever means Morton got there, however, in *Manitoba: A History* the progressive forces clearly emerged triumphant.

No evidence exists to suggest that James A. Jackson was bothered by any of the fundamental inconsistencies in his account of Red River in *The*

Centennial History of Manitoba. After an initial chapter on early exploration and the fur trade, Jackson prefaced his narrative account of Red
River with a detailed description of the buffalo hunt, which he called
"Manitoba's first processing industry and, as such, . . . almost the sole
raison d'être of the Red River settlement."[23] Despite this pronounce-
ment, Jackson wrote in support of the Selkirk settlers in their struggles
with the Métis buffalo hunters, accepting the massacre interpretation of
the Battle of Seven Oaks, for example. The merger of the two fur-trading rivals turned Red River into an "island colony," wrote Jackson, and
it enjoyed a "golden age"—the term is his—until it was reached by the
civilization of the East in the middle of the nineteenth century. Jackson
recognized that the years between 1821 and 1869 were "not entirely
idyllic."[24] But "social disparities" (presumably race and class) were mel-
iorated in the face of common obstacles, and gradually, "the disparities
became less significant and a gentle calm prevailed." This calm, in large
part "the result of good sense and a feeling of common humanity," was
broken by the intrusion of the outside world on the settlement. Jackson
did not deal explicitly with the implications of this perspective on the
inevitably progressive interpretation of the development of Manitoba
which his history otherwise embodied.

Unlike Morton, Jackson did not see the 1869-70 resistance in terms of
the preservation of traditional Métis values. Indeed, he specifically denied
that it was "one of race, language, religion, or political allegiance."[25] For
Jackson, the Métis resistance was "one for recognition of the ownership of
land," and when the Canadian government acknowledged this fact in its
negotiations with the delegates from Louis Riel's provisional government,
the Canadian annexation "was settled to the initial satisfaction of the new
Manitobans." For Jackson, the murder of Thomas Scott—perhaps the result
of Riel's incipient madness—was the great blemish on Riel's achievement,
depriving him of his proper role as the father of Manitoba. Jackson recognized that the arrival of the Wolseley Expedition resulted in the shedding
of far more blood than had occurred under the Riel regime, but he moved
quickly to describe in positive terms the new identity of Manitoba that
followed from Canadian annexation and Canadian settlement.

The Victim/Subordinate Tradition

Probably the first consistent attempts at portraying Red River and its people as innocent victims came in the course of the pamphleteering war
between the Hudson's Bay Company and the North West Company that
began around 1816. In that year, Dr. John Strachan of York published *A*

Letter to the Right Hon. the Earl of Selkirk, on his settlement at the Red River, near Hudson's Bay. In this work, Strachan excoriated Selkirk for practising deception on poor hapless emigrants. In his preface he wrote, "of the settlers who went to the Red River, many died at Churchill, in Hudson's Bay, from the severity of the climate and the quality of their food. Others seriously injured their health; and not one of those who have escaped, saw a joyful day, from the time they left Scotland till they began their journey to Canada." In a sense, Strachan's work was part of a larger literature that portrayed all Scottish Highlander emigrants to North America in the early nineteenth century as victims of unscrupulous promoters and speculators.[26]

A year after Strachan's screed appeared, John Murray of Albemarle Street, London, published a book entitled *Statement Respecting the Earl of Selkirk's Settlement upon the Red River, in North America; Its Destruction in 1815 and 1816; and the Massacre of Governor Semple and his Party. With Observations upon a Recent Publication, Entitled "A Narrative of Occurrences in the Indian Countries, &c."* The anonymous author of this work (actually Selkirk's brother-in-law John Halkett) attributed the destruction of Lord Selkirk's colony to the machinations of the North West Company, which had persecuted the settlement with violence from its beginning because of its efforts to control the fur trade against the legitimate charter monopoly of the Hudson's Bay Company. The Nor'Westers had involved the "savage" Métis as "hired banditti" in their campaign of destruction. The "Narrative of Occurrences" which this book sought to discredit had been prepared under the auspices of the North West Company. These works were only a small part of the controversial literature published by partisans of the two fur-trading companies in the second decade of the nineteenth century.[27]

Donald Gunn made much use of the pro-Nor'Wester material in writing his history of the early settlement, which was also an exercise in victimization literature, again within the larger context of Highland emigration. Instead of the nasty old North West Company as villain, Gunn offered the nasty old Hudson's Bay Company and its collaborator the Earl of Selkirk. Gunn's history was a fierce indictment of Selkirk for abusing, neglecting, and exploiting the settlers he recruited for his own nefarious purposes, and those of the HBC. But Gunn's account passed well beyond hostile partisanship into the realm of Highland mythology. The Highlanders recruited by Selkirk were duped into permanent exile (the label "exiles" is applied to the settlers continually) in a hostile land. Gunn described the feelings of the Kildonan party of 1813 as they sailed away from Scotland:

Some bade farewell forever to their native hills. Those who were engaged only for a few years, only buoyed up their sinking spirits with the thought that their time of service would soon expire, when they would return to their native land and once more enjoy the presence and society of those whom they had left behind. But few, very few, ever returned to realize the soul sustaining hope, which cheered their hearts in that hour. Little did those sad and heavy hearted exiles know, or even think, that there were far greater sufferings and heart-rending trials before them than those they had to endure on bidding a last adieu to their friends and to the land of their birth.[28]

Gunn managed to sustain a tone mixed of equal parts of anger and melancholy over several hundred pages. He pointed out, quite legitimately, that the settlement was well-armed but had no agricultural implements beyond the hoe. No wonder many of the earliest colonists in 1815 accepted the offers of the North West Company to transport them to Upper Canada, where they finally settled.

Just as Gunn's colonists were pawns in the larger machinations of Selkirk and the Hudson's Bay Company, so later settlers and indeed the entire settlement itself were seen to be buffeted by forces beyond their control. These forces, according to historians, were many and varied. The settlement was, throughout most of its history, little more than an unfortunate adjunct of the fur trade. A combination of geography and economics kept it an isolate. As such, however, it was coveted by the Americans and the Canadians, neglected by the British, and then finally annexed by the Canadians. None of the governments involved had any real interest in the settlers themselves. Whether the Hudson's Bay Company cared for the inhabitants of Red River is another matter.

Most of the fur-trade literature does not take Red River at all seriously as an independent player in western history. For the fur-trade historians, notions and movements of dissent are imported into the settlement rather than being generated locally. The result is a "colonial" history, in which all the impetus comes from without. Almost by definition, the settlement was dominated by the Hudson's Bay Company, in both an economic and a political sense. The problem is not necessarily that the Red River story does not get told, but that it gets told consistently from the perspective of the fur trade and external forces. In the hands of some of the fur-trade historians, the settlement's very existence weakens the fur trade. John S. Galbraith begins his chapter on "The Growth of Unrest at Red River, 1846-1853," with the assertion that:

The Red River colony was the anathema of the fur-trade monopoly. Free traders in liaison with American purchases demoralized the price system in southern Rupert's Land; the Company's efforts to restrict this allegedly illicit trade met resistance in the colony, and protests against its "injustices" reached England, where they were used by the Company's enemies to discredit it. The very existence of the settlement was evidence that agriculture could be carried on with hopes of success in at least part of Rupert's Land, and thus stimulated both Americans and Canadians to search for new land resources in British North America.[29]

E. E. Rich, in his *The Fur Trade and the Northwest to 1857*, in the Centennial History of Canada series, related the story of the settlement in two chapters which concentrate almost exclusively on its relationship with the HBC. Rich concluded that in the 1850s "the colony, born in the strife of fur companies, inextricably involved in their rivalries, and then placed under the control and protection of the coalition of the companies, had reached an equilibrium."[30] Because he ended his account in 1857, Rich was not obliged to take the story beyond this equilibrium. Rich had already told the rest of the story in the second volume of his *History of the Hudson's Bay Company, 1670-1870*, of course, where it became a tale of unwarranted attacks by a few, encouraged from without, on a defenceless HBC.[31] Most of the older fur-trade historians, reflecting the prejudices of their sources, have had difficulty in taking the Métis seriously, and Rich was no exception.

In his monumental history of early western Canada, Arthur Silver Morton treated the settlement almost entirely within the perspective of the fur trade, which was for him the unifying theme of early western history.[32] From the fur trade's point of view, of course, the period up to 1870 was not one of progress, but of demoralization and disintegration. Morton entitled a lengthy chapter on the post-1849 period "The Drift of Rupert's Land and the North-West Territory towards Confederation with Canada." He took most of his understanding of the period of the 1860s from Joseph James Hargrave's *Red River,* which saw the decade in terms of the decline of legitimate authority within the settlement. Thus Morton wrote about the "factors in the Settlement weakening the grip of the Company's system of government and working for disintegration."[33] Most of these factors were externally generated. Morton's overall interpretation was just the reverse of progressive. Its failure to allow for an internally generated local dynamic was in its own way just as limiting as the progressive view.

Most of the "Manifest Destiny" literature, virtually by definition, fails to comprehend anything much about the internal workings of the settlement itself, treating it basically as an inert object of external machinations. In the 1950s and 1960s American scholarship provided a series of studies of the relationship between Red River and the United States, culminating in A. C. Gluek's classic statement, *Minnesota and the Manifest Destiny of the Canadian North-West: A Study in Canadian-American Relations*.[34] What these studies demonstrated was that at least some Americans were willing to engage in both open and clandestine operations to facilitate the annexation of Red River to the United States, but they were essentially frustrated by an absence of enthusiasm for annexation within the settlement itself. These points received further confirmation in 1968, when Hartwell Bowsfield produced his edition of the letters of one of the leading American annexationists, James Wickes Taylor, who subsequently served for many years as American consul in Winnipeg.[35]

The principal loyalty of most of the population of the settlement, if not of the entire North-West, was to Great Britain. What the British had done to deserve Red River's loyalty has never been entirely clear. The British government had refused to intervene in an active way in the fur-trade war in the beginning of the century, though it was quite willing to facilitate the merger of the two fur-trading rivals in 1821 after Lord Selkirk's death, passing legislation giving the new Hudson's Bay Company a complete monopoly of the West. Great Britain never converted the settlement into a formal colony, although there was talk of such action in the late 1850s and early 1860s. It never intervened in the administration of the region on behalf of the inhabitants, whether settlers, Métis, or Aboriginals, although often pressed to do so by Alexander Isbister and the Aborigines' Protection Society. When Britain decided that the HBC monopoly had to go, it sought only to transfer responsibility to Canada. Under the circumstances, it is hardly surprising that historical analysis of the British role in Red River has been fairly minimal. A recent study by David McNab concludes that while British (i.e., Colonial Office) thinking about Red River—when it thought about it—was complex, the main ingredient was belief that the HBC had done a decent job with the Aboriginal population; alternatives would be much worse.[36] Furthermore, given the expense of running a colony in the West, the HBC was a cheap alternative. McNab also suggests that the attitudes of one deputy minister—Herman Merivale—may have been the major factor in Colonial Office thinking about Red River for much of the period.[37] Clearly Colonial Office attitudes to Red River were, well, colonial, featuring what amounted at best to benign neglect.

As for Canadian Manifest Destiny, its anatomy and meaning have been fully explored by Doug Owram in his *Promise of Eden: The Canadian*

Expansionist Movement and the Idea of the West, 1856-1900.[38] Owram demonstrated the continuities, real and imagined, between the early Canadian fur traders and later Canadian expansionism, as well as the way in which the images of Red River and the Prairie West were manipulated by Anglo-Canadians for their own purposes throughout the nineteenth century. Owram's work is, in a sense, devoted to illustrating how Red River was held hostage to, and made a victim of, Canadian expansionism. Such an analysis is particularly useful in reminding us how history gets massaged, especially by the victors, but it does not help very much in establishing what was actually going on in Red River.

Manifest Destiny did not always take political forms, as Debra Lindsay has shown in her work on the Smithsonian Institution and northern science in the 1860s.[39] Many traders and other employees of the Hudson's Bay Company—as well as Aboriginals—literally slaved away at the very base of scientific activity, collecting specimens for the Smithsonian, with little or no return. Red River had long served as a major—if somewhat unheralded—staging point for arctic exploration and discovery, mainly by British explorers and scientists. In this period the Americans began to compete with the British for scientific dominance in the Canadian North. Scientific imperialism was also at work in the establishment of several scientific expeditions in the 1850s to investigate the vast western territories of the Hudson's Bay Company. Eighteen fifty-seven—the year of the parliamentary inquiry into the HBC monopoly—saw the arrival of two scientific parties in the West. One was sponsored by the Royal Geographical Society and was headed by Captain John Palliser.[40] Another was sponsored by the Canadian government and was led by George Gladman and Professor Henry Youle Hind of the University of Toronto.[41] Each of these expeditions produced a major report; both emphasized the enormous agricultural and mineral potential of the region.[42]

Perhaps even more important and ubiquitous than science was technology, which also took a great leap towards Red River at the end of the 1850s. As is the case with the history of technology in Canada generally, there is precious little literature available on the subject, and most of what exists comes from the nineteenth century. In 1859 the settlement got its first steamboat and its first newspaper, as well as a reorganized postal system employing the American post office.[43] That same year the Transmundane Telegraph Company, with the support of Sir George Simpson, was chartered to build a telegraph line across British North America to connect with another line coming from Siberia. There was talk of a transcontinental railway as well. The possibility of a transcontinental telegraph line, constructed by the Atlantic and Pacific Transit and Telegraph Company, led to the reorganization and sale of the Hudson's Bay Company in 1863.[44] The Company ceased to be run by experienced fur traders, and instead was operated by London businessmen who would provide no obstacle to the ultimate transfer of western territory to Canada. These changes all occurred externally to the settlement, but obviously would affect it enormously in the years to come.

As early as 1856, Alexander Ross had commented,

> We are now occasionally visited by men of science as well as men of pleasure. The war road of the savage, and the solitary haunt of the bear, have of late been resorted to by the florist, the botanist, and the geologist; nor is it uncommon now-a-days to see Officers of the Guards, Knights, Baronets, and some of the higher nobility of England, and other countries, coursing their steeds over the boundless plains, and enjoying the pleasures of the chase among the half-breeds and savages of the country. Distinction of rank is, of course, out of the question; and at the close of the adventurous day, all squat down in merry mood together, enjoying the social freedom of equality round Nature's table, and the novel treat of a fresh buffalo steak served up in the style of the country—that is to say, roasted on a forked stick before the fire.[45]

Beyond the relatively brief discussion of this vast travel literature in Owram, we have absolutely no idea of what it reported, or perhaps more significantly, how the visitors and their reports may have influenced the settlement itself or were received in it.[46] As Ross implies, the visitors may have had some unexpected impacts, particularly on the Métis.

The Métis-Centred Tradition

After the merger of the two fur-trading companies, it quickly became apparent that Red River would become the centre of mixed-blood society in the Hudson's Bay Company territories. The existence of a substantial mixed-blood population in the West had already become evident even before this date in some circles, but it had not yet acquired a home base. Failure to identify the critical importance of the mixed-bloods was one of the factors leading to the downfall of the Selkirk Settlement. Despite the gradual recognition of the dominance of the mixed-bloods in Red River society, problems of identification and self-perception continued to bedevil the ranks of the mixed-blood peoples. The treatment of the mixed-bloods (or "half-breeds") in Alexander Ross's pioneer history, *The Red River Settlement*, suggests the nature of some of the problems.[47] Ross was a Scots-born fur trader who had married the daughter of an Okanagan chief and settled after retirement in Red River. His children were themselves mixed-bloods, which ought to have made Ross sensitive to the complexities of "méti-ness" in the settlement. At least in his book, it did not. In his chapter devoted to the "half-breeds," for example, he spent most of his space discussing the buffalo hunt and the buffalo hunters, ending up writing as if all half-breeds were plains-hunters. "Like the American peasantry," wrote Ross, "these people are all politicians, but of a peculiar creed, favouring a barbarous state of society and self-will; for they cordially detest all the laws and restraints of civilized life, believing all men were born to be free."[48] Ross's son James, who had achieved several gold medals at the University of Toronto, was certainly greatly disturbed by the characterization as semi-savages which the mixed-bloods received in his father's book.[49]

By the time of the resistance in 1869, most observers realized that not all the mixed-bloods were buffalo hunters. There was a tendency, however, to see the Catholic Francophone mixed-bloods (or Métis) as predominantly a people of the plains, and the Anglican Anglophone mixed-bloods as a more sedentary agricultural population. "Red River," really Joseph James Hargrave, wrote the *Montreal Herald* on 25 September 1869 that "the French half-breeds are a parcel of hunters, who have no taste for farming. Their rude and somewhat careless efforts do not deserve to be named as a serious agricultural experiment."[50] "Red River" had earlier observed that "the term 'half-breed' as applied to the English-speaking portion of the mixed population, is very apt to convey a false impression to a stranger. The number of those to whom the expression in its literal signification can be applied, is comparatively small, but the local custom prevails of speaking of every one, how remotely soever of Indian descent, as a half-breed. This section of the population is quite competent to hold its own in presence of any amount of immigration."[51] "Justitia," a *nom de plume* for Alexander Begg, explained to the *Globe* that the "French half-breeds are mostly given to hunting, fishing and trading for a livelihood."[52] The implication of the remarks of Begg and Hargrave was that the French mixed-bloods would not do very well in the Canadianized settlement. The Resistance, which was clearly led by the Métis portion of the mixed-blood population of Red River, had the effect of confirming the distinctions between the two mixed-blood groups. Even though Louis Riel managed to get most of the Anglophone mixed-blood leadership—which was horrified by the thought of an internal civil war—on the side of the provisional government, and despite the guarantee of mixed-blood lands on racial rather than religious or linguistic grounds, contemporaries plainly felt that the creation of Manitoba had been a Métis (i.e., Francophone Catholic mixed-blood) accomplishment.

The history of the Métis in the Red River Settlement, apart from the story of Louis Riel, was kept alive in the fifty years after 1870 chiefly by the Catholic historians. For the most part clerics, they told the Métis story from the perspective of the development of Catholicism, in works with titles like *Etablissement des Soeurs de Charité à la Rivière Rouge* or *Monseigneur Provencher et Les missions de la Rivière Rouge*—both by Father Georges Dugas—or *Histoire de l'Eglise Catholique dans l'ouest Canadian*—by Father A. G. Morice. In 1909 a group of Métis notables, including Ambroise Lépine, André Nault, Elzéar Lagimodière, and Joseph Riel, determined to produce a history of the period 1869-1885, partly to correct what they saw as the errors of the existing historical record. They obtained a number of documents, especially from the Riel family. This committee became the Union Nationale Métisse Saint-Joseph de Manitoba. They hired French-born historian August-Henri de Trémaudan to write their history.

Trémaudan began publishing scholarly articles about Louis Riel and the Métis in the early 1920s, based on new documentary material and the recollections of the Métis veterans.[53] Later in the decade, he retired to Los Angeles, where he completed in 1929 the manuscript which would eventually be published by the Union Nationale Métisse Saint-Joseph de Manitoba as *Histoire de la Nation Métisse*, a much-neglected pioneering historical work. Trémaudan was highly partisan in his sympathies, but he was a decent scholar who was familiar with the primary literature and especially with the oral traditions of the Métis people. Without that oral testimony, much Métis history was likely to be mostly indistinguishable from the history of the Church, which, unlike the Métis, had kept its written records intact. Even so, Trémaudan's illness and residence in Los Angeles kept him from writing a proper scholarly work, or one in which the Red River period was other than background to the years of resistance. His interpretation of the Métis in the settlement was fairly standard, focussing on the Catholic Francophones in a static portrayal.

The same year that Trémaudan published his history, the Anglo-Canadian scholar George F. G. Stanley brought out *The Birth of Western Canada: A History of the Riel Rebellions*. Stanley did not devote much attention to the Red River period. He recognized that there were both Anglophone and Francophone mixed-bloods in a "primitive society" which they dominated, at least demographically. "Economically and politically," wrote Stanley,

Red River "was a simple society and filled the needs of a simple people for nearly two generations."[54] He saw the Métis as unable to respond to change. His account of the last years of the settlement concentrated mainly on what was happening outside Red River that would eventually overwhelm it. The "half-breeds" (Stanley used the term without quotation marks) simply were not equipped to withstand the invasion of "an overwhelming white immigration and a competitive nineteenth-century civilization." Not surprisingly, faced with "the loss of their lands and their livelihood, the breakdown of their society, and the eventual effacement of their race," the Métis resisted the transfer to Canada.[55] They achieved some success in 1869–70, but then were tragically quashed in 1885.

Both Stanley's and Trémaudan's work suggest that the research of Marcel Giraud was somewhat less innovative than has sometimes been suggested. Nevertheless, it was the Frenchman who provided the influential scholarly synthesis of the prairie Métis that served as a major breakthrough in Red River historiography, chiefly by devoting a good deal of attention to the pre-insurgency period. Searching for a topic that was not hackneyed and would advance his academic career rapidly, Giraud researched in western Canada on a Rockefeller scholarship in the 1930s. He subsequently took an appointment in London which enabled him to research before World War II in the Hudson's Bay Company archives. Returning to occupied France during the war, Giraud wrote up his research in the midst of the chaos, and his finished book, a huge volume of nearly 1300 pages, was published in 1945 as *Le métis canadien* by the Institute of Ethnology at the University of Paris. The work was finally translated into English by George Woodcock and published in that language in 1986.

Giraud's work, while monumental in nature, had some limitations. His account of the early origins of the Métis relied heavily on fur-trade records, but for the nineteenth century he made much more use both of oral traditions and of the anthropological tendency to read back from the present into the past (the so-called "ethnographic present"). Thus, in the course of the work, Giraud's "Métis" increasingly became associated with the Francophone Roman Catholic population, and the Anglophone mixed-bloods were in later sections virtually ignored. Like many early anthropologists, Giraud had little sensitivity to the process of ongoing historical change. His view of the Métis as a people poised halfway between "savage" barbarity and civilization did not allow for a full spectrum of responses or for change over time. Moreover, his interpretation tended to see the Métis as the inherently imperfect and unstable products of racial miscegenation, lacking in moral fibre. Manitoba Métis society for Giraud was clearly in disarray after 1870 and the Canadian takeover; he used the term "decadence" to describe the post-1870 Red River group. Giraud has in recent years been charged with producing an interpretation of the Métis which was "in the mainstream of Anglo-Canadian discourse."[56] Whatever its imperfections, Giraud's work was eagerly absorbed by W.L. Morton, whose work on Red River—which represented the best scholarship of the day to both an academic and non-academic audience—was greatly influenced by the Frenchman.[57]

Morton dealt with the Métis in four major writings: his introductions to the Eden-Colvile letter-book and to the Alexander Begg journal, both published in 1956; his history of Manitoba, published in 1957; and his collaboration with Margaret Arnett MacLeod on a biography of Cuthbert Grant, originally published in 1963.[58] The four studies, taken together, encompassed the entire nineteenth century. The Grant study covered the early years, the Colvile introduction the middle years, the Begg introduction the first insurgency, and the Manitoba history—besides synthesizing the first seventy years of the century—also dealt with the post-1870 period. At the same time, although Morton knew more about Red River—and its records—than any historian before him, he never produced a full-scale study of the settlement. All four accounts were characterized by an interpretation of Métis society (and Red River history) which was heavily indebted to Marcel Giraud, although it may well be the case that Giraud merely strengthened Morton's own views rather than created them. Morton identified the "métis" with the buffalo hunt, with an "Indian concept of trade" and with "a nationalism that was French in its demand for equality with the English and *métis* in its sense of local corporate identity."[59] As with Giraud, Morton's *métis*—Catholic and Francophone—were uneasily poised on the bridge between savagery and civilization; he frequently used negative words to describe what he saw as their volatile temperament. Morton did not see Red River solely in terms of the *métis*, of course, but they were in his view the key to the settlement and its development up to the arrival of the Canadians in substantial numbers. He acknowledged the existence of the English-speaking half-breeds (the term for them he employed in most of his work), but did not take them very seriously.

Not surprisingly, the scholarly neglect of the Anglophone mixed-bloods soon produced its own corrective. John Foster wrote an M.A. thesis entitled "The Anglican Clergy in Red River Settlement, 1820-26" at the University of Alberta in 1966, and completed his Ph.D. thesis in 1972 at the same institution on "The Country-born in the Red River Settlement,

1820-1850." "Country-born" was the term Foster introduced into the scholarly literature to refer to the Anglophone mixed-bloods, most of whom were communicants of the Anglican Church in the settlement. Foster never published his thesis, but he advanced his views in a series of influential journal articles published in the late 1960s and in the 1970s.[60] These publications emphasized that there were two major groups of mixed-bloods in Red River, one Catholic and Francophone, one Anglican and Anglophone. Foster's work introduced a new level of social complexity into the mixed-blood element in Red River, one based on race and religion. Frits Pannekoek further emphasized the importance of religion, and especially the role of the Anglican church, in Red River in his doctoral thesis "The Churches and the Social Structure in the Red River Area 1818-70."[61] Pannekoek's thesis did not appear as a book until a revised version was published in 1991 as *A Snug Little Flock: The Social Origins of the Riel Resistance; 1869-70.*[62] But he had presented his main arguments in a series of journal articles which we will examine subsequently. Robert Coutts also focussed attention on the Anglophone mixed-bloods, in his work on St. Andrew's.[63]

In the later 1970s, Jennifer S. H. Brown began publishing journal articles which anticipated her book, *Strangers in Blood: Fur Trade Company Families in Indian Country.*[64] Brown's work not only distinguished two "linguistic solitudes," but explained their historical origins in the marriage patterns of the two fur-trading companies. The Francophone mixed-bloods had their beginnings in marriages between Native women and traders of the North West Company, while the Anglophones came from marriages of Hudson's Bay Company traders. Moreover, along with her colleague Sylvia Van Kirk, Brown introduced not only gender and family relations into the mixed-blood picture, but also a far more ambivalent and edgy notion of the racial tensions in Red River society.[65] The new scholarship also in general dealt more sympathetically with the Métis than had that of earlier generations. Irene Spry and Olive Dickason both offered new perspectives.[66] Lyle Dick's reconstruction of Seven Oaks both as an historical event and as an historiographical incident was particularly important in this regard, for it pointed out how unfavourably (and often unjustly) the Métis had been treated in most Anglo-Canadian historical writing.[67] Jacqueline Peterson and Jennifer S. H. Brown edited an important set of papers that emerged out of the first conference on the Métis in North America, which had been held in 1981 at the Newberry Library in Chicago.[68] Barry Cooper's biography of the "country-born" mixed-blood Alexander Kennedy Isbister demonstrated that his subject was an important figure in reform circles in

Britain in the mid-nineteenth century, especially active in Aboriginal matters.[69] Rehabilitating a nineteenth-century mixed-blood as a major intellectual and moral force was a substantial advance. It clearly was becoming increasingly difficult to sustain the old Anglo-Canadian in-terpretations in the face of the new scholarship, as Gerald Friesen showed as early as 1984 in his regional study, *The Canadian Prairies: A History*.[70] In his chapter "The metis and the Red River settlement 1844-1870," Friesen saw changing views of "race, respectability, and progress" as products of and evidence for the emergence of a new industrial capitalism in North America. The Métis were at a disadvantage in this new world, Friesen argued, but "they responded to this adversity with the pride and inde-pendence of a self-reliant people." The Métis at first held their own, but eventually, when they found that the expansion of Europe was "irresistible," they precipitated an insurgency.

The question of the nature of mixed-blood society in Red River was reopened in 1986 by Brian Gallagher in an important, unpublished M.A. thesis, somewhat misleadingly entitled.[71] Gallagher insisted that most his-torians of Red River, beginning with Morton and Stanley, and continuing through John Foster, Frits Pannekoek, and Sylvia Van Kirk, had exagger-ated racial and religious differences among the mixed-bloods. He argued that Foster had ignored the common Cree heritage of most mixed-bloods in Red River and created in the "country-born" a term not often em-ployed by contemporaries. Both Foster and Pannekoek to a considerable extent had magnified religious strife in the settlement, Gallagher claimed, and Pannekoek had taken matters one step further by erroneously recast-ing the Protestant mixed-bloods as the loyalist supporters of Canada in 1869-70. Gallagher was equally critical of the work of Sylvia Van Kirk, insisting that her work was built on the assumptions of Foster and Pannekoek. Later Red River was not divided by marriage patterns in which mixed-blood women were excluded.

While academics were busy revising the scholarly view of mixed-blood society in the Red River Settlement and beyond, a new spirit of con-sciousness was emerging among Native peoples in Canada. This new po-litical awareness produced rejuvenated Métis organizations with conscious agendas. Several issues seemed important to the Métis organizers. One was the negative reputation which the Métis held, both in much of the histori-cal literature on Canada and in Canadian society generally. Not only was the general reputation negative, but the Métis had never been properly recognized within Canada as a distinct people, particularly by the Depart-ment of Indian Affairs, which accepted the need to renegotiate rights with the Aboriginal peoples but did not accept that the mixed-bloods had any rights worthy of negotiation. The Métis response took two forms. The first was a general consciousness-raising through books that concentrated on Métis history, many of them subsidized by Métis organizations and published by Métis publishing houses, such as Pemmican Publications in Winnipeg.[72] The second was the modern reintroduction of Métis land claims into the complex picture of Aboriginal rights in Canada. In this latter business, the first shot was fired by Emile Pelletier in his *Exploitation of Métis Lands* in 1975.[73] Gradually, the lead on the land claims business was taken by the historian Douglas Sprague of the University of Manitoba, who was employed by the Manitoba Métis Federation beginning in 1978.[74]

The Métis land claims question is one which begins as a Canadian political issue in 1870 and thus is for the most part beyond the scope of this survey. Nevertheless, it obviously has its origins in the Red River period, for it was here that the people awarded land by the federal government in and after 1870 had their genesis.[75] Moreover, a large part of the historical debate over land claims has turned on the question of what happened to the Manitoba mixed-bloods after 1870, a problem which, to a considerable extent, involves a discussion of demographic and other trends that began or did not begin long before Confederation and did or did not carry on for many years afterwards.[76] More to the point, Sprague and his collaborators have insisted that the Red River Métis were a stable and persistent population in the Red River period, and their rapid disappearance from Manitoba after 1870 was, according to Sprague, the result of a government policy of dispossession of their land rights. Gerhard Ens has maintained, on the other hand, that there was a continuity of Métis behaviour between the pre-and post-1870 periods. The Métis—or at least some of them—Ens has argued, did not move because of their failure to adapt to new ways or because of a government conspiracy, but because of their continuing adaptation to new economic conditions. Ens has also insisted that the invidious distinction between Métis and mixed-blood agricultural practice has been greatly exaggerated. When examined carefully, there was little difference between the groups.[77]

Gerhard Ens expanded his views in his book *Homeland to Hinterland: The Changing Worlds of the Red River Metis in the Nineteenth Century*, published in 1996, making clear the extent of his disagreements not only with Sprague but with Giraud and Morton.[78] Instead of being victims of progress, many Métis did their best to adapt to it and share in it. The mixed-bloods were not dispersed after 1870, for they had been moving westward since 1840. Instead of monolithic mixed-blood groups, Ens saw a continuum across the linguistic/religious divide, particularly in terms of responses to economic opportunity. Not all Francophones supported Riel; some Métis were able to co-operate with their Anglophone cousins in a variety of ways, including an insistence on their rights as heirs of the Aboriginals to land claims in the region. The buffalo-skin trade was preferred to subsistence agriculture not because the Métis were primitive hunters, but because it was more profitable. The decline of the buffalo meant that the Métis may have made a bad choice, but buffalo hunting was not in and of itself a sign of their "savage" heritage.

One of the contemporary issues involving the Métis at Red River was whether they were legally entitled to any share in the Aboriginal inheritance, whether they had "Aboriginal rights." Despite the beginnings of serious investigation on the matter, the whole question of Aboriginal rights, particularly in Red River, needs to be reopened and reinvestigated, as does the place of the Aboriginal peoples in the life of the settlement.[79] Little has been written specifically or recently on the Aboriginal peoples in Red River. Most of the literature is really concentrated on the role of the missionaries.[80]

Given the obvious importance of the decline of the buffalo, one might have expected more recent scholarly attention to be paid to the natural environment in and around Red River. The major work on the buffalo remains F. G. Roe's *The North American Buffalo: A critical study of the species in its wild state,* originally published in 1951 and republished in a second edition in 1970. Roe is much better at rejecting the Aboriginal and mixed-blood peoples as responsible through over-hunting for the extermination of the buffalo than he is with explaining what forces should be put in their place. It is worth emphasizing, however, that the focus of modern environmental science has been on total ecosystems, and furthermore, that the ecosystem of the Red River Valley, beginning with its climate, altered dramatically in the second half of the nineteenth century.[81] We need to know considerably more about the natural environment in Red River and its history in the nineteenth century.

The Internal Dynamic

The first thing that has to be said about the internal dynamic is that we know remarkably little about how people actually operated in the community of Red River—about the quality of existence, about the routine of daily life, about their amusements or their addictions. Most of the daily life literature is very old and nostalgic. Much of the modern historical discussion about the nature of Red River society exists on some highly abstract level well above the mundane rhythms of everyday life, although references are often made to them. Many of the generalizations are either deduced from what the historian wants to believe or are derived from the remarks of a few outside observers. Virtually all Red River students would have been well advised to begin with the police blotter—or what passed for one in the settlement, the records of the court of quarterly sessions. Curiously enough, nobody appears to have examined the court records thoroughly, on either the civil or the criminal side, for what they tell us about how people lived, any more than anyone seems to have read carefully the pages of the *Nor'-Wester*, certainly few students of Red River have ever managed to spell the name of its newspaper correctly—it has both an apostrophe and a dash. Most legal history of the settlement has focussed on the recorders (i.e., judges) or anecdotally upon controversial cases.[82]

As has already been suggested, there are two main streams of interpretation of Red River society. One sees the settlement as an oasis in a wilderness, at least until the serpent in the form of modern technology/capitalism/immigration intrudes. As Owram has pointed out, in some hands in the generation or two after 1870, Red River actually became a "garden of eden" or a "utopia." What historians have meant precisely when talking about periods in Red River of "stability" or "tranquility" or "equilibrium" has never in detail been entirely clear, but often such times of peace appear to have been characterized by an absence of racial tension in the settlement. Alexander Begg wrote in 1894, for example, that "socially there was much good feeling existing between all classes of the community, and a more hospitable or happier people could hardly be found on the face of the earth."[83] As well, the good times occurred before "intercourse with civilized mankind" intruded upon an idyllic existence. The high point of this approach was probably reached by Frank Larned Hunt in 1902, in a paper entitled "Britain's One Utopia." There were no "cursings and obscenities," claimed Hunt. There were no political parties and hence no politics. The settlement was inhabited by nomadic pastoralists who lived "under conditions of excellence unthought of by themselves until they had passed away."[84] But Alexander Begg had already come close to this interpretation as early as 1869, in his first "Justitia" paper for the *Toronto Globe*, which became the opening pages of his journal for 1869-70.[85] His villains were the *Nor'-Wester* and the Canadian Party. The notion that a semi-idyllic pastoral life at one time existed in Red River has been common to many of its historians. This notion must be distinguished from the insistence of historians like Gallagher that there were not great amounts of racial and religious strife before 1870. Gallagher merely wants to resituate strife, rather than to eliminate it. If a tranquil period existed, it must have been extremely brief. But it enables some historians to distinguish some part of the post-1821 period from the period after 1859 or 1860, when the outside world made its appearance in Red River and life apparently suddenly changed. Those few historians who have dealt with cultural institutions have not so much commented directly on the idyllic nature of Red River society as they have marvelled that this small isolated community was capable of producing such a high level of energy and activity.

Whether the churches of Red River were actually instruments for the creation of social order in the settlement is an interesting question. Certainly both Protestant and Catholic clergymen sought to convince their flocks to become agriculturalists, partly because farming was more "civilized," partly because sedentary agriculture produced better communicants. But particularly among the Anglican clergy, infighting was an ongoing problem.[86] Both Father Georges Belcourt at Pembina and the Reverend Griffith Owen Corbett at Headingley were notorious critics of the HBC regime.[87] Corbett's conviction in 1863 on charges of the attempted abortion on a young, lower-class, mixed-blood servant girl whom he had impregnated hardly reassured anyone about the Anglican clergy.[88] Those who believed the charges could but marvel at Corbett's hypocrisy. Those who refused to believe in Corbett's guilt could blame the Church for persecuting him. Father Noel Ritchot was notorious for his active involvement in the insurgency of 1869-70.[89]

It could be argued that what changed after 1859 was not so much Red River, but the extent of the documentation of the less idyllic side of life, thanks to the founding of the newspaper and improved levels of record-keeping by the courts, as well as the influence of the much underrated book *Red River* by Joseph James Hargrave. In any event, not all scholars have accepted the view that Red River could ever have been a society free from tensions, given its racial and religious ingredients, superimposed as they were on a patriarchal society. Jennifer Brown and Sylvia Van Kirk have pointed to the "turning off" of Indian wives of the leading traders, which began with George Simpson in the 1830s, as an important straw in the wind, although Gallagher has insisted that after 1845, young HBC officers married exclusively within the ranks of mixed-blood (rather than European) women. Joseph James Hargrave in his *Red River* certainly saw the growth of tensions, especially as revealed in the courts, as contributing to the loss of authority by the Hudson's Bay Company during the decade. But no historian has gone as far as Frits Pannekoek in building the growing tensions of the 1860s into a crisis that would also become a civil war in 1870, turning Anglophone mixed-blood Anglicans against Francophone Métis Catholics. For Pannekoek, the Riel insurgency was at least in part created "by a sectarian and racial conflict that had roots deep in Red River's past."[90] Whether or not one agrees with Pannekoek's interpretation, it is hard to argue with his insistence that the internal dynamic of the settlement is the one which is so crucial and so relatively neglected. There are many unanswered questions and under-explored subjects.

Despite some interesting work, the role of women in the Red River Settlement certainly falls within the under-explored category. There is only one general book-length study that concentrates on the settlement, W. J. Healey's aged and totally anecdotal *Women of Red River*, first published in 1923. The fact that this book has been reprinted three times, in 1967, 1977, and 1987, suggests the continued demand for a discussion of the subject.[91] Sylvia Van Kirk's *Many Tender Ties: Women in Fur-Trade Society*, ends up in Red River but does not pretend to be a general survey of women in the early settlement. The most concentrated attention on women has been placed on the Catholic nuns and their educational activities.[92] There are several scattered articles on Métis women, including Jennifer S.H. Brown's brief "Women as Centre and Symbol in the Emergence of Métis Communities"; Van Kirk's sketch of the notorious Foss-Ballenden affair; and Erica Smith's study of the young mixed-blood girl Maria Thomas as victim in the Corbett trial of 1863.[93] By the 1860s there were certainly in the settlement some women of spirit and independence who were not intimidated by patriarchal society, such as Annie Bannatyne, Victoria McVicar, Elizabeth McKenney Mair, Eleanor Kennedy, and Agnes Campbell Farquharson Schultz, but we do not really understand how these figures fit into the larger picture.

One important question is not simply whether there were deep social tensions and divisions in Red River, but the extent to which they were exacerbated by events of the 1860s. Gerald Friesen has insisted that a view of the 1860s as a period of instability "exaggerates the weaknesses of the community and underestimates the abilities of its residents." He claims that a "truer picture would give greater attention to the regular performance of daily duties and the development of political interest groups in these years."[94] As Friesen suggests, we need to know far more about daily life in the settlement. For Friesen, there was an ordered continuity, although he admits that the small group of Canadians introduced another dimension. An alternate interpretation, never seriously explored, is that the continuity running throughout the existence of the settlement was of a constant high level of tension and instability. In such a view, the 1860s would be no worse than or no different from previous decades, except perhaps in the publicity afforded to the cracks in the fabric by the presence of a newspaper.

There is also the issue of where to locate the sources of tension and instability. As we have seen, most scholars who see an unstable Red River would emphasize racial and sectarian differences. Perhaps only Brian Gallagher, building to some extent on the studies of Philip Goldring on the HBC labour force beyond Red River, has sought to situate the underlying conflict in class rather than in race or religion. For Gallagher, there had developed in Red River by the 1860s a polyglot mercantile oligarchy which included most of the influential leaders of government and business. Its marriage patterns were exogamous. Most of the population married endogamously, however, less because of race and religion than because of geographical location and the absence of social mobility brought about by the creation of a capitalist labour market in the settlement. Most mixed-blood farmers were subsistence farmers who found it hard to leave the agricultural community and join the buffalo hunt. Louis Riel's supporters came mainly from tripmen residing in the settlement. Gallagher has not offered a full-scale class-based analysis of Red River, but his thesis that the real divide in the settlement was between the elite and the "majority of simple commodity producers existing at a subsistence level whose ranks also afforded the Company with an abundant reserve of casual labour" certainly deserves further investigation.

Another important question is whether—or in what ways—Red River was different from any other isolated community in British North America during the first two-thirds of the nineteenth century. Like almost all other regional historians, those of Red River have always taken the exceptionalist approach to their subject. With the possible exception of an article published some years ago by Wendy Owen and myself, which briefly explores some social comparisons between Red River and Prince Edward Island— both isolated island colonies in the mid-nineteenth century—virtually no comparative work has been done on Red River.[95] There are nevertheless three colonies in British North America which simply cry out for comparative study: Red River, Prince Edward Island, and Vancouver Island. All three are, of course, exceptionally isolated island settlements. All three have to deal with landed proprietors and complex land problems. Further abroad, comparative study of Red River and Tasmania (or Van Diemen's Land) would hardly be farfetched, and might prove extremely revealing. I suspect that such a comparative analysis might actually support the notion of continual underlying social tensions that were more related to class than to race and religion.

As the foregoing discussion has suggested, while much research has been done, there is much still left to do, especially on the social history of Red River in the larger context of similar communities in British North America and even within the British Empire. Nevertheless, the most crying need is for full-fledged scholarly syntheses of the entire history of the settlement, from its establishment in 1811/12 to its transmutation into the province of Manitoba in 1870. Until one or more such histories has been produced, we are a bit like the blind men who tried to picture the buffalo (or was it the elephant?) by a careful examination of various small parts of the beast's anatomy.

ANOTHER LOOK AT THE FOUNDER:
LORD SELKIRK AS POLITICAL
ECONOMIST

T HOMAS Douglas (1771-1820), Fifth Earl of Selkirk, is usually characterized as a founder of colonies and a philanthropist—if one is favourably disposed—or as a self-seeking opportunistic speculator—if one is not. Often forgotten is that he has some credentials also to be remembered as an early political economist, of the same sort if not in the same league as Adam Smith and Thomas Malthus. The reasons for Selkirk's lack of prominence in the annals of political economy are not hard to find. He was a member of the Scottish nobility, not normally a breed to be taken seriously in intellectual terms. His written work was scattered and not clearly focussed, some of it privately published and some never published at all.[1] Perhaps most crucially, Selkirk—when he is remembered at all—is associated with Highland emigration to British North America and a disastrous colonization venture that foundered when caught in a fur-trade war in the middle of the continent. Ironically enough, the links between Highland emigration, the fur trade, and political economy were close and direct. Selkirk, unlike his early co-toilers in the fields of political economy, thought of himself as an experimental rather than a speculative philosopher. Although he was not a major theorist, his involvement in North America was an extension of his political economy. Throughout his life, Selkirk attempted to combine the scientific emphasis on careful experimentation with the philosophical spirit of Dugald Stewart that maintained that virtue and morality were epitomized by selfless dedication to the improvement of society.

Selkirk and the Scottish Enlightenment

The relationship between the Scottish Enlightenment and early political economy was a close one. Among early writers of political economy,
few had better Enlightenment credentials than the Fifth Earl of Selkirk.
His father, Dunbar Hamilton, Fourth Earl of Selkirk, was a favourite
pupil of Frances Hutcheson at the University of Glasgow and later in life
was a close friend of Dugald Stewart. His eldest brother Basil (Lord
Daer) was active in circles of radical political reform in Scotland and
Britain in the 1780s and early 1790s. Thomas himself attended Palgrave
School, where he came under the moral influence of Mrs. Anna Laetitia
Barbauld, and at age fifteen went on to the University of Edinburgh.
There he lodged with Dugald Stewart and became a member of several
Edinburgh student clubs, including an informal one that had as fellow
members Walter Scott, William Clerk, Adam Ferguson, and George
Abercromby, and the more formal Speculative Society of Edinburgh.
His first paper before the Speculative Society was on "The Territorial
Tax," a topic that demonstrated his student interest in the realm of po-
litical economy.

In April of 1791 Thomas Douglas left Edinburgh for revolutionary Paris
with his brother-in-law, Sir James Hall of Dunglass. Sir James was a highly
regarded scientist of the time, particularly renowned for his pioneer work
in chemistry.[2] He had travelled extensively in Europe in the 1770s, form-
ing contacts and friendships with a number of leading French scientists and
philosophes, including the chemist Antoine Lavoisier. Hall was able to renew
these contacts in 1791. The visit to Paris was well beyond the usual languid
tour of picture galleries and eminent ruins associated with the foreign part
of a young British gentlemen's education. Hall quickly established contact
in Paris with his friends Lavoisier and LaRochefoucauld. Within days of
its arrival, the Hall party (including Thomas's two eldest brothers) were
circulating at a soiree attended by Dupont de Nemours, Condorcet,
and LaRochefoucauld. Daer left the party at this point to take lodgings
at the Grand Hotel du Vendome. Hall, Thomas Douglas, and his brother
John eventually settled at the Grand Hotel de Vauben, Rue de Richelieu.

Sir James Hall kept a journal of the Paris visit, providing us with consid-
erable detail on the activities of his party.[3] Its members dined regularly with
Lavoisier, heard about the revolution from Condorcet, listened to
Robespierre and other debaters in the National Assembly, and attended
plays and operas. On 13 May brother John returned to England, leaving
Hall and Thomas together, to be joined frequently by Daer. On 7 May,
John Paul Jones (who had led an American raiding party on the Selkirk

estate in Kirkcudbright in 1778) called on the visitors at their hotel, having met Daer the night before at a soiree. He refused to be drawn on the Selkirk raid, however. That same evening Hall and Thomas dined "at home" with Abbe Sieyes, Condorcet, and Lavoisier. The last took his coat off after dinner to help the young Scot with a chemical experiment of some sort. A few days later, Thomas entered into a discussion with a dinner guest on the question of Locke's insistence on the relationship of government to the protection of private property. Hall had initiated the subject by remarking that the estate of a man without children should be distributed among the poor, recording in his journal, "T.D. supported me in this by saying that to employ a man's estate on his death for the public service was making a present to those who paid the taxes, that is, as we all agreed to the landed proprietors—to the rich and not the poor." The pair subsequently adjourned to dinner with a number of prominent republican leaders, including Brissot de Warville and du Chastellet.

The summer months of June and July 1791 passed quickly. The times were exciting, and the revolution had not yet turned nasty. The little party of Scots enjoyed a constant round of social engagements, as well as visits to the countryside to study agricultural practice and survey the temper of the people in a period of change. Lord Selkirk himself joined them in late June, at the same time that Louis XVI was carried by the "mob" to Paris. Regular visits by the Scots continued to the National Assembly to listen to the debates, mainly over the future of the monarchy and France's overseas colonies, and on one occasion Thomas observed that "the republican spirit of the country" seemed greater than that to be found in Paris itself. On 3 July, on the eve of the anniversary of the American Declaration of Independence, the party dined at home with Thomas Paine as principal guest. Paine was full of stories and anecdotes, admitting his understanding of French was quite imperfect. A few days later the Scots "supt" at Condorcet's rooms with du Chastellet and Paine, discussing the "fable about maintaining bees," as well as emigration and education. On 7 July Hall recorded, "Abbe Sieyes has written a monarchial letter in the Moniteur & Payne who goes to England tomorrow with Daer means to have an answer to it." The next day Daer set out for England with both Thomas Paine and the manuscript of *The Rights of Man* accompanying him.

After Daer's departure, Hall and Thomas were thrown even more closely together. By this time events in Paris were moving at a breakneck pace, and the two men spent much time crowding into public gatherings to observe and listen. They still managed to find time for regular dinner parties with the leading intellectuals of Paris, usually discussing some aspect of political economy. Although they occasionally visited with members of the British community, including British Ambassador Lord Gower, they found their compatriots "remarkably cool," doubtless because the Selkirk group had become notorious as "violent friends of liberty." A Paris newspaper reported that Robespierre was plotting with two Englishmen whose names—M. D'Ark and M. le Chev'r d'Ark—obviously conflated Daer and Selkirk. Such publicity probably hastened the departure of the little party from France. They were back in London by 27 July. A few days later Hall and Thomas called on Sir Joseph Banks and Josiah Wedgewood, subsequently meeting Mr. and Mrs. Barbauld at dinner, where they "disputed much about French politics."

For young Thomas Douglas, the visit to Paris had been largely an opportunity—given to few of his generation in Britain—to observe and listen. In a short space of time he had been exposed to the leading *philosophes* of revolutionary France, and had listened to them discuss politics and economics in an informal setting. He had witnessed the turmoil of the French Revolution at first hand, and had, if nothing else, been made to appreciate that intellectuals could also be men of action, that ideas were not necess-arily mere academic exercises. Throughout his later career, Thomas would insist on the need to translate ideas into action, on the need to test social and economic theories experimentally. Paris in 1791 was not the only influence upon him in this regard, but it was undoubtedly a critical one. The city was far more alive with a spirit of social experimentation than was the staid and perhaps more speculative Edinburgh that had been his previous exemplar.

Selkirk's Early Political Economy

As a fifth son, Thomas Douglas was hardly expected to inherit the family title. Given his interests in political economy, it is hardly fanciful to think that he might well have ended up teaching at one of the Scottish universities, perhaps even the University of Edinburgh. Instead, a tragic series of deaths among his elder brothers during the 1790s brought him constantly closer to the title. By 1797 he was Lord Daer, the acknowledged heir. As Lord Daer, he spent much of his time managing the family estate for his father, who had become quite infirm. Apart from his family responsibilities, he became involved in two projects, one related to his interest in political economy, the other to his interest in public service. The political economy project was undertaken for the Board of Agriculture, organized in 1793 by Sir John Sinclair, that industrious compiler of social statistics and research information.[4] The board was a quasi-public agency funded by Parliament but organized as a voluntary society, with the noted agriculturalist Arthur Young as secretary. It never really found a satisfactory niche, but its most successful activities were those connected with county-by-county agricultural surveys and reports, many of which were published. The report for Galloway was to be the responsibility of Thomas, Lord Daer, and the young man went about the task of gathering information on agricultural practices with his usual energy, concentrating particularly on sheep husbandry. By early 1798 the report was in a rough form, ready to be perused by Sinclair but "not yet in a state for the public."[5] By this point, however, the Board of Agriculture had lost its impetus for existence, and the Galloway volume was never completed. The rough notes for it remain in the surviving Selkirk papers, however.

Considerable connection existed between agricultural investigation and relieving the Galloway poor. Lord Daer undoubtedly became involved in the latter problem as a major landowner, although the question clearly fascinated him as a political economist and reformer. The late 1790s were a period of agricultural distress, caused by poor harvests and wartime inflation. Food was in short supply and expensive. As the Fourth Earl of Selkirk's old friend Charles James Fox once trenchantly put it, "the great majority of the people . . ., an enormous and dreadful majority are no longer in a situation where they can boast that they live by the produce of their labour."[6] Contemporaries saw few solutions. One was enclosure to increase production, especially of grain. Another was the notorious Speenhamland System, by which in England especially low wages were supplemented by poor relief. Minimum wage laws would infringe the sacred right of property—including the right of an individual to sell his labour at the market rate. Regulation of the grain trade ran counter to the "system of natural liberty" of Adam Smith. The question of the regulation of grain in periods of extreme shortage had been a hotly debated one throughout the eighteenth century. Most economic thinkers preferred an open market, but some drew the line when the poor really suffered. One especially sharp discussion had come in France at the end of the 1760s. It pitted Galiani, Diderot, Voltaire, Necker, Grimm, Linguet, and Mably (for regulation) against Quesnay, Baudeau, Roubaud, Dupont, Mecier, Morellet, and Condorcet (against regulation).[7] A similar debate had also erupted in Scotland in the 1770s, with James Steuart on one side and Adam Smith on the other. In 1798 Thomas Malthus had his essay on population published anonymously.[8]

Could the poor be cared for with a minimum of public regulation, thus reconciling moral concerns with the continuation of the free market? This question led to Selkirk's first publication, an anonymous and untitled pamphlet describing the 1799 relief system in Galloway, which had obviously been implemented at his instigation. The only known copy of this pamphlet survives in the Dugald Stewart Collection at the University of Edinburgh, in which the authorship is attributed—in Stewart's own hand—to Lord Selkirk. It is not clear whether the pamphlet was printed before or after Thomas Douglas's accession to the title in 1799. The specifics of the Galloway scheme outlined in the pamphlet are less important for our purposes than the general philosophy enunciated by its author. Here several points stand out. In the first place, Selkirk approached the problem as one of political economy, attempting to use the occasion to provide—in his words—"experimental proof" of the efficacy of the particular methods employed. To the modern reader, the dispassionate and coldly analytical tone of the pamphlet may strike a discordant note. Consumption of grain was not only to be calculated, monitored, and regulated at the level of the individual family, but amounts of barley were to be added to the grain to allow broth to go farther while still providing the necessary nutrition. Count Rumford's "An Essay on Food, and particularly on feeding the poor, exhibiting the science of nutrition and the art of providing wholesome and palatable food at small expense" was several times cited enthusiastically, but there is no evidence that the author had read Malthus's recently published essay on population.[9] Selkirk plainly thought of himself here as a social scientist, although he would not have used such a term, rather than as a philanthropist.

At the same time, the second point emerging from the pamphlet is its author's clear sense of the social responsibility of the upper classes for the poor. Smith's invisible hand of the market (restated by Malthus) was not good enough. The pamphlet advocated voluntarism and opposed taxation for relief of the poor on the grounds that the poor would not feel gratitude if "the only aid they receive is extorted from the rich without their consent." Such relief would lead the poor "to believe that the assistance given them is their right" and any hardships suffered would be "considered as an injustice." Poor rates, opined Selkirk, "will spread a profligate dependence on it among the poorer classes; the money that would otherwise be laid up for the support of age and infirmity, will go to the whisky shop; poverty and misery continually increasing, will continually add to the demands upon public charity." Such a policy not only undermined the spirit of industry, it perpetuated the cycle of poverty it was intended to relieve. Despite its limitations, Selkirk's pamphlet did represent a real effort to find—

in experimental practice rather than in intellectual speculation—a middle ground between the natural liberty of the market and the "right to subsistence" of the labouring poor. The author's solution was voluntary intervention by the landowners, designed to draw "closer those bonds of union between the different classes of society, on which the stability of social order so essentially depends." In later years Selkirk would find in emigration an alternative way to aid the poor while preserving the principle of self-help. He continued to be obsessed throughout his life with reconciling and unifying the classes.

Soon after his inheritance of the title in 1799, Selkirk became involved in various schemes to recruit potential settlers for a colonization venture in North America. In February of 1802 he prepared the draft of a memorial to the British government proposing that he lead a colony of Irish Cath-olics to Louisiana. Selkirk's life-long involvement with North American colonization had begun.[10] The British government found the Louisiana proposal—and a revision proposing to relocate the scheme to the territory where the waters which fell into Lake Winnipeg united with rivers draining into Hudson Bay— unacceptable. Selkirk was prepared to change locations, subsequently offering Upper Canada or Prince Edward Island as well, but was more stubborn about the source of his colonists. Lord Hobart, secretary of state for the colonies, suggested that Selkirk shift from Irish to Scottish families, and the Earl eventually took up this idea with enthusiasm. Thus was he brought into the midst of the Highland Emigration Crisis, which was becoming a major public issue in Scotland. Characteristically, he plunged into the centre of the "emigration mania," doubtless pleased to be able to become active in such an important public matter.[11] He was soon in the Highlands of Scotland, especially the Hebrides, actively recruiting settlers. When in late 1802 a number of books and pamphlets began to appear, criticizing the Highland operations as unscrupulous promoters of North America, Selkirk was a principal target. Matters became more complicated when his negotiations over land concessions with the British government broke down late in 1802, forcing him to buy land in Prince Edward Island on the open market. The passage of parliamentary legislation regulating the emigrant trade in the spring of 1803 was really a godsend for Selkirk, for he was the only promoter whose project seemed likely to survive the stringencies of the legislation. He acquired many new recruits as a result. In the end, Selkirk sent more than 800 Highlanders to Prince Edward Island aboard three ships in the spring of 1803, and, as he had agreed, he accompanied the party to the Island. It proved to be his only successful colonization venture.

Selkirk spent a month on Prince Edward Island organizing his settlement, and then headed for a tour of the United States and Upper Canada.[12] As the diary he kept of the tour indicated, he acquired large amounts of first-hand information by talking with almost everyone he met. Much of his knowledge of the United States came from lengthy conversations with Alexander Hamilton.[13] The fur traders of the North West Company would later accuse him of acquiring his interest in Red River through discussions he held with his hosts at the Beaver Club in Montreal. According to Nicholas Garry, Selkirk's interviewing techniques were a bit unusual. Garry wrote just after his death, "Lord Selkirk had the Custom of taking down in Shorthand on his Nails the Conversations he had with People, which he did unobserved. His Nails were very large."[14] In Upper Canada he had plans to create a personal estate at "Baldoon" that would breed the finest possible sheep for North America.[15] He left Baldoon in July 1804, just before the arrival of 102 settlers who would experience a devastating malaria epidemic.

The "Observations on the Present State of the Highlands of Scotland"

Upon his return to Britain, Selkirk began work on the manuscript that would become *Observations on the Present State of the Highlands of Scotland,* his major contribution to political economy and to the debate over emigration and public policy for the Highlands. The manuscript was prepared somewhat hastily in the spring of 1805 against a backdrop of changing developments in British politics and on Selkirk's North American lands. On the public front, Henry Dundas, the government's Scottish political manager and opponent of Selkirk's family, fell from political grace. It is likely that Selkirk was spurred on in his composition by the possibility for public office opened by the Dundas demise. Although the resultant book was less a work of reflection than of large-scale pamphleteering, Selkirk clearly attempted to write in the broader context of political economy, facing the larger issues of his subject squarely and directly. Those issues included emigration, but only as a consequence. The real Highland question revolved around change and development. To the contemporary discussion over public measures to develop the Highlands and to arrest emigration to North America, Selkirk interjected a completely fresh perspective that actually created the basis for a debate.[16]

After a brief introduction explaining his activities over the past few years, Selkirk turned to an analysis of the Highland problem as he understood it. In long appendices that took the place of footnotes, the author demonstrated his familiarity with the standard literature on the Highlands. He quoted the usual travellers' accounts, Sir John Sinclair's *Statistical Account of Scotland,* the various works on the Highlands in the Board of Agriculture series, and a number of published and unpublished contemporary writings on emigration—including the manuscript reports of the Highland Society of Edinburgh. As was characteristic of his writing, Selkirk did not often in *Observations* cite explicitly the general theorists in political economy, although at one point in his discussion on the consequences of Highland overpopulation he did refer "to the valuable work of Mr. Malthus on the Principle of Population, in which these arguments are traced to such uncontrovertible general principles, and with such force of illustration, as to put skepticism at defiance."[17] At several points he also referred to Adam Smith's *Wealth of Nations,* but for details rather than for general theory.

For Selkirk, Highland overpopulation was a consequence of the long-standing feudal structure of the region, which for centuries had placed emphasis on the perpetuation of large numbers of military retainers rather than on the maximization of agricultural production. The value of land in the feudal period was reckoned not by rents but by the number of men it could send into battle. Thus the country was subdivided into holdings that barely supported its occupiers, whose principal occupation was not its cultivation. The great change came after the rebellion in 1745, when the military power of the chieftains was finally broken and they began to discover that their rentals were "far below the real value of the lands." The shift to "real rentals" would inevitably displace much of the ancient population, for "where there is no employment but what arises directly from the cultivation of the land, the country is more or less peopled according to the mode of cultivation." In a region where most of the land was in grass, numbers would be further reduced. The essential questions were what employment could be afforded and under what mode of management would the land be most profitable to its occupier. Comparing the Highlands with other similar regions in Britain, Selkirk concluded that the most profitable employment of land was in rearing young cattle and sheep. Even in areas that could sustain cultivation, fewer people were required than occupied the lands at that time.

Thus it was inevitable and unavoidable that most small occupiers in the Highlands would be dispossessed. Selkirk applauded the great public works recently undertaken in the north of Scotland, but insisted that although they might in the short run employ some of the population, they would not "essentially alter the circumstances of the country." Excess population and low wages were the only advantages the region could offer a manufacturer, and few would attempt an enterprise without additional incentives. Even if the public works encouraged manufacturing, however, the typical Highlander would find confinement in a factory most unpleasant. Since the Highlander was simply not trained to "habits of regular and steady industry" and had no experience of "sedentary employment," he would end up doing no more than the demeaning drudge work of the day labourer. The best (and indeed only) alternative for the Highlander, Selkirk argued, was removal to North America, where he could continue his agricultural way of life. The Highlander himself recognized the logic of this choice, which explained his propensity for emigration.

Selkirk then turned to the local opposition to emigration. He focussed his attention on the inconsistency of the opponents of emigration, who simultaneously acted to improve the Highlands in ways "most conducive to the pecuniary interests of its individual proprietors" while offering no real solution to the problems inherent on the dispossession of the ancient inhabitants. It was clear, he maintained, that the process of change had already gone too far to be reversed. With improvement, "in no part will cultivation require all the people whom the produce of the land can support." Proprietors could not be expected to concede to a population possessing land at a rent much below its potential value. Therefore most of the Highlanders would need a new means of livelihood. Clearances for sheep were only the most spectacular dispossessions, not the root cause of the difficulties of the Highland region. But since dispossession was inevitable, what options did the Highlander have? He could join the labouring force in the manufacturing towns, largely outside the region, or he could continue his traditional pastoral ways by emigrating to America. Emigration, Selkirk insisted, was "most likely to suit the inclination of habits of the Highlanders," since it promised land and outdoor labour.

The loss of the supply of soldiers would pose a real danger to the nation, Selkirk admitted. But he insisted that opposition to emigration would not "add a single recruit to the army." The real threat to the nursery of soldiers, to the continued recruitment of hardy peasants loyal to their clan leaders and well-disciplined because they were serving among their friends and neighbours, was the change occurring in the Highlands. Emigration was only the consequence. With change the Highlands would cease to be feudal, and regiments composed of the region's manhood could be "no longer composed of the flower of the peasantry, collected under their natural superiors." As to the argument that emigration carried off labour required for agriculture and manufacture, Selkirk asserted that, paradoxically enough, production had been increased by the exodus of people from the region. In the north of Scotland, the traditional population existed as "intrepid but indolent military retainers," useful only for unskilled labour. While the state was entitled to regulate the loss of skilled labour, he observed, "there is perhaps no precedent of regulations for obviating a deficiency of porters and barrowmen and ditchers." The merchants and manufacturers of Paisley and Glasgow had not instigated emigration restrictions.

A point which Selkirk emphasized was that the same interests which had been responsible for regulatory legislation in 1803 were also producing the changes underlying emigration. It was quite unfair, he argued, to deny the same rights to their tenantry that they themselves were demanding. If public welfare was the issue, why not a restriction on the proprietors as to the disposal of their lands, instead of a brake on the population as to the disposal of their bodies? Selkirk allowed that the exodus could be avoided by returning to the old ways (i.e., feudalism), but if the old ways were not acceptable, then the consequences must be followed to their logical conclusion. Attempting to be sympathetic to the lairds, Selkirk speculated that the landlord's aversion to emigration sprang partly from the unjust criticism levelled against him for improvement. Instead of defending their own actions as just, the proprietors had turned instead to lash out against the emigrants and the promoters who had allegedly deluded them. He then examined the activities of the Royal Highland Society and Parliament regarding emigration regulation. He was extremely sceptical and critical of the published reports of both. But Selkirk reserved the full force of his fury for the legislation itself, the inconsistencies of which he attempted to expose.

Selkirk had carefully read the minutes of the Highland Society, and in *Observations* pointed out that the basis of the legislation—the abuse of the emigrant—was not well documented by either the society or the Select Committee of Parliament that had recommended the Emigration Act. He maintained that the food allowance specified in the legislation bore absolutely no relationship to the normal living standards of the Highlander at home. Moreover, he questioned that legislation would keep the price of passage out of the reach of the average Highlander, for he was not as impoverished as Parliament believed. Selkirk argued instead that the increased cost of passage resulting from the legislation would in most cases be met by emigrants out of the cash reserve that they needed to settle at their destination. "What is to be thought, however," he wrote scathingly, "of the super-abundant humanity of the Highland Society, of which this is all the result—which to save the emigrants from the miserable consequences of being as much crowded on ship-board as the King's troops themselves, and of living there on the same fare as at home, reduces them to land in the colonies in the state of beggars, instead of having a comfortable provision beforehand?" The society, he maintained, represented "one class of men, for whom they appear as advocates at the bar of the public." Such a characterization was not designed to increase his popularity among the Highland lairds.

When Selkirk finished his analysis of the Scottish scene and moved on to that of North America, he offered two related propositions regarding Highland emigration: first, that the presence of Highlanders would help prevent British North America from falling to the Americans; and second, that to take full advantage of what Highlanders offered, the newcomers (like other ethnic groups) should be concentrated in what he called "national Settlements" in order to preserve their language, culture, and manners. In his various colonization activities, Selkirk always attempted to maintain the old culture. But he did not elaborate here on the concept of national settlement, moving quickly on instead to describe his efforts on Prince Edward Island. These were seen as a concrete experimental test of how Highland settlers could best be assisted so as to increase their chances for success in a strange environment. Selkirk concluded, "the experiment that has been detailed, may perhaps be useful as a preparatory step, and serve to point out the principles, on which effectual national measures might be grounded— measures which, if followed up on an extensive scale, while the object is within our reach, might secure to the empire most important advantages."

Selkirk's book was initially greeted most enthusiastically by the reviewers, who unanimously recognized the force of his arguments. The *Critical Review* commented: "we think that he has combated the prejudice and censured the weakness of some leading movers of the late transactions of the Highland Society with considerable success; and that his publication will have a powerful effect in removing such embarrassing and untoward obstacles to the adoption of a just system of policy."[18] The *Scots Magazine,* traditionally hostile to Highland emigration, grudgingly acknowledged that Selkirk "certainly appears to us to be guided by such sound and enlarged views of policy, and has explained these in a manner so clear and forcible, as to leave hardly any room for contesting the important conclusions which it is his object to draw." Moreover, added the reviewer, "of all the persons affected by the present state of things, the

Highland proprietors are certainly the last that have any title to complain, since it is their own work."[19] The *Farmer's Magazine* opined: "We hope that every Highland proprietor will peruse this work; not that we wish it to have the effect of inducing them to drive their tenantry from their estates, but of persuading them to adopt prudent measures in the management of their properties, that the people may have time to prepare, and may leave them without shewing any discontent."[20]

The heartiest applause for *Observations* came from the influential *Edinburgh Review,* which found the question so well-handled that the work merely needed to be summarized at length. This review—published unsigned at the time—is the only one for which we know the author. It was Francis Horner, one of the leading political economists of his day. He concluded his review by observing that political economy must not mistake "as symptoms of decay and devastation, the movements occasioned by the growth of wealth, enterprize, and industry," adding that Selkirk had "contributed a new article, very nearly finished in its form, to the general elements of political administration, and . . . cast light on one of the most intricate parts of the science of oeconomy, that in which the theory of wealth and the theory of population are examined in connexion."[21] In private correspondence, Horner observed that the book was "a valuable piece of descriptive history, as well as political economy," noting that the critics had experienced a "concurrence of opinion" on its importance.[22] Like the other reviewers, however, Horner failed to comment on the experimental rather than speculative nature of Selkirk's work.

A second round of less favourable comment on *Observations* was published in the opening months of 1806. Three full-scale critiques of Selkirk and his book appeared in print, one by Clanranald factor Robert Brown and two by anonymous writers.[23] None of these works dealt with Selkirk's book as political economy. All three responses were characterized by ad hominem arguments, combined with a reiteration of the optimism of improvement and hostility to the overseas empire. Selkirk was accused of romanticizing the culture of indolent Highlanders, of the outsider's ignorance of "true conditions" in the Highlands, and of pecuniary self-interest. All three authors insisted that there was room for even more people in the Highlands, by opening wasteland for cultivation and shifting much of the population to crofting. Maintaining that America was not really a land of opportunity, they advanced the arguments that Highlanders were required at home as soldiers and as labourers in the south. The reviewers were relatively unimpressed with these critiques.[24] If there was a case to be made against Selkirk, these authors had not succeeded in making it.

Selkirk as Political Economist

Despite the obvious attention and approval of political economists excited by *Observations* at the time of its publication, posterity has not followed the lead of the contemporary reviewers in placing Selkirk's book in the canon of early political economy. There are a number of reasons for the failure of the book to continue to be taken seriously. In the first place, the immediate issues addressed by Selkirk rapidly shifted, altered to some considerable extent by the force of his own arguments. The book came to be seen as a tract for the times rather than as a general statement of theoretical principles. This assessment was encouraged by the nature of the subsequent attack upon it and its author by spokesmen for the Highland lairds. More importantly, however, Selkirk failed to pursue his ideas further in print, at least in ways that gave his thinking greater coherence. Selkirk's subsequent publications were occasional and issue-oriented, thus helping to disguise his own emphasis upon the need for system.

Perhaps the critical factors in Selkirk's failure to achieve prominence as a political economist, however, were inherent in the threads he was attempting to combine and reconcile. Methodologically, Selkirk was trying to mix the historical study of society with economic theory and scientific experimentalism. Intellectually, Selkirk was attempting to find some way to moderate the invisible hand he seemingly accepted. At first glance Selkirk appeared to be expounding the standard liberal notions of the Scottish Enlightenment, arguing for freedom from restraint and the encouragement of natural and inevitable processes of change and modernization. But he was not simply another laisser-faire liberal, for he was committed both to appropriate intervention and to its utilization for the preservation of important human values. He recognized that human nature had to be taken into account in the process of modernization, and moreover, that human nature was simply not as adaptable as was the marketplace or the economy. Undoubtedly the most interesting feature of Selkirk's book on emigration was his simultaneous insistence that traditional Highland culture and personal psychology were inimical to modernization, and that the Highlander had a legitimate right to avoid progress if he chose. For Selkirk, the traditional ways of Highland life could in large measure be preserved in land-rich British North America, and he even offered a series of arguments that found strategic advantage for the colonies in the perpetuation of traditional cultures. He was hardly the only contemporary who concerned himself with the human cost of progress, but he was one of the few who accepted the inevitability and even desirability of change at the same time as he sought practical alternatives for the victims. It would appear that few readers of *Observations,* either at the time of its publication or later, recognized Selkirk's ingenious reconciliation of natural progress and traditional rights. In many senses Selkirk was more a pioneer sociologist than political economist, but insufficiently clear (and unfashionable) about what he was doing to impress sociology's historians any more than those in political economy. Nevertheless, if a concern with "social stratification, social conflict, social change, and the social role of the division of labour" are the marks of the "essence of sociological inquiry"—as one historian of sociology has suggested[25]—then for *Observations on the State of the Highlands of Scotland* Selkirk certainly deserves a consideration he does not currently receive.

In 1806 the Fifth Earl of Selkirk was elected to the House of Lords as one of the eighteen representative peers from Scotland. Almost immediately he took the lead in an attempt to reform the political situation of the peerage of Scotland, an effort which resulted in his next publication, *A Letter to the Peers of Scotland by the Earl of Selkirk,* which appeared in 1807. Selkirk's major concern in this pamphlet was to demonstrate the disadvantageous public position of the Scottish peerage. Eighteen peers could serve in the House of Lords, but the remainder were totally shut out of politics because they were not eligible to serve in the House of Commons. The present system, he insisted, excluded many capable men from public life and the pursuit of "honourable ambition." Party voting for representative peers had excluded men of talent in favour of lesser figures. "From such exclusion, my Lords," he warned, "none of us, in the present state of our elections, can flatter himself with being exempt: today the vindictive *ostracism* may fall on the head of our adversaries; to-morrow it may light on our own."[26] Men defeated by party machinations in the Commons could find another seat, but Scottish peers had no alternative, being the only individuals in the Kingdom who "in spite of the most distinguished and acknowledged merit, may be sunk in oblivion and condemned to obscurity." Moreover, Selkirk noted that some peers might find the Commons a preferable theatre for the display of their talents. Whether such service degraded the peerage was surely a matter each peer could judge for himself. Only by enlarging on political opportunity could the Scottish peerage be true to its traditions. "It is no longer the ferocious valour of the feudal chieftain that leads to the highest honours of the state, but the talents of the statesman and the orator. The senate, in short, is now the *arena,* in which individuals have to struggle for personal consequence and distinction."

Despite his eloquent arguments, Selkirk's campaign for peerage reform was not successful. The existing system was too entrenched.

In March 1807, Selkirk had been appointed Lord Lieutenant of Kirkcudbright, a traditionally ceremonial military position which during the years of the Napoleonic Wars actually brought with it responsibilities and authority. The Lords Lieutenant were civilians of importance who were charged with home defence for their counties. They supervised not only the militia within their jurisdiction but also the various volunteer companies organized through local initiative and accepted by the War Office.[27] Kirkcudbright was not a particularly likely target for French invasion, but it had to be prepared. Selkirk did his homework. Instinctively he elaborated a rational system for home defence, which he unveiled in a debate in the House of Lords discussing the government's Militia Transfer Bill, which proposed to raise 44,000 militia men across Britain by use of a ballot. On 10 August 1807 he rose in the House to deliver a long and carefully argued speech on home defence, the text of which was subsequently published as *Substance of the Speech of the Earl of Selkirk, in the House of Lords, Monday, August 10, 1807, on the Defence of the Country*.[28] Selkirk thus weighed in on yet another long-standing controversy, which had reappeared in the Scottish Enlightenment, over the question of standing armies.[29] There was much hostility in Scotland, as in England, to standing armies.[30] As "True Whigs," Selkirk's father and elder brother had always opposed them. On the other hand, from the perspective of the new political economy of Adam Smith, standing armies merely reflected the division of labour of the commercial society and could hardly be avoided.[31]

In his speech Selkirk protested that the proposed bill was insufficient, for French invasion was a distinct possibility and preparedness the only deterrent. "It is not to the Channel that we must look for security," Selkirk proclaimed, "but to the hands of Englishmen fighting for their liberties, for the glory and independence of their country." If there was to be a citizen army, it required a "permanent system." Selkirk called for the creation of a well-trained force of reserves, led by "the principal landed proprietors of the country," insisting that "in the process of time the whole people will have gone through a course of discipline; we shall become, like our enemies, a nation of soldiers; and then England will assuredly be invincible." Particular criticisms of the existing ad hoc arrangements, especially the volunteers with which Selkirk was doubtless familiar as Lord Lieutenant, were accompanied by references to the "valuable speculations of Mr. Malthus," as Selkirk used demography to argue his case. He insisted that calculations from "approved tables of the ordinary duration of human life" demonstrated that Great Britain could put half a million men between the ages of fifteen and twenty-five in arms as part-time soldiers, and could form a second reserve from those between the ages of twenty-five and thirty. He scathingly condemned not only the volunteer system but the existing milita system, arguing that training was effective only "when the men were assembled in quarters at a distance from their homes, and kept in permanent duty under military law."

Selkirk returned to home defence in a revised and expanded version of his speech, which appeared under the title, *On the Necessity of a More Effectual System of National Defence, and the Means of Establishing the Permanent Security of the Kingdom.*[32] In this work he attempted to enlarge upon his earlier proposals for a reserve army, here labelled the "Local Militia," rather "for the purpose of illustrating the general principle, and of showing its practicability, than with any idea of exhibiting a perfect system." Once again he demonstrated his preoccupation with demography by calculating the number of young men who could be involved in his scheme of required national military training, using data first published by Dr. Richard Price. A lengthy series of statistical tables were appended. He wrote favourably of the "internal energy, resulting from that happy connection which subsists between the different orders of society." Going still further, Selkirk insisted that what needed to be imparted to his citizen soldiery was less experience in the use of arms than "habits of strict obedience." He justified his proposal in a variety of ways, including the argument that such military service would "operate in an indirect manner in favour of the whole body of manufacturing labourers, by withdrawing the competition of a large portion of the younger workmen, and throwing the employment that remains into the hands of those who are more advanced in life, and more generally burdened with families." He suggested a separate system for Ireland and explained it in equal detail.

In his conclusions, Selkirk emphasized the importance of universality. Although he obviously was no democrat, insisting as he did on the replication of the "natural order of society" in the command structure of his citizen army, he also recognized that his plan would be totally subverted by "any exemption in favour of the higher ranks of society, or any which can be purchased by pecuniary sacrifices." Moreover, he wrote, "to lay the burden of compulsory service upon the poor, and not upon the rich, would be contrary to the spirit of that constitution which it is our ambition to preserve." The opportunity to employ substitutes had subverted the existing system. Once again, Selkirk was searching for middle ground. In the advocacy of universal military training, Selkirk was, as in so many other matters, "ahead of his time."[33] But as was typical of his work, he wrote less in general terms than as an advocate of a concrete proposal of policy, elaborated in substantial detail. Had he written a book examining the general utility of universal military service instead of one proposing a detailed programme, his ideas might have received more notice, at least from posterity, than they have enjoyed.

After the publication of *National Defence*, Selkirk became increasingly involved in the Hudson's Bay Company and the creation of his colony at Red River, activities which remained his principal concerns for the rest of his life. He published only three more works of general interest, most of his later writings defending his conduct in the Red River business. In 1809 he did produce a brief pamphlet, *A Letter Addressed to John Cartwright, Esq. Chairman of the Committeee at the Crown and Anchor; on the Subject of Parliamentary Reform.*[34] This little piece, which was reprinted several times, took advantage of an invitation to take part in a meeting of the Friends of Parliamentary Reform to repudiate formally the radical principles of his family and his own earlier career. Characteristically, Selkirk broke with radical reform not through a restatement of Burkean principles but because, he said, the situation in America demonstrated that it did not work. Democracy produced only demagoguery. He cited his own experiences in the United States and the "Peter Porcupine" writings of William Cobbett. Alexander Hamilton was not mentioned by name, but Selkirk's diary for 1803-4 indicates how influential that American statesman was in formulating Selkirk's critical views of American democracy.[35]

After the letter to Cartwright, Selkirk published nothing until around 1814, when there appeared a small pamphlet printed by J. Brettell— Selkirk's favourite printer—on Indian education in North America. In its only surviving copy it has no title page, but despite its brevity it has all the earmarks of a Selkirk production. In it the author called for the establishment of a school for young Indians in the Hudson's Bay Company territories. This school, teaching English to serve as "a common medium of communication," must not in its course of instruction over-educate its charges. Its young pupils were to be sent back to their people with all the Native skills of hunting and fishing fully developed, and with additional accomplishments that would be valued. Reading and writing were less important than knowing how to mend a gun. In general, the school should inculcate habits of industry and the advantages of farming. The school could profit from the new monitorial systems of education, demonstrating that its author was familiar with the writings of Joseph Lancaster.

If the pamphlet on Indian education might be attributable to Selkirk, there was no doubt about *A Sketch of the British Fur Trade in North America; with Observations Relative to the North-West Company of Montreal,* published in London early in 1816.[36] Like many of Selkirk's works, it was frequently reprinted in its own time. It was also translated into French and printed in Montreal in 1819. The subject of the fur trade provided Selkirk with a perfect opportunity to cast a political economist's eye on a distinctly North American enterprise. By the time the work was written, however, he was far too embroiled in the fur-trade war with the North West Company to provide any measure of dispassionate analysis. His righteous indignation had been kept under control in *Observations on the State of the Highlands,* but it spilled over in *A Sketch of the British Fur Trade.* As the reviewer in the *Quarterly Review* justly pointed out, the book was less "a history, than a Bill of Indictment against the North-west Company—an angry attack on the provincial administration of justice—and a panegyric on the Hudson's Bay Company."[37] The review was on the whole sympathetic to Selkirk, but it emphasized that he had allowed his benevolence to become sullied through his involvement with an economic struggle in which "almost any species of outrage and aggression" was acceptable. After this work, Selkirk's subsequent written efforts consisted exclusively of narrative attempts to defend his conduct in the fur trade.[38]

On the whole, the image of Selkirk as a man trapped between his benevolence and his economic self-interest is the one that posterity has come to accept. He is usually viewed as a somewhat eccentric (perhaps philanthropic) exponent of emigration and colonization in British North America, who eventually became involved in a tragic fur-trade conflict totally outside his previous experience. Forgotten in this picture is the more scholarly Selkirk, author of a number of books and pamphlets that confronted some of the principal issues of his time from the vantage point of Scottish political economy, attempting to moderate and even reconcile its extreme positions. Had he not become so wrapped up in the Canadian West and in defending his own role in its development, Selkirk might well have blossomed into a major figure in the history of political economy. In any case, he deserves to be remembered in its annals, and to be treated in Canadian history as more than merely a misguided or self-interested colonizer.

THE SWISS AND RED RIVER
1819-1826

NE of the early components of the Red River Settlement was people from Switzerland. Their story has never properly been told, partly because of the nature of the historiography on Red River, and partly because of the fact that their sojourn in the settlement was relatively brief and they did not make a lasting impact on the region. The Swiss settlers are mentioned but briefly in most historical accounts of the early settlement, where they are treated mainly as people ill-suited to be settlers, who experienced great privations, and who departed Red River as soon as possible. Since there are no detailed modern historical accounts of early Red River, it is hardly surprising that the Swiss get little attention. Adding to the problem, much of the evidence for the Swiss involvement is available only in manuscript or in material not readily available in Canada. As is usually the case with early settlement in Canada, however, there is an alternate version of the Swiss story told in contemporary documents and nineteenth-century publications, and also carried forward by the American descendants of the settlers themselves. This story does not acknowledge that the settlers were ill-chosen, but insists that they were certainly badly deceived and ill-used by Lord Selkirk and the colony.[1] Like most settler accounts of Red River, those of the early Swiss are tales of survival against overwhelming obstacles. They have not entered Canadian mythology because their storytellers did not persist in Canada, but rather either returned to Switzerland or moved on to the United States.

The Red River Swiss were not the first of their nation to immigrate to British North America. In 1751 and 1752 large numbers of Swiss were included in an immigration of 2700 souls recruited in Europe and sent to Nova Scotia. These immigrants were composed of 40 percent adult men, 25 percent adult women, and 35 percent children; most of the adults were under the age of forty. The largest single occupational component—well over 60 percent—described themselves as farmers, but there were over fifty other trades and professions represented, including carpenters, surgeons, watchmakers, schoolmasters, and clergymen. Few unskilled labourers appeared on the passenger rolls. The government of Nova Scotia had nothing but trouble with these settlers. They complained from their arrival about conditions at Halifax, and were eventually sent fifty miles west to Merliguish (renamed Lunenburg), where they continued to be turbulent and mutinous for many years.[2] The Selkirk executors obviously did not know of this earlier Swiss history.

Although the Swiss Red River story is a brief one, it is an instructive and significant one in a variety of ways. It demonstrates yet again how difficult it was to establish settlement along the Red River, given the obstacles of climate and geography. It further suggests that the executors of Lord Selkirk did not immediately abandon attempts to strengthen the settlement after his death. The Swiss emigration of 1821 owed little to Selkirk's efforts. It was, nevertheless, a relatively well-planned and expensive effort to nurture Red River. Its almost inevitable failure, however, marked the end of an active role on the part of the Selkirk estate in the affairs of the settlement, and once again demonstrated the difficulty of transplanting Europeans directly to North America.

Two groups of Swiss were active in early Red River. The Swiss first became involved in Red River in 1816, when Lord Selkirk recruited a number of demobilized soldiers from the de Watteville and de Meuron regiments (which had been disbanded in Canada) as settlers for Red River. Selkirk deliberately selected mercenary soldiers as settlers, calculating that they knew how to fight if it were necessary to oppose the machinations of the North West Company. He led nearly 100 of these mercenaries west in 1816, where they captured Fort William and, early in 1817, recaptured Fort Douglas. Although a number of the soldiers left the West at the expiration of their one-year contracts, a number remained in Red River and accepted land grants along what became known as "German Street" (which suggests the linguistic preferences of the soldiers). About fifty de Meurons and a few de Wattevilles remained in the settlement. They were not entirely happy in their new situation, partly because of the difficulties the settlement experienced with grasshoppers and other natural disasters, partly because of the general shortage of almost everything in Red River, partly because of an

A contemporary sketch of "types of Lord Selkirk's settlers in 1822," including at the left a Swiss colonist and his wife and child.

internal power struggle between Captain Frederick Matthey (their leader) and Alexander Macdonell, which the latter won. Most of these soldiers had spent a lifetime as mercenary warriors and had no other profession. They were not experienced farmers and had trouble settling down, not least because of a terrible shortage of eligible women to enable them to marry and begin to raise families.

Organizing a Swiss Emigration

Lord Selkirk himself had begun the process of attempting to find additional German-speakers for the settlement. Females from Switzerland would have been ideal, but he could not simply import unmarried women. In 1819, Selkirk sent Frederick Heurter (who had actually joined the NWC in 1816 but defected to the HBC at Red River later that year and testified against the NWC in the Canadian trials) to Europe to try to recruit a few new settlers. A memorandum to Heurter about terms suggests that Selkirk was hoping to attract settlers to large tracts of land, who would receive favourable terms if they brought servants with them. The memo pointed out that in Red River there was little risk of servants running away from their engagements, more than a bit of hopeful exaggeration.

Heurter arrived in Coblenz on 2 April 1819, and began to explore possibilities. Selkirk also contacted a C. Gehnpfening in Dusseldorf to enquire about German recruits for the settlement. Gehnpfening was initially hopeful about obtaining German workmen, but later informed Selkirk that the German government would only allow people to emigrate who had fulfilled their military obligations. Moreover, Germans were being too well paid to want to leave for America. In ill health, Gehnpfening wrote that he could not be of further service. Heurter himself wrote from Bertrich in August of 1819 that when he had reached Cologne, he discovered hundreds of emigrants had passed him going in the other direction. Most were Swiss heading to Brazil to settle at the expense of the King of Portugal. This major emigration would make recruitment of settlers for Red River difficult, he suspected.

On 4 September 1819, a former de Meuron half-pay captain named Rudolf de May, who had served for many years attached to the British army, wrote to Selkirk from London on the suggestion of Captain Proteus D'Orsonnens, a friend and another of Selkirk's de Meuron officers. A native of Bern, de May offered his services to procure settlers from Switzerland, adding that there was a great surplus of population in the country and the cantonal governments wished to reduce the excess. By this time Selkirk was very ill and planning a journey to the Mediterranean for his health, so the negotiations with de May were taken over by Andrew Colvile. De May offered to deliver at Rotterdam as many settlers of both sexes and every class wanted by Selkirk. In Switzerland there was no opposition to the recruitment of emigrants, de May emphasized, and he thought the Swiss peasantry would make excellent settlers for North America. Colvile and de May met in London in October 1819 and came to an understanding which led de May to return to Bern to begin organizing a recruitment.

Andrew Colvile had a considerable reputation as an astute businessman, but this emigration operation proved well beyond his capacities in a variety of ways. The chief problem, of course, was that Colvile had control of the situation at neither end, but had to rely upon distant agents to fulfill fairly tight deadlines and difficult requirements. Neither Rudolf de May in Europe nor Alexander Macdonell at the settlement were able to meet Colvile's expectations. For his part, Colvile was from the beginning much too sanguine about the possibilities of having things work out. Selkirk's earlier problems with North American colonization ought to have told his brother-in-law that what could go wrong would go wrong. To some extent, Colvile may have misled himself into thinking that the earlier problems in Red River had been caused by the origins of the settlers (from the Highlands of Scotland), the exigencies of the fur-trade war in North America, and perhaps even Selkirk's lack of attention to business detail. Colvile certainly expected the Swiss to be more steady and successful than the Highlanders. Although he began his negotiations with de May before the final resolution of the conflict between the HBC and the NWC, long before the dispatch of the first emigrants in the spring of 1821 Colvile knew that the fur-trade war was over. He was appropriately cautious in his business dealings. None of this made any difference. The emigration venture was from beginning to end a disaster.

In mid-December of 1819, Colvile sent a packet of papers to de May in Switzerland. The package included a power of attorney and descriptions of the country.[3] Selkirk would provide transportation to the settlement and provisions for twenty pounds sterling per adult, no inconsiderable sum in the years after the Napoleonic Wars. Colvile understood this point, but he privately believed that such settlers who could pay their own way would be more successful than the people Selkirk had previously sent. He admitted to de May that he thought the Swiss more likely to be steady than those available in Britain in the wake of the war. Although he was dealing on behalf of Selkirk, Colvile managed to sound as if the HBC was also involved, writing that the Company considered the establishment of a flourishing settlement at the Forks essential to its affairs. He wanted between 160 and 180 settlers at the beginning, with few children under ten, although he held out the promise of further immigration in succeeding years. He described the accommodation in the overseas vessel in some detail. It was fairly sumptuous by contemporary standards, with the principal deck fitted with bed places six feet long and six feet wide, each designed for five adults. A bulkhead would separate men and boys from women and children. He asked de May's advice about appropriate provisioning and an accompanying clergyman. The papers had obviously been discussed at the October meeting of the two men, for before the end of December de May was writing about the papers, which had not arrived. Without them, he insisted, he could not prove that the scheme was anything but "a bubble of my own creation and invention."[4] The papers arrived by Christmas.[5]

De May wrote a detailed letter to Colvile from Bern in mid-January 1820. In it he reported that he had prepared a prospectus of the plan, which he would print locally.[6] He had made some alterations in

Colvile's proposal, he wrote, especially by promising both a house and a barn at Selkirk's expense on each settler's lot. Ominously, he noted that one of the returning de Meuron soldiers, Frederick de Graffenried, was not enthusiastic about the project. De Graffenried had informed de May that there was much dissension at the colony, and the settlers could not get their earlier promises fulfilled. Moreover, there was no wood for building around Fort Douglas, and a better location would be about 100 miles higher up the river, around Pembina, where the climate was better and there was easier access to the buffalo. De Graffenried further insisted that there were few agricultural implements in Red River, and de May quite properly pointed out to Colvile that without proper tools the newcomers could hardly succeed. Moreover, the governor would have to have sterling qualities, wrote de May, for "in these turbulent times the lower classes of every country spurn at authority." The governor would have to treat the settlers with kindness, and especially fulfill every promise made to them. De Graffenried's remarks had made de May more than a bit dubious of success, but the Swiss did not withdraw from the project. Instead, he negotiated with the government of Bern permission to recruit in its jurisdiction. The Bern people had more reservations, he reported to Colvile. The price for land was too high, and it was not clear what would happen to the settlement after Selkirk's death.

In his reply to de May, Andrew Colvile complained about any alteration in the terms he had proposed.[7] He pointed out that he might personally have to fulfill every promise, and insisted that he be consulted about any alterations in what was offered settlers. The settlement was far different from it had been when de Graffenried had been there, Colvile insisted. Tools and tradesmen were now on the scene. Timber could be rafted to the settlement. He thought his governor—who was now Alexander Macdonell —could do the job. Pembina was objectionable on several grounds. Colvile merely observed that it was low ground and flooded every seven to ten years, not bothering to point out that it was probably outside British jurisdiction south of the forty-ninth parallel agreed to as the international boundary in 1818. He warned against making minute promises to the settlers, which would only lead to difficulties. In a subsequent letter, Colvile argued that American land prices were deceiving and that the land when ploughed produced fever and ague, that in Red River it was much healthier.[8]

In his response to Frederick de Graffenried's criticisms of the settlement as reported by Rudolf de May, Andrew Colvile had fallen prey to the disease of the promoter, that is, minimizing and denying difficulties that were in truth real enough. Timber was in short supply at the Forks, as were agricultural implements and people to make or mend them. The government was in disarray, at best, and Colvile's suggestion of rafting timber to Fort Douglas was more difficult to achieve than it sounded on paper. It could be argued on Colvile's behalf that because he had never been to Red River, he was both willing to believe what he had been told by those in charge of the settlement, and prepared to judge obstacles by European rather than by local standards. But both these tendencies were egregious faults for a man who sought to build a successful settlement. Colvile would later attempt to place the blame for the failure of the Swiss colonization upon de May, but the agent's sanguine promises and exaggerations were only encouraged by Colvile himself. Despite his posture of hard-nosed businessman, Colvile had joined his brother-in-law Lord Selkirk in the fantasy business. As for de May, in a letter of 16 February, he backed off the "alterations," although he still argued that they were essential.[9] The good captain added, however, that "the plain common sense of most country people is generally equal to the acuteness and penetration of the most cultivated understanding."[10] In short, the people were understandably sceptical. How de May would deal with their concerns would make or break the project.

Recruiting Settlers in Switzerland

Colvile in early March of 1820 conceded that the settlers could finance part of their payment on credit, although he insisted on Protestants.[11] He would later grumble that he could get all the settlers he wanted in Britain if he did not insist on cash in advance.[12] De May responded in succeeding letters by accepting what he described as "discretionary power," and reported the difficulties he was having in recruiting. Official obstacles still remained, and there was competition from the Portuguese, who were recruiting for Brazil and offering much more generous terms.[13] He reported that the Bern government would assist in the transportation of forty inmates of an "institution which is a medium between a parish work house & a house of correction," and was making this a condition of their support for the entire scheme of emigration. Colvile had hardly wanted to be in the business of transporting paupers and petty criminals, and he ought to have backed off at this point, if not earlier. Instead he accepted forty such immigrants, providing they were "not really criminals."[14] This decision probably put Colvile beyond the point of no return, although both he and de May came to the same conclusion in April of 1820, which was that time was too short, and the emigration should be postponed until 1821. Colvile used the excuse of the death of Selkirk for this decision, although he emphasized that in the long run this would make no difference to his Swiss ventures.[15] For his part, de May emphasized the difficulties in arranging transportation to Rotterdam, and introduced the problem of leases, which he insisted were contrary to the landholding customs of his country. A seigneurial arrangement involving the transfer of land in return for ground rent would be acceptable, but, he cautioned, the word "lease" could not be used in any dealings with the settlers.[16]

The caution about leases was likely in anticipation of objections to the recruiting pamphlet which de May published in French and German in Bern in late spring of 1820.[17] As promotional publications for emigration ventures to new territories went, de May's effort was hardly extreme. He described the positive features of Red River in glowing terms, and either downplayed or conveniently forgot about the negative ones. This was standard strategy for promoters of North American emigration in the early nineteenth century. The rich soil of the prairies, not covered with thick forest, was extremely fertile and well-suited for grain and other crops. There were "boeufs sauvages" literally waiting to be hunted; the lakes and rivers abounded in fish; the settlement was well-supplied with houses and a fortress; conditions for raising Merino sheep were ideal. The climate was moderate and very healthy, with winters neither very cold nor very long. No mention was made of the isolation of the place, nor of the difficulties of getting to it (or away from it).

However utopian the description of Red River sounded, it was seemingly confirmed by the commitments which the Earl of Selkirk was prepared to make to the settlers, to be embodied in a formal contract. Upon payment of ten louis in advance, and another eleven louis to be repaid within four or five years at 5 percent interest, Selkirk promised to transport the potential settlers to Rotterdam and then to Hudson Bay on a ship with sufficient provisions of good quality. At the Bay the settlers would be transported in boats to the colony, where they would be placed in houses already constructed until they could build their own with materials supplied by the settlement. They would be furnished with provisions to supplement food obtained by hunting and fishing; these provisions would only be made available if the settlers had hunted and fished. They would be advanced seed grain and potatoes for planting. They could buy furniture, cooking utensils, and farm equipment on credit at reasonable prices. Each head of family would get 100 arpents of land "en toute propriété et pour toujours pour lui et ses decendans" in return for an annual payment of a moderate and reasonable cens, beginning the second year and gradually rising to fifty bushels by the fifth year. The settler could commute his cens on payment of

500 bushels of wheat. These rentals, it transpired, were well beyond the capacity of the settlers in Red River. Selkirk would sell additional lots of 100 to 500 acres.

The promises in the prospectus published by de May were made without reservations about local conditions or availability. In dealing with its earlier settlers, Red River had already experienced enormous difficulties in measuring up to advertised expectations and in fulfilling promises made to settlers.[18] But earlier promises paled in comparison with those guaranteed to potential Swiss settlers by de May in 1820. These commitments demanded resources at the settlement well beyond the capability of Red River to provide, although in fairness to Captain de May, Andrew Colvile had assured him that the resources were in place. Moreover, although Colvile complained about a lack of precision in the printed prospectus, he wrote de May that the only material error the pamphlet contained was the promise to enclose the lands. At this point he was prepared to stand by the prospectus minus the enclosure promise.[19] Colvile might well have to back up the prospectus, because, according to de May, the people he was dealing with in Baden insisted on guarantees of the printed promises.[20]

The promises of the prospectus were supposed to be condensed by de May into a single-paged, printed document, to be signed by both parties. A copy of what appears to be this agreement survives in the Bulger Papers at the National Archives of Canada. The commitment of Selkirk in this agreement is slightly different from that in the prospectus in one important respect. Settlers were now allowed to choose their lands wherever they wished.[21] The real difference between the agreement and the prospectus, however, was in the statement of the obligations of the settlers. The prospectus had not mentioned obligations. But the printed document made clear that as well as financial commitments, the settlers promised to "behave as quiet, thoughtful, peaceful and honest citizens." They engaged not to become involved in the fur trade; to help maintain the roads and highways of the settlement; to contribute six days' labour per year for the upkeep of a minister and a schoolmaster; to become part of any defence of the country against enemies within and without; and in future to open their homes to new settlers until they could build their own dwellings. These responsibilities showed the fine hand of Andrew Colvile, who obviously felt he had learned much about emigration from the earlier Scots ventures in Red River.

Over the summer of 1820, de May reported that he had engaged a Mr. de Salis as an observer who would accompany the emigrants and report back to the Swiss government on their treatment and progress. De Salis had not come cheaply. He insisted on a free passage, a berth in the gentleman's cabin and feeding at the captain's table, as well as £100 to be paid when the settlers were assembled.[22] Colvile grumbled about the terms with de Salis, but agreed that his participation was absolutely essential in order to persuade both governments and prospective future emigrants that the scheme was working properly.[23] He obviously had continued great faith in the success of the venture. In the autumn of that year the exchange of correspondence between Colvile and de May heated up considerably. There was considerable remanoeuvring for position between the two men. De May continued to insist on concessions for the amount of cash to be paid in advance by the emigrants, insisting that "these good and honest people will most faithfully repay their debts."[24] For his part, Colvile had backed off earlier statements about wanting up to 500 settlers, and was insisting on no more than 200 for the first year.[25] De May complained about the reduction in numbers, but had to admit that he had only 100 actually committed on paper. His concern was for those who were already selling their property in preparation for the journey, but who had not yet formally signed the agreement.[26] Ever the businessman, Colvile responded, "I am not to be told that every man who offers is to be taken or that *any* family is to be taken until an actual agreement is made with them until this is done there is no obligation on either side and I trust you will not engage more than I have already named without my concurrence."[27]

On 19 January 1821, Colvile wrote a letter to one F. Riser in Bern, obviously in response to a letter he had received from this correspondent. He had instructed de May, wrote Colvile, "to keep strict faith with the people who are engaged to go to Red River—and to make no promises which cannot or are not intended to be fulfilled." At the same time, he could not be held responsible for private bargains between de May and the settlers.[28] In a letter that same day to de May, Colvile wrote that he had received a complaint from a person in Bern that de May was demanding an additional louis on top of the contracted terms. This would destroy the plan, and shook his confidence in de May as his agent. He never intended that the authority he gave de May should include "raising a capitation tax on the people who engaged to migrate to Red River."[29] It is hard to know how to explain the tone of this letter to de May. One interpretation would be that Colvile had long harboured suspicions of his agent's duplicitous behaviour, which he had now found to be true. Alternatively, he wrote undiplomatically without thinking about the consequences, for it was true that he chastised de May without confirming the accuracy of the Riser charges.

De May's response to the letter of 19 January was one of wounded indignation. He would have thought that Colvile would hear both sides before pronouncing judgment and that personal character would count for something, he wrote. He admitted to charging the fee but justified it as necessary, given his constantly escalating costs, all the time complaining about Colvile's having given credence to "the accusation of an unknown, and without waiting for an explanation on my side." De May admitted that he should have informed Colvile earlier about the extra charge, but insisted it was necessary to cover expenses.[30] In any case, whatever mutual confidence and trust had existed between Colvile and de May was now shattered. Colvile had caught de May in, at the very least, keeping secret part of the arrangements he was negotiating with the emigrants, while de May felt that Colvile ought not to have responded so judgmentally without hearing his explanations. Once again there was an opportunity to call off the emigration, but neither man chose to take it. Instead, this question continued to surface in the correspondence, especially on the part of de May. For his part, Colvile wrote that he accepted de May's explanation, but still thought the head tax objectionable "on principle." Colvile also reiterated what was for him a standard line: "the difficulty arose in great measure from your undertaking the business without knowing precisely the difficulties which were to be encountered."[31] The two men agreed not to engage settlers beyond 1821 until they had a clearer idea of the expenses of the venture, and also concurred that there was no need to send either a schoolmaster or a clergyman with the first contingent.

On 24 February 1821, Andrew Colvile wrote to his governor in Red River, Alexander Macdonell, announcing that 250 to 260 settlers, mostly from Switzerland, would arrive in Hudson Bay in the autumn, and would require transportation to Red River. They would have to be brought to the settlement and at least partly provisioned over the winter. He trusted that a good many 100-acre lots had been laid out with proper boundary posts.[32] This extraordinary letter was the first definite word the settlement had been sent of the arrival of a substantial number of new settlers, who would have to be transported, fed, housed, and provided with land. Even were the letter to be sent to Montreal rather than to the Bay and thence across the continent by express canoe, it could not have arrived in Red River much before August of 1821. More likely, it would be first read by Macdonell when he received his mail at York Factory in September of 1821 off the same ship that was bringing the emigrants. Under such circumstances, it was unlikely that proper preparations for the arrival of the Swiss could possibly have been made.

The fallout from the head tax continued through the spring of 1821. In March, de May wrote Colvile that in Neuchatel a meeting of settlers had been held, at which a letter purportedly from Colvile had been read. It stated that the settlers need pay nothing down and that all the cash upfront which de May was demanding was improper.[33] De May followed this letter with another enclosing two abusive letters from the Neuchatel meeting, both insisting that the agent honour the commitments which Colvile had made in personal correspondence to one of the settlers, presumably Riser, of a cash down payment of only one pound per head.[34] Colvile was forced to supply a copy of the letter he had sent to Riser, subsequently adding that either the Neuchatel people had misunderstood or were merely looking for an excuse to get out of their engagements.[35] In still another letter, Colvile insisted that the trouble was not the letter to Riser, but the extra louis demanded by de May. In any event, he was becoming concerned about the "unlooked for difficulties."[36] But the ship had been chartered and would sail for Rotterdam on 1 May.[37]

Despite the "difficulties," Rudolf de May carried on. The people used the charge of the extra louis, which de May had told them they need not pay, as an excuse for paying nothing. Some prospective emigrants complained that the down payment was not filled in the contract, but he refused to do so until they paid it. Some planned to write again, and he hoped Colvile would answer differently, seizing "this opportunity to repair the errors you have committed in your first letter to them." He still thought that only the good-for-nothings would be lost and he could still fill the ship.[38] De May was disappointed to learn that the Dutch government would not waive customs duties for the settlers on their way to Rotterdam, and requested Colvile to arrange matters with a substantial local merchant house; Colvile did so. De May reported that he was building two large boats, seventy feet long by fourteen feet wide, to convey the settlers; the boats would be sold at the end.[39] He also contracted for provisions from Switzerland to Rotterdam at the rate per day of one pound of bread, eight ounces of meat, two pounds of potatoes, three ounces of flour, one-half ounce butter, and one-third ounce salt.[40]

Meanwhile, Andrew Colvile was dealing with questions from Swiss officialdom about the emigration.[41] The difficulties continued to mount. More prospective settlers drew back in the fallout from the dispute over the head tax and the amount of the down payment. De

May told Colvile any losses experienced "must be attributed entirely to the unfortunate letter you have wrote to these people." The prospective observer, Mr. de Salis, was let go because of questions about his character, and he was threatening a lawsuit.[42] A Mr. "Huser" (Walter von Hauser von Clarus) was appointed instead. De May wanted to pay both men to avoid trouble.[43] The Swiss agent saw all the extra expenses as a further justification for the head tax, claiming he would lose money over the emigration.

The Departure for Red River

To everyone's surprise, the journey down the Rhine to Rotterdam went extremely smoothly. De May left Bern for Basel in early May 1821, and subsequently left Basel with 169 settlers bound for Holland. Most of the Neuchatel people did not go in the end. Despite disappointment with the final numbers, de May wrote Colvile that "a better chosen & better composed party of Settlers never left Europe for America."[44] On 23 May, de May arrived at Rotterdam with two boats carrying 172 persons, including 64 adult males and 44 adult females. William Todd, the surgeon appointed by Colvile to accompany the passengers to Hudson Bay, complained to Colvile that their chests were much too large to be transported from the Bay to Red River. Todd suspected that the chests were full of extra clothing.[45] The *Berner Wochenblatt* on 30 June 1821 published a letter from the emigrants reporting their safe arrival at Rotterdam and the good quality of their provisions for the journey. It also offered thanks to Captain de May, who "has told us many good and lively things about our new fatherland, so it seems that the achievement of our undertaking cannot be doubted."[46]

The fourteen-week voyage across the Atlantic in the *Lord Wellington* also went without serious mishap, quite in contrast to several of the earlier ones carrying Highland Scots to Red River. According to a later account published in Switzerland by one of the settlers, Rodolph Wyss, bad water on shipboard was the biggest problem with the provisions. The bad water was a severe hardship, he wrote, for Swiss accustomed to "pure spring water." The ship, now joined by two other HBC ships, became stuck in ice off the entrance to Hudson Strait, enabling the passengers to trade with the "Eskimos" and hunt for polar bears. One Swiss girl fell into the icy water, but was retrieved without long-term ill effects. The passengers on the ice-bound vessels were able to visit each other via the ice, and held several dances on it. The Swiss were joined in these amusements by young Scots from the other ships. Two children were born and two died (one of them newborn) on the voyage. The ship carrying the emigrants was rammed by another vessel after passing through the Hudson Strait, and limped into York Factory with its pumps running continually.[47]

On 5 September 1821, George Simpson wrote from York Factory to Andrew Colvile that the Swiss had arrived. He was impressed with "Mr. Dehouser" but not with the settlers, Simpson reported. "The present batch has been most injudiciously selected, men of bad character some taken out of Jails and others out of Work & Mad houses; instead of useful hardy agriculturalists they are of all ages and unaccustomed to labourers work being chiefly Watch makers Jewellers pedlers &c &c. Your Agent Capt'n [de] May has certainly not done his duty conscientiously; I do not know how he is paid but conceive from the rabble he has sent out that it must be by head, many without looking to their abilities habits or morals."[48] This assessment—and its criticism of Captain de May—is undoubtedly the most frequently quoted comment on the Swiss who arrived in Red River. As Simpson subsequently acknowledged in a later letter not usually cited, however, his initial impressions had been unwarranted, and most of the Swiss settlers were really quite responsible people. Perhaps de May had not done that bad a job. Later observations by residents of Red River that the Swiss were "generally intelligent and well-to-do persons, some of them possessed of considerable means," were probably as accurate as Simpson's initial assessment.[49]

In the Bulger Papers at the National Archives of Canada is a document dated 31 July 1822 and entitled "The State of the Swiss Colonists at Red River." It was probably prepared by Walter von Hauser, who had spent a year with these people observing their progress. According to his name-by-name assessment, all but fourteen of the settlers were of the Reformed Church (there were six Catholics, two Lutherans, and six unspecified). Nearly half of the male heads of families were over the age of forty, and one-third were over the age of fifty. Men of this age, particularly if normally engaged in sedentary occupations, would not fare well in the rough life of Red River. The party contained only nine farmers and two vine growers. Apart from these agriculturalists, who represented just over one-quarter of those for whom occupations were listed, there were twenty-one other trades represented. The percentage of individuals who farmed was thus consider- ably lower than in the 1751-52 immigration to Nova Scotia, although the range of non-agricultural skills and trades was similar. Six settlers were indeed clockmakers, but the remainder included a variety of individuals, most of whose skills would be useful to a new colony, including a joiner, a master carpenter, a locksmith, a nailmaker, a physician, a midwife, three weavers, and a schoolmaster. The problem with the party does not appear to have been in the occupational mix. On the other hand, Walter von Hauser was not much impressed with the character and morals of many of his fellow passengers, although we do not know on what basis his assessments were made. In any event, he described thirty-three (40 percent) of the adults as bad or worthless, twenty-seven (33 percent) as fair, and twenty (24 percent) as good or very honest. One passenger was described as crazy and another as simple-minded. All but one of the clockmakers—not watchmakers, it would appear—were of bad character. In short, von Hauser was favourably disposed to less than 60 percent of the passengers on grounds of character and morals.

Simpson was doubtless led to his early assessment of the overall nature of the emigrants by a handful of troublemakers, whose vices were almost immediately apparent. One had tried to stab von Hauser and was sent out of the country, while another died of drink the day after he had landed. Simpson reported that Nicholas Garry, an HBC governor who was present at York Factory, was fluent in German and was able to read the printed prospectus. That document, insisted Simpson, was "rather highly coloured and leads them to expect more than can be realized in the present state of the Colony. I take the liberty of mentioning this as it may be the ground of future complaint." That there would exist a discrepancy between what the Swiss had been led to expect in Red River and what they found was, of course, a bit of an understatement. Even Walter von Hauser was disappointed. In his letter from York Factory of 1821, Alexander Macdonell pointedly commented about the "strange Gentlemen . . . thrown upon us . . . who are in the habit of living well and obliged to put up with our Country & not pleased, I am told this foreign Gentleman from Switzerland even did not consider York Factory very good in the eating & drinking way."[50] In the event, virtually none of the promises made to these settlers were ever fulfilled.

Rodolph Wyss recounted in some detail the tale of the journey from York Factory to Red River. By local standards it was a relatively normal and uneventful one, although for Europeans unfamiliar with the hardships of the region it seemed harsh and frightening. One adult male and two children died before the party arrived at Lake Winnipeg. The Red River people wrote Andrew Colvile that the settlers had far too much baggage, most of which had to be left at York Factory.[51] Wyss reported that the settlers had to endure 300 hours of upstream travel in small boats, the men frequently dragging the boats with ropes from the shore. When the dragging was done, the rowing—as in galleys, Wyss observed—began. The boats often had to be carried between navigable waterways. Halfway through the journey, the snow began. The HBC postmaster at the head of the lake was not very helpful with provisions, claiming that he was short himself. He gave the settlers enough barley and fish for four days, although it took them eighteen to cross Lake Winnipeg, just ahead of freeze-up.

Arrival at Fort Douglas brought little improvement for the newcomers. They were greeted with cannon and each was given a glass of rum, but then they were informed that the grasshoppers had destroyed the crops and food was in short supply. From the beginning, the Swiss arrivals told the Red River authorities that they could not remain under such conditions. According to Wyss, the de Meurons took in many of their fellow countrymen and shared what little they had. Wyss thought much of their interest was in marriage with the young women in the party, and within a week nine young women had become engaged. Over the winter of 1821-22, fifteen marriages of Swiss women to men of the settlement were celebrated.[52] Governor Alexander Macdonell reported the arrival of the settlers to Andrew Colvile by remarking that the newcomers were very inadequately clothed for the winter. He added that the newcomers "are the greatest eaters I have ever seen." Some of the young Swiss were put to work fulling buffalo wool, and others were put into service.[53] Most of the Swiss wintered at Pembina.

George Simpson subsequently wrote that the winter of 1821-22 was an unpleasant one for the settlement. The buffalo virtually disappeared, and food was in very short supply. Even Simpson admitted that how the Swiss had managed the winter and spring was "inexplicable."[54] According to a paper found at Red River, provisions dispensed to thirty-two heads of families over the winter of 1821-22 consisted of 17,789 pounds of fresh meat, 5,350 pounds of dried meat, 12 pounds of tongue, 151 pounds of potatoes, 55 pounds of wheat, 71 pounds of barley, and 120 of fish.[55] Rodolph Wyss acknowledged that meat was distributed regularly until shortly after New Year's, but then became in short supply because of the movement of the buffalo well away from the fort. On 26 February 1822, a paper was signed by fourteen Swiss and transmitted to Governor Macdonell. It complained about ill treatment, insisting that the houses were in ruins, and that the people were treated like slaves, being largely confined to the fort.[56] A few of these settlers attempted to leave Pembina over the winter, and according to Rodolph Wyss experienced great hardships after getting lost on the prairies.

In December of 1821, Andrew Colvile wrote to Rudolf de May from

London. He reported that the emigrants had arrived safely and were on their way to Red River. He enclosed a letter from Walter von Hauser. "It appears that the people were not a good selection," he added, "few of them being adapted for a new Colony." Colvile doubted that this lot of arrivals would encourage more to come, and he had thus determined to wait for Mr. von Hauser's final return and report before resuming the project. He complained about de May's financial dealings and concluded, "In point of fact I am in advance this transaction near 2,000 pounds besides the expense that must be incurred for these people after their arrival at York Factory, and after all I fear I have got some pretty indifferent people for the Colony."[57] A few days later, Colvile wrote to Captain Proteus D'Orsonnens at Freibourg that he doubted the Swiss authorities were interested in any emigrations except those that exported paupers.[58] That same day, de May wrote to Colvile from Bern. He had no idea of the difficulties of getting to Hudson Bay until he read von Hauser's report, he began. As for the selection of the people, all had good recommendations, and they seemed an orderly lot on the journey down the Rhine. Some were probably soured by the length and difficulty of their voyage, he argued. Except for three or four watchmakers—not clockmakers—of the better sort, the entire party was composed of cultivators, he insisted. In any event, the contingent was as good as he could get under the circumstances.[59]

A further correspondence between de May and Colvile ensued, beginning by arguing over financial matters and moving to responsibility for the debacle.[60] Andrew Colvile insisted that he had never seen de May's prospectus, which he heard had given too favourable a colouring on many points. He maintained that he had always wanted nothing said which was not correct, and had never described Fort Douglas as a fort in the European sense.[61] De May responded that he had written of the climate, the beauty and resources of the country, and its fertility on the advice of Captain Matthey. He was not to know, he protested, that the fort, the houses, and the mills were not completed. He had not only told the emigrants that they would receive tools and household implements at the settlement, but had written this into the printed agreement which Colvile had approved. In this exchange, Rudolf de May definitely had the better case. Colvile had accepted the printed agreement. De May added, quite correctly, that the real problem was lack of proper administration in the settlement, and no promises could ever be honoured if orders could be given and not executed.[62]

The Discontent of the Swiss Settlers

While Andrew Colvile would probably never have acknowledged the point to Rudolf de May, by 1822 he had recognized full well the administrative problems at Red River. All the evidence had been available for years, and the wonder is that he had pushed ahead with the Swiss emigration in 1821 in the face of it. In any event, Governor Alexander Macdonell was relieved of his duties in the spring of 1822. By the summer of that year, ex-soldier Andrew Bulger had arrived as head of the settlement, accompanied by John Halkett as representative of the Selkirk executors.[63] Within a few weeks Bulger was describing his "life of slavery and exposure to the insults and threats of some of the most worthless of God's creatures, in one of the most miserable countries on the face of the earth."[64]

Part of Bulger's responsibility was dealing with the mess surrounding the arrival of the Swiss settlers, and on 4 August 1822 he wrote a report to Colvile which included a lengthy discussion of their situation. He and Halkett had examined the printed prospectus, and it was clear to them that "these wretched people have not been fairly dealt with," he wrote. The country was certainly not as represented. Moreover, Bulger had also seen correspondence between one of the settlers and Captain de May, which suggested the agent's chief concern was for all the money he could obtain. Certainly de May promised support to these people "which Mr. Macdonell had no means of fulfilling," argued Bulger, who doubtless did not realize that Andrew Colvile had himself approved those commitments.[65] Not surprisingly, the settlers had petitioned Mr. Halkett to be assisted to leave Red River.[66] Given their debt to the Selkirk estate, this was impossible, Bulger observed, but their contracted indebtedness was abated. He and Halkett had been unable to fulfill their other demands for cattle, but he hoped soon to do something about the baggage left at York Factory, as well as about land allotments, which by their contracts they could choose where they think proper. John Halkett had told them that if they were dissatisfied, they were at liberty to leave the settlement, obviously willing for the estate to cut its losses. Bulger forwarded to Colvile a thick wad of documents on the Swiss emigration, copies of some of which ended up in his papers. In any case, it was clear that in the summer of 1822, the Swiss settlers were nowhere near receiving what had been promised them.[67] Their letters home apparently reflected their discontent and despair.[68]

While Andrew Colvile and Captain de May continued to correspond over the winter of 1822-23 about past finances and future emigrations from Switzerland, Colvile had no serious intention of resuming the project. Indeed, he and George Simpson had already decided to end European migration to the settlement and find new settlers among fur traders and their families made redundant by the merger of the Hudson's Bay Company and the North West Company. This decision was undoubtedly taken in large measure because of the Swiss debacle, which had cost thousands of pounds and clearly had provided only a legacy of discontent and hatred among the settlers. In the settlement itself Andrew Bulger found it necessary to investigate efforts by the Swiss settlers to depart Red River. To finance their departure, the settlers began selling the cows they had recently been given by Bulger. The Swiss intended to walk away from their substantial debts to the Selkirk estate. On 10 February 1823, David Louis DesCombe testified before Bulger and witnesses on why he sought to leave the settlement: "The promises made to us in Switzerland have not been fulfilled. We were not nourished the first year, as was promised. Our Baggage was left at the Sea, and even this Year the greatest part of it was left there also. We gave almost all we had last Winter for Provisions, and we suffered much misery. This Country is not what the Prospectus stated that it was. The winters are too long. We can never become farmers here. We cannot live here. We are not hunters, to obtain a little meat we run the risk of being killed by the Indians, or of being Frozen." DesCombe had been a tenant farmer in Switzerland who had paid forty-four louis d'ors over the past winter for provisions. He was forty-three, with three children. He did not know exactly where his family would go. "We have everything to dread—we may die on the road, or be drowned or killed by the Savages," he confessed, "but we cannot remain here."[69] That same day, John Dubach was also examined. He concurred that he could not continue. The land was good but the vegetables froze. He was "not accustomed to that way of life," he added. He had paid Rudolf de May nearly fifty pounds for nothing but broken promises.[70] Andrew Bulger decided to do nothing, and the Swiss who so desired were quietly permitted to depart.

By the summer of 1823, the authorities of Red River, led by George Simpson, regarded both the de Meuron and Swiss residents as a discontented time bomb only waiting to go off. Conditions did not improve. According to Rodolph Wyss, the houses of the settlers were of wood, daubed with mud and clay. Only a few had wooden floors and most lacked glass for windows. In the summer of 1823 heavy rains soaked almost all of the houses so that many had to be abandoned. Not one sawmill was yet in operation. Wyss insisted that those in charge of the settlement put Selkirk's money in their own pockets while sending glowing reports on progress to the executors. The Swiss had no clergyman and could not understand enough English to attend services at the fort; some converted to Catholicism. The promise of a clergyman was yet another promise broken, of course. Swiss settlers constantly trickled away from the settlement in small numbers for the United States. In 1824, Wyss and others, having paid for the cost of passage back to Europe, left Red River for York Factory. In London, Wyss visited the Swiss consul who had earlier corresponded with Andrew Colvile, and pleaded for government assistance for his colleagues still in North America.

The final straw for the disappointed Swiss came in 1826. The winter of 1825-26 had been another difficult one, food was again in short supply, and there were constant rumours of armed rebellion by the Swiss and the de Meurons.[71] Then came a new menace. The local rivers flooded and washed away everyone's houses. In the wake of this disaster, about 250 Swiss and de Meurons decided to leave the settlement forever. Governor Simpson provided no opposition, having always regarded their discontent as unsatisfiable and their role as one of troublemaker. Most of these Swiss ended up eventually in St. Louis, Missouri, although some settled first near Darlington, Wisconsin.[72] Only one or two people of Swiss origin remained in the settlement as remnants of this initially optimistic emigration venture. For most of the residents of Red River, as for many of the settlement's subsequent historians, the Swiss sojourn on the banks of the Red and Assiniboine rivers was virtually forgotten. The only Swiss settler occasionally remembered by name in Canada is Peter Rindisbacher, the artist.[73]

Assigning responsibility for the failure of the Swiss emigration to Red River is no easy matter. Virtually all those involved must bear a share of the blame. Andrew Colvile should have known better than to think that in 1821 the settlement could support or supply such an influx of people. Rudolf de May should have been less glowing in his descriptions of Red River, and done a better job of securing responsible emigrants. The emigrants themselves should have had less exalted expectations of what they would find in British North America. The authorities in Red River, while not initially responsible for the broken promises to the Swiss, should have been able to do a better job of putting the settlement back on its feet in the early 1820s and fulfilling their needs. As a case study in what could go wrong with an early, well-financed settlement venture to the Canadian prairies, the story of the Swiss and Red River is hard to beat.

EARLY FLOODING IN RED RIVER
1776-1861

T HE Red River Valley had both many attractions and many disadvantages for European settlement. The soil was rich and fertile. It did not have to be cleared of very many trees, thus avoiding a major expense of settlement in much of eastern Canada. But the region had one drawback even more unpredictable and possibly more catastrophic than its capricious climate and its invasion by insect pests such as grasshoppers. Located on a flood plain, it had an enormously high potential for serious springtime flooding. Undoubtedly, recurrent floods occurred during its habitation by Native peoples before the arrival of Europeans in substantial numbers—the flood of 1776 was of vast proportions and part of the oral tradition of the region—but the Aboriginals did not attempt to live year-round at river's edge.[1]

Not until a permanent colony had settled on the banks of the Red and Assiniboine rivers in the early years of the nineteenth century did the flooding of the river valleys become recognized as one of the natural hazards of life.[2] In October of 1811, Governor Miles Macdonell reported to Lord Selkirk that an extraordinary inundation of water on the south branch of the Red River had occurred in the spring of that year. The river had overflowed its banks for four miles on either side.[3] Selkirk's response was to write, "the flood of the Red River is a serious consideration, notwithstanding the rarity of the occurrence. I had imagined the upper banks to be quite out of the reach of the water."[4] He suggested that the settlement might be better placed at or near the mouth of the Dauphin River, insisting that being on the Red River "does not appear to be essential." This location was never further pursued because events pressed in too quickly on Macdonell. Had the settlement been differently located, however, much trouble could have been avoided, both from the North West Company and from flooding. Because of the unpredictability of the occurrence, a major flood automatically became a disaster of substantial proportion. The three greatest floods in Manitoba which have left historical records behind all occurred in the nineteenth century between 1826 and 1861. This concentration of high water, really before the region had been fully settled, tended to recede into the back of the minds of those who came after 1870.

The Flood of 1826

The first devastating flood in the post-settlement Red River basin came in 1826, occurring as the culmination of a series of man-made and natural disasters that had plagued Lord Selkirk's infant colony since its establishment in 1812. The fur-trade war between the Hudson's Bay Company and the North West Company had resulted in the virtual destruction of the colony in 1815 by bois-brûlés and the subsequent bloody incident at Seven Oaks in 1816.[5] Lord Selkirk himself visited the settlement in 1817 to supervise the orderly restoration of the Highland settlers and the establishment on the land of the discharged mercenaries, mainly Swiss from the de Meuron regiment, whom he had brought west with him in 1816.[6] In 1818 and 1819 the crops were overrun by locusts (or grasshoppers), and not until 1820, the year of Selkirk's death in France, was a normal harvest gathered. The merger in 1821 of the two warring fur-trading companies, made possible by the exhaustion of both sides and the convenient demise of Selkirk—whose offended sense of honour made compromise difficult, if not impossible—signalled a new era for Red River. Andrew Colvile wrote with satisfaction to a correspondent on Prince Edward Island: "I am convinced it was the only means by which the peace of these countries could be preserved or an end put to the waste or property & all the mischiefs of a contest & considering that the Colonial Office was hostile to us & that the N.W. Co. in fact yield up the power to the HBC, I think it is a very good finish to a very troublesome business."[7]

Even before the formal union of the companies, a process of population drifting to the banks of the Red and the Assiniboine had begun, as Métis freemen, retired European fur traders and their mixed-blood families, and an occasional French Canadian joined the Highland Scots and European soldiers originally recruited by Selkirk. Roman Catholic missionaries had arrived in 1818, and an Anglican missionary in 1820. Churches and schools were founded. By 1821 there were 221 Scots, 65 de Meurons, and 133

Canadians scattered along the banks of the forks of the Red and Assiniboine, with 500 Métis concentrated around Pembina. By the spring of 1822, there were 126 houses and 160 garden plots.[8] After Selkirk's death, executors on behalf of the earl's minor heir administered the colony separately from the HBC. The chief trustee was Andrew Wedderburn-Colvile, Selkirk's brother-in-law and long-time business associate, who also dominated the management of the HBC. George Simpson was Wedderburn-Colvile's man in western Canada.

Over the 1820s, Simpson came increasingly to run the colony and the fur trade in tandem, as integrated rather than separate entities.[9] He quickly recognized that many of the redundant employees of the newly amalgamated trading rivals would have no place to go without abandoning their Native families. He encouraged those people he "retired" as part of the rationalization of manpower to accept land in the colony. Simpson also appreciated that the buffalo hunters must be controlled. Through Cuthbert Grant the process began of attracting the Métis north of the 49th parallel into some form of semi-sedentary existence on the river lots originally laid out by Selkirk.[10] Swiss settlers, recruited as part of the earl's attempt to increase population, arrived in 1821 after his death.[11] They proved a considerable problem. For the most part inexperienced farmers, they complained a good deal (often with considerable justification) about conditions and treatment, particularly when the Selkirk estate cut back on credit and ceased assistance to the newcomers.[12] Both to save money and to reduce problems of adjustment to prairie conditions, Simpson recommended to the Selkirk estate that recruitment of European immigrants effectively cease.[13] A small wilderness settlement, after all, needed only so many watchmakers. The colony would be peopled from the West itself, not from abroad. This policy was finalized in a sense by the flood of 1826.

Years of tribulation appeared finally to be ending in 1825. John Pritchard could boast of "a line of well built houses" from the White Horse Plain to Netley Creek, of "an abundance of domestic cattle," and "a prospect of wheat exceeding anything heretofore produced in this Country."[14] But the winter of 1825-26 was an exceptionally hard one, providing most of the classic climatic conditions for a flood. It was, recalled Alexander Ross, "unusually severe, having begun earlier and continued later than usual. The snow averaged three feet deep and in the woods from four to five feet. The cold was intense, being often 45 degrees below zero; the ice measured five feet seven inches in thickness."[15] Catholic bishop Provencher noted that the ice did not break until 5 May. It was until late April "as strong as in January."[16] The previous September and October had been unusually rainy. By the end of October, noted Donald Gunn, "not only the rivers but even the great lakes assumed their winter covering." The great depths of snow, Gunn added, made hunting difficult, particularly on horseback. A great December snowstorm "such as had rarely seen in these parts" drove "the buffalo before it beyond the reach of the hunters and killed a great many of their horses."[17] The result, reported Bishop Provencher, was a winter famine at the settlement which caused much suffering. Many settlers were eating their dogs and horses.

Despite the severity of the winter, the leaders of the colony were feeling extremely optimistic in early 1826. Donald McKenzie, the Company's chief factor at Fort Garry, wrote to Andrew Wedderburn-Colvile on 6 February that the settlement was finally prosperous and tranquil. A new grain mill had been put into operation and 1,600 bushels of wheat were in store for Norway House.[18] George Simpson was even more enthusiastic in a report entitled "Red River Colony" penned on 10 February.[19] In it he argued that flax culture and livestock rearing were the most profitable aspects of agriculture for the settlement. He projected a scheme for supplying livestock to the Company in which the profits "may in my humble opinion be made even to surpass the Fur Trade in value." Such enthusiasm was considerably dampened (pardon the pun) by the developments of the spring of 1826.

The settlers did not share in the Company optimism. By early April, there were many rumours of plots involving the Métis, Canadians, and Swiss settlers, especially the de Meurons. Some planned to sack Fort Garry, others to attack the rich in Kildonan.[20] The HBC offered grain to those who kept the peace, and insisted that the Catholic clergy keep its people quiet. Whether these efforts would be enough was not clear, but the coming of the flood ended all thoughts of mob action. Thawing came suddenly at the end of April, ice jams occurred, and rain fell heavily. By 3 May the water was overflowing the banks of the Red, and during the next twenty-four hours rose five feet at the Forks. The water was still held in restraint by the ice, however, until the ice gave way suddenly about 2 P.M. on 5 May "with an awful rush, carrying away cattle, houses, trees and everything else that came in its way."[21] Forty-seven dwelling houses were carried away in the first half-hour by the tidal wave. Others soon followed. Only at the last moment were perishable goods and property taken to higher ground, or placed in scaffolding in the trees along the banks. John Pritchard wrote to his brother, "when the ice broke up in our neighbourhood, it was late in the evening. The night was dark and stormy accompanied with rain. The flood at once rose higher than ever known by man. The crashing of immense masses of ice was loud as thunder; neither the tallest poplar nor the stoutest oak could resist its impetuosity. They were mowed down like grass before the scythe."[22] According to Francis Heron, clerk of the HBC at Fort Garry and keeper of a journal which is our best source for the 1826 devastation, even before the valuables could be fully removed by the inhabitants, "their houses and part of their furniture, were swept off before their eyes by the icy deluge. The havoc was terrible." On 7 May the ice in the Assiniboine broke up. The sudden discharge of vast quantities of water made the preservation of property virtually impossible. People were happy to have escaped with their lives. The breakups of ice in 1826 produced sudden inundations of tidal-wave proportions rather than the gradual advance of water normally characteristic of Red River flooding. Donald Gunn wrote that "the water rose so suddenly that, in some cases, its rushing into the houses roused the inmates from their beds."[23] The maximum flow, estimated at 260,000 cubic feet per second, was the highest on record.[24]

The Company's boats were kept busy over the next few days "snatching" people from "watery graves," often off the rooftops of their houses. As the waters continued to rise and spread, the settlers were forced into constant retreat to higher ground. Most houses were wrecked and floated downstream, while the population huddled on a few pieces of higher ground far from their property. Even Fort Garry, on the highest ground available around the confluence of the rivers, was under eleven and a half feet of water. The heavy loss of buildings was in part attributable to their impermanent construction and in larger part to the rush of waters connected with the ice breakup in early May. Francis Heron wrote, "the pickets and the chimneys of the houses are falling daily, as well as the plastering of the walls, and even the houses themselves begin to totter on their foundations."[25] Livestock was also particularly vulnerable and much was lost. One of the few bright spots of the inundation was the destruction of much of the vermin of the settlement.

Not until 22 May did the waters crest, and then took over a month to recede completely. According to John Pritchard, "you may form some idea of the extent of this flood by considering the river whose usual breadth may be compared with the Severn at Shrewsbury having expanded itself over a surface of more than seventeen miles; which is the distance between the hills on which the settlers took refuge."[26] Planting was begun in small quantities on new ground away from the river banks, and continued until early July, although damp ground made it impossible to plant the quantity of land cultivated in 1825. Not surprisingly, the mosquito invasion was severe that summer. Loss of life had been surprisingly light given the property devastation caused by waters which rose as much as forty feet above ice level, and which produced a lake seventeen miles wide extending from Pembina to Lake Winnipeg. Light casualties would be a characteristic of Red River flooding, however. People usually had time to get out of the path of the water. Francis Heron recorded five deaths. One de Meuron settler was drowned on 21 May while questing his cattle. A man and three children—probably Métis—were killed when their canoe overturned. But the damage to property was extensive. Not only were houses, outbuildings, and personal possessions destroyed, but the loss of livestock was considerable. The slow process of building breeding herds of sheep, cattle, and horses, accumulated at great expense from the United States over the preceding half-dozen years, was interrupted, if not destroyed. Contemporaries found some solace in a circumstance John Pritchard observed in his letter to England: "the three churches, the residence of the clergy and the house of our social prayer meeting, with the exception of the windmill," were "the only buildings which have not been carried away or so much injured as not to deserve notice." These structures had apparently instinctively been built on higher ground, although Pritchard insisted that their sites were not deliberately so chosen.[27]

On 14 June 1826, George Simpson produced his first report on the colony's calamitous state for his employers, writing, "nothing short of ocular demonstration can give a correct idea of the present suffering state of its wretched inhabitants who have but Death staring them in the face whatever direction they look. All former reverses are scarcely worthy of notice compared with the present and this I consider an extinguisher to the hope of Red River ever retaining the name of a Settlement."[28] Simpson was not a man given to exaggeration, although his pessimism on this occasion was perhaps unwarranted. Doom and gloom were typical sentiments of those who surveyed the damage caused by a major flood in the Red River Valley. Simpson found the colonists in the "greatest consternation and distress," but refused to advise them to remain, because they would demand assistance either as free gifts or in the form of credit.[29] Eternally the bookkeeper, Simpson's dejection was coloured by his fears of the expense of rebuilding. Not surprisingly, the Swiss and de Meuron settlers, always the most restive and discontented, decided to move south into the United States. About 250 of them departed the colony with no opposition from Simpson, who had always regarded them as troublemakers. Most of the Swiss went eventually to St. Louis, on the Mississippi River, but some settled first near Darlington, Wisconsin.[30]

Despite Simpson's trepidation and the exodus of most of the Swiss and Germans, the settlement sprang back to life very quickly. By 5 July Francis Heron noted, "the people of the settlement employed enclosing their farms, and building new houses, with as much enthusiasm as if no misfortunes had ever befallen them."[31] John Pritchard added in August that despite the departure of many, "the old residents still remain and are actively employed in re-establishing things as heretofore; so that I expect next summer the remembrance of the flood alone will be retained." [32] An exceptionally warm summer enabled crops not planted until July to flourish. By 21 August wheat and barley were in full ear and potatoes were big enough for the table.[33]

Nevertheless, the flood had made its impact, particularly on Simpson and on the least-committed and most marginal of the European settlers. The loss of livestock was a heavy blow to many. The exodus of the Swiss and Germans not only removed an entire ethnic component—one that was armed and restive—from Red River, but also marked another step toward the emergence of the mixed-bloods as the dominant demographic element of the community. At the same time, the long-term response to the 1826 flood had its negative as well as positive side. The extent of the devastation and the spread of the water was quickly pushed to the background. Settlers resumed their occupation of low-lying land that was otherwise so attractive. No serious efforts at flood protection were undertaken. The inhabitants of the Red River Valley would have to relearn their flood lessons with every inundation.

The flood of 1826 left some vivid impressions on those who subsequently resided in the Hudson's Bay Territories. In 1880 novelist Robert Ballantyne, who had been in Red River in the 1840s, published *The Red Man's Revenge: A Tale of the Red River Flood*.[34] Ballantyne assumed that his readers were familiar with the propensities of the Red for flooding and, given the state of development he describes in the settlement, somewhat anachronistically set the novel in 1826. The author included a cast of Aboriginals, a "motley crew of Red River half-breeds" for the annual spring buffalo hunt, described in some detail, and some rather genteel settlers, headed by the Ravenshaws.

Ballantyne's book reaches its climax with the great flood, which forms the backdrop for the last half of the novel. The Ravenshaws are driven to the upper storey of their house, while other settlers scurry for higher ground. Families are divided and separated. A footnote to one of the graphic descriptions of the inundation reads: "Twenty-six years later, in 1852, Red River Settlement was visited by a flood very similar in its main features to that of 1826, above described; and it is a curious coincidence that only one man lost his life during the latter flood; also, that the waters of the flood of both years began to subside on exactly the same date." There are in the course of the book some hair's-breadth escapes, but eventually the water recedes and the lovers (who have been separated by the flood) are reunited and married. Everyone lives happily ever after.

According to the later calculations of the engineers, based on Sanford Fleming's data, the flood of 1826 would have created a water flow of 225,000 cubic feet per second, a maximum elevation in feet at the Forks of 764.5, and an elevation in feet above city datum at James Avenue of 37.3.[35] Such a flood would occur every 460 years.[36] The 1958 Flood Cost Benefit Commission estimated the loss to 1957 Winnipeg of a flood of 1826 proportions at $852 million.[37] Not only was the Flood of 1826 the "benchmark flood," it was also the disaster that finished the Red River Settlement as a personal fiefdom of the Selkirk family. Lord Selkirk, the son of the founder, would not actually sell the settlement to the HBC for another decade, but the estate and the family lost all interest in Red River after 1826.

The 1852 Flood

Over a generation would pass before the Red River basin was again seriously affected by flooding conditions. The 1852 flood waters did not crest quite as high or remain quite as long as in the 1826 flood. The engineers later calculated the maximum discharge of the 1852 flood at 165,000 cubic feet per second, the maximum elevation at the Forks at 762.5 feet, and the elevation above datum at the James Avenue Pumping Station (which is the standard place for measuring elevations in Winnipeg) at 35.2 feet, with a probable frequency (again understated) at once every 150 years.[38] Large sectors of the region, especially well below the confluence of the Red and Assiniboine rivers, were completely spared. At the same time, the colony was far better established and prosperous than in 1826. Property damage was more extensive.[39] Dislocation was felt far more acutely, particularly among the less prosperous elements of the population, who tended to cluster residentially in the low-lying areas. The disaster of 1826 had affected everyone in the colony. That of 1852 was far more selective.

Weather conditions had been building toward a major inundation for years.[40] Summer and autumn rainfall had been heavy since 1848, and the rivers had overflowed their banks in the springs of 1850 and 1851. In 1852 a heavy March snowfall was followed by a cold April which delayed the breakup of the ice until the end of the month.[41] Unlike 1826, however, the rise of water was gradual, beginning on 25 April. There was a sudden rise in water level on 9-10 May, probably caused by the cresting of the Assiniboine. In his journal of this flood, Bishop David Anderson reported on 9 May the eerie sound—audible all across the region—of "the pouring of water over the plains."[42] It sounded like a distant waterfall, he wrote. Mgr. Provencher reported another sound: "Day and night, I could hear the waves, whipped by a strong wind, beat against the walls of my house."[43] On 12 May, a ceremony in the Catholic chapel was punctuated by the sound of the waves beating under the floorboards.[44] According to Governor Colvile, the rise was gradual, varying from five to eleven inches per day.[45] The waters began receding around 20 May, allowing the fields in many places to dry by early June.[46] For most inhabitants there had been more than sufficient warning to remove valuables and livestock to higher ground. In Pembina, the postmaster, George Setter, began living from 30 April on board a boat "with all his trading goods on board."[47]

Bishop Anderson's journal, subsequently published in London, provides a poignant account of one flood victim's tribulations. Water began trickling into the manse on 12 May, soaking his papers, which were supposed to have been stored safely. A day later, the family said prayers in the kitchen in three inches of water. A boat was unable to remove the piano because the waves were running too high on the water. Anderson and his sister remained on the second storey of the house until 14 May, initially refusing evacuation because of the property of others stored there. The bishop was reunited with his children on his six-year-old's birthday. "He said his little presents were not to be given to him until he returned home, as he called the old house, now almost a wreck."[48] This note of pathos was perhaps the most poignant struck in the entire journal.

While many buildings had their main floors covered with water, few were actually swept away. The major property damage in most areas—apart from houses which had to be dried and cleaned after having their floors covered with six to twelve inches of muddy slime—was to fencing and outbuildings. Bishop Anderson reported seeing pyramids of clay in front of all the houses, as their inhabitants shovelled out the mud and the remains of their collapsed chimneys. The loss of fencing was particularly severe, since it was difficult to keep livestock out of planted fields without it. A relative shortage of timber made it expensive to replace. That fencing was a substantial item of damage distinguishes 1852 from 1826; in the earlier flood there was little mention made of lost fences. Agricultural practices had changed and progress made over the years. Some planting was delayed or prevented, but the settlement experienced only one death—David Lowe, a servant of Bishop Anderson, was drowned—due to the flood.

While estimates of property damage ran as high as £25,000—Bishop Anderson reported driftwood caught by the trees included "a motley assemblage of wheels, hay-carts, tables, doors, chairs, &c."—the flood was but one more natural disaster with which settlers coped. As one old Métis who had lost his home commented, "C'est le bon Dieu qui afflige."[49]

According to Bishop Anderson, who had obtained a copy of a report to the Church Missionary Society on the 1826 flood before attempting the comparison, the inundation of 1852 was simultaneously more and less serious than the earlier devastation.[50] The total value of property losses was higher in 1852, admitted Anderson, but the settlement's resources were not so totally destroyed as in 1826. More was left with which to begin again, he argued. Losses to livestock, in particular, were proportionately much lower. People were able to carry off their property in boats rather than on their persons. "Instead of a few solitary settlers, unknown and almost forgotten by their fellow-men, they are now parts of a mighty system, linked more closely by sympathy and interest to other lands."

Perhaps the most serious aspect of the 1852 flood was the differential way in which damage was inflicted. The areas that experienced the greatest flooding were those along the Red just south of the Forks on both sides of the river, and along the lower part of the Assiniboine, although the land north of the Forks around St. John's Cathedral was also inundated almost to the second storey of the Anglican bishop's manse. These districts were hit by the highest water and also by whatever surges of water were released by the breakup of the ice and the cresting of the rivers. Most buildings removed from their foundations were in these areas. The most affected section on the Red was inhabited by Métis, and that around Fort Garry by British army pensioners who had come to the colony in 1848 and 1850.[51] According to Alexander Ross, 3,500 inhabitants were forced to flee their homes for higher ground. Most settlers went to either Stony Mountain or Little Mountain, in the northwestern corner of present-day Winnipeg, where tents were set up by the military for their temporary residence.[52] The tents included stoves and adjacent kitchens, so the refugees were not completely uncomfortable. Rations were supplied by the Company to the pensioners, "to be repaid by small monthly stoppages from their pensions."[53] The Scots and mixed-blood settlers in St. James and St. Andrew's districts were virtually unaffected. Their ground was high enough to escape the water entirely. The Scots were reported to have saved all their wheat on hand, up to a three-year reserve. According to Governor Colvile, the wheat reserve was 16,000 bushels.[54]

Governor Eden Colvile commented that the improvident "will have in great measure to trust to the produce of the gun and the net," but he failed to add that the chief of their improvidences had been their choice of residential location along the low-lying banks of the rivers.[55] The Métis were simply replicating earlier Canadian patterns of settlement along the banks of rivers, ignoring the fact that in Red River those rivers were susceptible to spring flooding. The pensioners had clustered around the low-lying land near Fort Garry because no one else had much wanted it. They were forced to evacuate their homes *en masse,* and were of course disheartened by the experience. Even among the pensioners, however, only three houses were actually lost. Although most dwellings required some repair, Governor Colvile did not regard the repairs as extensive, at least to render them habitable.[56] Bishop Anderson insisted that several of the residents of the flooded houses or shacks sold them for a pittance while they were under water.[57] Governor Colvile reported that these people were settled on un-usually low ground purchased from a settler rather than the Company.[58] Better construction than in 1826 was credited for the survival of the dwellings. Fortunately the pensioners' garden plots were largely spared.[59]

Food prices were temporarily raised by the flood, although the 1852 harvest was less a disaster than had been predicted. As usual, a warm summer followed a flood. So did the mosquitoes. By 23 May, Dr. William Cowan reported in his diary that the mozzies had "become very troublesome."[60] Seed wheat was distributed to those who had no 1852 crop. As expected, those without capital resources—the "improvident"—probably increased their reliance on hunting and fishing. By early September, Governor Colvile reported that "no apprehension need be entertained as to scarcity."[61] The 1852 flood, even more quickly than the 1826 one, receded into memory. Had the waters run as high for as long as in 1826, however, memories might have been different, since settlement was much more extensive in 1852 than it had been a quarter-century earlier.

The Flood of 1861

Only nine years later—in 1861—the Red River Settlement was again visited with a major flood. By this time the colony had its own newspaper, the *Nor'-Wester,* begun in 1859 by James Ross. The *Nor'-Wester* was highly critical of the Hudson's Bay Company regime in the settlement. It loudly advocated annexation to Canada. Despite this stridency in its editorial policy, the newspaper was actually quite a good one. It published a good deal of local news and opened its pages to budding writers at every opportunity. Its pages provide much of our information about the 1861 disaster.

As usual in flood years, a heavy snowpack, increased by April snow-storms, was followed by a late and sudden thaw at the end of the month.[62] There was an ice jam at the Forks. By this time, residents had come to expect this ice jam, and even tended to think that all flooding on the Red was caused by the ice. According to the *Nor'-Wester,* "at last came the winter *finale.* With a loud crash the ice was rent; and driving it before them in wild confusion, the liberated waters rushed down."[63] The water continued rising, as much as a foot between sundown and sunrise. Many along the rivers were forced to evacuate their homes. The crest was lower than in 1852, although the waters drove all the settlers along the Red north of Upper Fort Garry from their homes. As Henry Youle Hind had recognized in 1858, "Above Mill Creek, on Red River, there does not appear to be any rise of land sufficient to afford security against extraordinary floods, such as those of 1826 and 1852."[64] Flooding ulti-mately forced many as far as Middle Church to evacuate. Many resi-dents moved all their possessions to their second storeys, and toughed out the high water there. Point Douglas was under water and St. Boniface surrounded by it, but districts to the south of the Forks appear to have been less affected than in 1852.[65] The 1861 inundation was also experi-enced south of the border. According to "G.W.N." in the *St. Cloud Demo-crat,* "from the mouth of the Sheyenne to Lake Winnipeg—the valley at one time resembled an immense sea, to which, looking from any point on Red River, no boundary could be defined, excepting perhaps to the eastward, in which direction the heights of the Mississippi could be faintly discerned."[66]

No lives were lost in 1861, and few if any houses were seriously dam-aged, apart from the usual layer of muddy slime on the floors and walls. Aside from fencing, the most serious damage was to the various mills lo-cated along the rivers.[67] Despite the initial inability of the mail-carrier to navigate the swollen rivers, the *Nor'-Wester* reported with some satisfaction that "even during the flood the mails have come and gone with all regu-larity."[68] As in 1852, those with no grain stocks on hand or those who had been unable to move their grain to higher ground suffered most heavily. Many refugees, mostly mixed-bloods, retreated to Pembina Mountain and St. Joseph. But loss of livestock was low, at least in Red River. Reports further south suggested that a great many horned cattle had perished.[69] Because of the freshness of the 1852 experience, most settlers took precautions when it became clear that the water was rising. As in 1826 and 1852, planting was delayed. "G.W.N." insisted in June that "farming in the Red River valley below the Red Lake River is utterly impossible this season."[70] Nevertheless, S.P. Matheson observed in the autumn of 1861 that "nature seemed to adjust itself to our needs and mishaps, with the result that both grain and vegetables matured in time to supply adequately our wants."[71] American observers were nevertheless convinced that "buffalo hunting will be more profitable than cultivating Red River mud."[72] This turn to hunting was reinforced by reports of immense herds of buffalo heading onto the eastern plains of Dakota and a rise in the price of pemmican. In any case, Red River would experience a famine only a few years later, in 1868, caused by drought rather than by flooding.[73]

Despite the 1861 experience, recent arrivals in the settlement began to build the houses and shops that would become the village of Winnipeg. Henry McKenney, a Canadian who had arrived in 1859, constructed the first house and shop along Main Street in 1862. He was soon joined by others, and within ten years Winnipeg was a thriving little village, its main street located almost entirely along the Red River.[74] In 1869, newcomer Charles Mair was struck by the extent of the swampy marsh to the south of the Forks, chiefly in present-day St. Norbert and St. Vital.[75]

The early floods, while establishing record discharges and elevations for Red River flooding which were not challenged until 1997, also occurred in a settlement which was far less built-up than the Red River Valley was in 1950 and thereafter.

Table 1: Six Greatest Red River Floods to 2000 A.D.

Year	max. discharge Redwood Bridge cfs	max. level above datum James Ave.
1826	225,000	37.3
1852	165,000	35.2
1997	160,000	24.5 (after floodway)
1861	125,000	32.3
1979	106,000	24.0 (after floodway)
1950	103,600	30.3

As a result of the relative lack of development, the actual extent of devastation possible by such flooding was considerably masked. Only historians were conscious of these floods by the second half of the twentieth century, and it was virtually impossible to visualize how they would affect the modern city and valley.[76] For modern Manitobans, their most important feature was that they had not reoccurred since settlement in the province had begun in earnest.

THE COLONIAL OFFICE, ABORIGINAL POLICY, AND RED RIVER 1847–1849

NE of the many problems faced by the Red River Settlement and its inhabitants was that of achieving some sort of recognition and standing with the British government, particularly with the Colonial Office. The settlement was never a formal colony, under the jurisdiction of the Colonial Office, but in its early years a proprietary colony and then later merely an adjunct to the operations of a chartered trading company responsible for half a continent. From the British perspective, one of the chief roles of the Hudson's Bay Company was as guardian of the Aboriginal population of the vast region under its control. This role was quite different from that as governor of the Red River Settlement. When the people of Red River tried to call themselves and their situation to the attention of the British authorities in the 1840s, the supposed friends of Red River proved more part of the problem than of the solution. The protests against the Company's political behaviour in Red River were not only subordinated to complaints about the Company's Aboriginal policy, but it is doubtful whether the Colonial Office ever realized exactly what the political complaints were. While the Colonial Office worked its way toward a decision that there had been no serious abuse of the Aboriginals, the complaints about Company political behaviour were lost in the process. A detailed account of the process of dealing with the Red River protests in the 1840s tell us much about the problems of getting grievances redressed at the Colonial Office. It also is illuminating about the nature of official British policy towards the North American Aboriginal. The whole process tells us very little, however, about Colonial Office thinking about the rights of the people of Red River.

The Free-Trade Agitation

In 1843, the American-based fur trader Norman Kittson, on behalf of the American Fur Company, constructed a trading post at Pembina, on the Red River just south of the international border. The post, on the site of earlier posts of the North West and Hudson's Bay companies, soon drew a number of mixed-blood traders from the British territory at Red River.[1] A commerce with the Americans quickly began to flourish. The Hudson's Bay Company, always sensitive to threats to its trading monopoly, was soon planning counter-strategy. The Council of Assiniboia began to enforce the customs duties, and Recorder Adam Thom recommended a series of "negative" measures, including a land-title deed that if taken seriously virtually put its recipient in feudal thralldom to the Company.[2] Simultaneously, Sir George Simpson began to lobby the British government for a military force, ostensibly to defend the British West against the Americans, but more particularly to enforce the laws of the Red River Settlement, including the prohibitions on trade.[3] A tougher governor of Assiniboia was also appointed by the Company, in the person of Alexander Christie. Christie issued several proclamations on 8 December 1844, including one requiring all importers to guarantee that they would not use their goods in the fur trade, and another making all mail liable to Company inspection.[4] The importers, in their turn, refused to pay the customs duties and their goods were detained, although nobody was actually arrested.

Escalating matters, the Governor and Council of Rupert's Land passed a series of regulations on 10 June 1845 that limited the traders to the importing and exporting of goods only if the governor of Red River "reasonably believed" that they "have neither trafficked in furs themselves since the 18th day of December 1844, nor enabled others to do so by illegally or improperly supplying themselves with trading articles of any description."[5] By this point, both sides were organized for a confrontation. The traders were understandably unwilling to treat the Company's policy and actions as mere commercial regulation. Having chafed for years under Company restriction, they sought the highest possible political and moral ground for their opposition. On 29 August of that year, the mixed-blood James Sinclair, on behalf of nineteen other traders, wrote to Governor Christie with a series of fourteen hypothetical questions dealing with the fur trade.[6] It began by declaring "a very strong belief that we, as natives of this country, and as half-breeds, have the right to hunt furs in the Hudson's Bay Company's territories whenever we think proper, and again sell those furs to the highest bidder." The subsequent questions dealt with particulars of this assertion of "Aboriginal rights." Christie answered swiftly.[7] He denied that the half-breeds had any such privileges, but merely "as British subjects," had the same rights as anyone born in England or Scotland, and these were limited by the Charter.

In February of 1846, the traders met again in the shadow of Upper Fort Garry at the house of Andrew McDermott to draw up a request for relief to the British government. The details of the meetings and their immediate outcome are not clear. Earlier, in October of 1845, Andrew McDermott's nephew, John McLaughlin, had generated a petition to the American government signed by 1,250 "half breeds and Canadian settlers." McLaughlin had left Red River, according to Sir George Simpson, "for the purpose of laying it before the authorities there."[8] The petition prayed "to be admitted as settlers within the Iowa territory, and to be allowed the priveledge [sic] of hunting. . . ."[9] According to W. L. Morton, the February meeting of the traders drew up two petitions, one in French and one in English, but waited to dispatch them until they knew the outcome of the McLaughlin petition.[10] This account seems most unlikely, for the results of the McLaughlin initiative could not be known for some months, and James Sinclair was already preparing to depart for England. Moreover, there never were two petitions in addition to the McLaughlin one. Instead, there was one undated petition in French, and a set of instructions in English "addressed to the Delegate in charge of the Petition."[11] As it transpired, McLaughlin proved a useless emissary. Instead of presenting the petition in person, McLaughlin merely posted it in the mail to the American Secretary of State, James Buchanan, who sent it on to the War Department. There it died an ignominious death.[12] The HBC was able to use the dispatch of the petition as evidence of the settlement's flirtation with the Americans, but it otherwise had no effect.

The Isbister Memorial

The second act of the free-trade agitation would be played out in London. The most detailed accounts of this affair have quite different understandings of its nature.[13] According to John Galbraith, the basic problem was that the major complaints against the HBC of Aboriginal abuse could not be substantiated. According to Barry Cooper, Alexander Isbister was outmanoeuvred by the unsportsmanlike machinations of the Company in collusion with the Colonial Office. Both interpretations are partially true. But the real problem was that Isbister had out-manoeuvred himself. He presented a case about Company treatment of the Aboriginals that could not be proved and could in part be refuted, rather than concentrating on the Company's political machinations in Red River, where the abuses—if properly presented—ought to have been quite palpable and disturbing to any liberal government or politician.[14] In the process, Isbister succeeded in confusing both the Colonial Office and subsequent historians as to the nature of the charges being advanced against the Company, thus allowing the HBC off the hook, at least temporarily.

James Sinclair had taken his instructions to London in the spring of 1846.[15] The "Copy of Instructions to the Delegates by the Members of the Committee" emphasized that the delegates had been elected by "the people" and were acting "in conformity with the desires and unanimously known interests of the people."[16] This document included a series of complaints that "the people" wished redressed. The complaints were that the Company was forcing settlers to pay for lands without giving them a legal contract; that the Company's bills of exchange were redeemable only in London; that silver money be put into circulation; that the Company be required to carry all exports in Company ships; that if the Company continued to have a monopoly, that it pay a reasonable price for everything that the inhabitants had to sell; that given the monopoly, the Company should operate an adequately stocked shop in the settlement; that the Company had extended its claims too far in suppressing the fur trade; that the Company be bound by any prohibitions on the sale of intoxicating liquors. This list accepted the Charter and the monopoly and raised no principles except equity under the Charter.

Sinclair apparently did not actually carry the French petition; it probably arrived in London much later. Sinclair headed south to St. Louis, and then by rail to New York, where he boarded a swift packet ship which crossed the Atlantic in a mere five weeks. In London, Sinclair went immediately to the home of old friend Alexander Isbister. Like Sinclair, Isbister was a "country-born" mixed-blood.[17] Born at Cumberland House (Saskatchewan), he was the son of an Orkney clerk of the HBC and a mixed-blood daughter of Alexander Kennedy and his Cree wife Aggathas. He was originally schooled in the Orkneys, but returned to Rupert's Land to attend Red River Academy from 1833 to 1837. He entered HBC service in 1838, but was unhappy at the lack of advancement granted to mixed-bloods. Isbister resigned from the Company in 1841 and left for Great Britain in

1842, attending King's College (Aberdeen) for two years and the University of Edinburgh for one year.

Isbister was one of those Anglophilic British Americans who became more British than the British. He was fascinated with London and later lived within the Temple at Bolt Court. Tall (he stood six feet, three inches) and well-mannered, often described as being of "aristocratic bearing," he had not yet settled into a career in Britain. But he had recently become associated with the Aborigines' Protection Society, an organization which lobbied on behalf of Aboriginal peoples around the British Empire. Isbister advised Sinclair that the process of petitioning the Crown could take years, but he readily agreed to shepherd a memorial through the necessary stages. Anxious about his family and his business, Sinclair returned to North America early in 1847, leaving the Red River business solely in the hands of Isbister. Why it took Isbister until 1847 to begin the memorializing process is not clear from the surviving documents. Most of the papers in the case were published in 1849 by the British government as a "Blue Book."[18] However, as we shall see, some of the most interesting and revealing material did not make its way into print, and subsequent historians have had some considerable difficulty in making sense out of what was published.

On 6 February 1847, Alexander Isbister informed Earl Grey, the secretary of state at the Colonial Office, that he was about to receive a petition "for presentation to Her Majesty," from "the native and half-caste Indians" of the Hudson's Bay Company territory.[19] Isbister signed the letter "A. Koonaubay Isbister," thus using his Indian name. He subsequently forwarded a "Memorial of the undersigned Deputies from the Natives of Rupert's Land, North America" to "the Right honourable the Secretary of State for the Colonies"—signed by Isbister, T. Vincent, J. Sinclair, D.V. Stewart, J. McLeod, and J. Isbister—which was dated 17 February 1847.[20] Thus began the confusion. The Memorial was not the Petition mentioned on 6 February, however, nor was it, as W. L. Morton has suggested, a document generated in Red River.[21] The "Memorial" was accompanied by another letter from Isbister which noted that there was another document from the HBC territories, this one "signed by upwards of a thousand names of the leading Indians and half-breeds, who having been drawn to the little settlement on the Red River from all parts of the Indian country, may be considered as fitly representing the general body of their countrymen." Isbister noted that it was meant to submit the Petition and the Memorial together, but did not explain why this had not occurred. The most likely explanation for this failure is that he did not actually have it at hand at the time he submitted the Memorial.

The Petition signed by 977 "inhabitants of Red River" had been generated earlier by Father Georges Belcourt, at the behest of a large number of Métis, who had initially sought more strenuous action against the government.[22] Later historians have commented on its elegant French. Belcourt had counselled obedience to authority, however evil it was, and recommended a legal means of achieving justice. The priest would subsequently insist that his action in drafting the Petition had prevented a serious confrontation, and he may well have been correct. The Petition employed rhetorical excess. It claimed that Lord Selkirk's promises— the colonists' "commodities, etc., would be sold at a satisfactory price, fixed in the said contracts, and that the toil of the laborer would not be paralyzed by his inability to sell his productions"—had been evaded and frustrated. It insisted that the HBC monopoly had "weighed heavily on us for about one hundred and seventy-six years." On the other hand, the Petition did concern itself with Aboriginal policy and had provided a fairly straightforward series of requests. First, the petitioners asked to be governed according to the principles of the British constitution. Secondly, they wanted the liberty of trade that prevailed elsewhere in the Empire, so that they would not continue to be "reduced to a kind of slavery." Finally, they wanted land sold to new immigrants, with the proceeds used to improve transportation. "We are near the boundary line; we can go over to the neighbouring territory," the Petition concluded, "but we admire the wisdom of the British Constitution, and we desire its privileges." Unfortunately, these requests were never really considered by the Colonial Office, partly because Isbister had treated them as an afterthought rather than as the core of the complaint. The desire on the part of the Métis to become an equal part of the British political system would continue through Confederation. This Petition was not placed in the hands of the Colonial Office until May 1847, and while it was reprinted in French in the 1849 Blue Book, it would not serve as a major component of the charges of complaint.[23] Galbraith wrote that the "petition contained an element of fact and a mass of exaggeration and falsehoods," but he thought this Petition and Isbister's "Memorial" were the same document.[24]

The Memorial was an ingeniously phrased document, described by Barry Cooper as "a fine piece of forensic rhetoric, combining moral exhortation and factual allegation with a set of political and economic assumptions calculated to appeal to the liberal predispositions of the recipients.[25] Unfortunately, the liberal predispositions appealed to were humanitarian rather than strictly political. The Memorial began by complaining of the "harsh administration of the Hudson's Bay Company." Its monopoly of trade had impoverished the Natives and amassed a "princely" revenue, while doing little or nothing for the moral and religious improvement of the Native inhabitants. Instead, the Company's policies and behaviour consigned the Natives "to pass their lives in the darkest heathenism." The Company had evaded all its responsibilities in favour of making money. It traded in spiritous liquors and exposed the Natives to "the most frightful destitution." The HBC's agents were "loose moralists" whose "deity is gold, to obtain which they trample down Christianity and benevolence."

Significantly, this Memorial did not directly argue the question of the validity of the Charter, but instead insisted that even if the Charter were still valid, "none of its provisions are or can be binding on the natives to trade with the Company exclusively, or can prevent them from carrying their furs or other property out of the country to the best market." Nevertheless, the HBC insisted on enforcing its monopoly. The Memorial pointed out that the Americans were offering to provide American citizenship for the hunters of the Red River. The Company sought to mislead the British government, said the Memorial, and as evidence it contrasted Simpson's 1842 published report with Alexander Simpson's published *The Life and Travels of Thomas Simpson*. The Company sought the greatest possible revenue, in the course of which it overlooked all "considerations of humanity and religion." While the document was well-designed not only to get the attention of the Aborigines' Protection Society and the Colonial Office, but to require that the latter take some action on the allegations, its rhetorical excesses would eventually tell against it.[26] The Memorial's broad attack on the Company's Aboriginal policy—Isbister himself described it as "professedly occupied with the effects of the Company's system of trade on the Indians of the interior"—rather than directly on the tyrannical administration of Red River, was probably ultimately a mistake.[27] Isbister seemed to think that since the mixed-bloods of Red River were Native Aboriginals, their problems with the Company could somehow be combined with those of the people of the vast territories administered by the HBC.

The Hudson's Bay Company Response

On 5 March 1847, Benjamin Hawes, Earl Grey's parliamentary undersecretary, acknowledged to Isbister the receipt of his letter, adding that "I am to inform you, that his Lordship has called upon the Governor of the Bay Company for a report upon the statement advanced in your memorial."[28] That statement did not include any of the documents from Red

River, however. That same day, Isbister wrote again to Grey with what he said was "additional information" on the condition of the Indian tribes.[29] One document he enclosed was a report of the Rev. Henry Beaver, who had been briefly stationed on the Columbia River. This report, originally published as a tract by the Aborigines' Protection Society in 1842, charged that virtually no effort had been made to civilize the Indians of the Pacific Slope. Infanticide was common, wrote Beaver, and "infidelity in Indian women living with their natural husbands is of rare occurrence; that of those living with the lower servants of the Company notoriously common." Worse still, the Company held many Indians "in a state of slavery" and tolerated much violence against them.[30]

Another of Isbister's enclosures provided a list of the prices the HBC paid for furs in the Mackenzie River District, and a gloss by Isbister on the reports of the Company to the British government in 1837 seeking a renewal of their trading monopoly. Isbister insisted that in 1837 the Company had applied for renewal on three grounds: (1) the alleged improvement in the state of the Native population; (2) the improvement of the country through agricultural settlement and the establishment of an export trade; and (3) the advantages to British commerce of the monopoly. He then produced a table which in parallel columns compared the HBC statements of 1837 with the evidence of Beaver and Alexander Simpson.[31] A final document was a legal opinion on the validity of the HBC charter, which Isbister insisted "most clearly and conclusively demonstrated that this instrument, on which the Hudson's Bay Company found their extraordinary pretensions, has long since lost its force." Whether this newly forwarded information was in recognition of the fact that the Memorial would be sent to the HBC is not clear, but it seems likely. The complaints from Red River had still not been sent to the Colonial Office, however.

The Hudson's Bay Company responded with alacrity to Grey's request for a report. On 24 April 1847, Sir John H. Pelly, Bart., the governor of the HBC, sent his "observations" on the Memorial.[32] In contrast to Isbister's obvious moral earnestness, Pelly adopted the tone of an experienced man of business, as indeed he was. After sailing in his youth for the East India Company, he was elected a director of the HBC in 1806 (his father transferred stock to him to enable him to be elected). He rose rapidly in the ranks to deputy governor in 1812 and governor in 1822, the same year he became a director of the Bank of England. Pelly was highly regarded for what John S. Galbraith described as his "ability to arrive at sound policies founded upon realistic appraisals of the facts."[33]

Pelly began his defence of the Company by alluding to the agitation at Red River, emphasizing that some settlers at Red River had lately been trading "in violation of the Hudson's Bay Company's chartered rights, and of the covenants under which they hold their lands." The chief agents in this traffic were the settlement's half-breeds, he said, who were thereby "diverted from the cultivation of the soil, acquire habits which render them averse to the sober pursuits of industry, and exert a baneful influence on the other settlers of mixed race." The complaints against the Company's administration, especially of the Indian population, were thus politically inspired by the turbulent half-breeds. No greater calamity could befall the Indians, pronounced Pelly, "than to have the Red River half-breeds let loose upon them." Since the memorialists offered mainly "vague and general assertions which do not admit of specific answers," Pelly produced his own table of parallel statements, in which the words of the Memorial in the left-hand column were refuted in the right-hand column. Much of his comment was, at best, disingenuous, and nearly all of it manifestly demonstrated contempt for both Indians and mixed-bloods, who were themselves held responsible for whatever victimization occurred.

Pelly commented upon the ambiguity of the term "natives" in Isbister's Memorial. "Natives" was "sometimes employed to denote half-breeds, or persons of mixed race, and sometimes the Indians or aboriginal inhabitants," he observed. His report would use the term exclusively for the Indians, he wrote. Naturally the half-breeds were discontented with Company policy, although "with even moderate industry, they have within their reach more of the comforts of life than are enjoyed by persons of their station in almost any part of the world." Pelly brushed aside a discussion of the merits of the Charter, which he took for granted. In answer to the charge that the Company had a "princely revenue" of £250,000 per annum, he insisted that the "revenue which they derive from the trade enables them to divide £40,000 per annum on a capital of £400,000 with an occasional bonus, which together do not exceed the ordinary rate of mercantile profit."

The HBC's governor denied the allegations about the Company's responsibility for the Christianization of the Indians. The Charter made no mention of this; "its sole objects were trade, and the discovery of a Northwest passage." Nevertheless, although the Company was not obliged to do missionary work, it had not neglected such objects. Pelly emphasized that the HBC saw its interests and those of the Indians as inseparable, maintaining that the Company would settle the Aboriginals agriculturally if possible. But the failure to do so would not "surprise those who know how difficult it is to overcome the instinctive repugnance of the

North American Indians to any employment requiring the application of steady and persevering industry." The Charter equally placed no obligations on the Company for improvement of the country "by opening up its mineral and agricultural resources." Moreover, Pelly observed that the Red River Settlement, the region best suited for agriculture, was "700 miles from the nearest port, which is ice-bound nine months out of the twelve." The Company would improve the land if it could, he insisted.

Turning to the charge that the Company had resumed trading in spiritous liquor with the Indians, Pelly indignantly denied it. He insisted that the diminution of the resources of the country would be greater if not checked by the Company; moreover, the Native population was increasing rather than declining. The Company did not prevent missionaries from going to the most northern parts of the territory. What held the missionaries back was "the obvious impossibility of their doing any good if they went." If the Natives were occasionally reduced to great distress, the cause was chiefly in their "want of foresight and . . . habits of indolence; the active hunter being always able to maintain himself." The HBC certainly often alleviated distress by importing goods from districts of abundance. Pelly offered a mini-disquisition on Indian life in the northern regions, where agriculture was impossible. The Natives could be transplanted to a more "genial region," but how was this to be done? Not the prices of the HBC but Native lack of industry was responsible for their poverty. Credit was "an unavoidable consequence of an improvidence inherent in the Indian nature." Pelly had nothing but praise for the Company's officers, who "in point of mental and moral cultivation . . . are, at least equal to those of their own rank in this country."

Pelly now addressed Red River and the half-breeds directly. The argument that the mixed-bloods had a right to trade with the Indians regardless of the Charter was "quite untenable," he wrote. "The circumstance of their being born in the country may entitle them to call themselves natives, but it neither conveys to them any privileges belonging or supposed to belong to the aboriginal inhabitants, nor does it divest them of the character of British subjects, all of whom are precluded by the Company's charter from trafficking in furs within its limits without a license from the Company, and the Red River settlers are additionally bound, by the covenants under which they hold their lands, to abstain from such traffic."

In his insistence that the mixed-bloods were nothing but British subjects, Pelly apparently did not recognize the potential inconsistency of his position, and it was not brought to his attention by anyone. After all, the people of Red River were also attempting to gain their full rights under the British constitution, although Pelly had been sent as yet no documentation on this point. As Barry Cooper has pointed out, "If the natives, whether Indian, Half-breed or European, were British subjects they were in the unusual position of being governed by a trading company, and were inhabitants of a 'plantation' in seventeenth-century legal language. None of these questions were ever settled by a competent judicial body."[34] Nor were the complaints of the Natives of Red River ever really considered by the Colonial Office in this round of consideration. If the Natives were British subjects, why were they not entitled to the traditional "rights of Englishmen"? Pelly did insist with some justice that the Company had not actually imprisoned anyone for illicit trading. If the Americans warned off the mixed-bloods, this was no misfortune, he wrote, since properly interpreted it would lead them to abandon the chase and apply themselves more usefully to agriculture. The governor categorically denied that the Company had any claim to the proceeds of the buffalo hunt. He argued that Alexander Simpson had an animus against the Company. In his conclusion, Pelly claimed that if the mixed-bloods "have any grievances to complain of, and remedies to propose, due consideration will be given to them." The statement more than implied that there was nothing to be taken seriously in the existing memorial, which in some ways was true, since the real complaints of the settlers were expressed elsewhere.

Pelly then turned to Isbister's letter of 5 March and its accompanying documents. The HBC governor went straight after the two main "authorities" employed by Isbister, Herbert Beaver and Alexander Simpson. Beaver had been dismissed by the Company and had departed it a "disappointed and discontented man." His letter to the Aborigines' Society was a mélange of exaggeration and misinterpretation. He had not actually witnessed any of the abuses he described. Pelly complained that Isbister would not give the Company any credit for bringing peace and tranquility to the Indian country. He reproduced Isbister's set of parallel columns and added a third to disprove Isbister's use of Simpson and Beaver. Pelly included an appendix with lengthy extracts from Thomas Simpson's manuscript journal, with passages omitted by his brother restored.

Finally, Pelly also included a blank copy of the land deed which the Company had been giving the settlers.[35] Even in this mock-up, the date 1840 appeared at the very beginning, which ought to have suggested that this legal form had not been in use for very long but was a relatively recent innovation.[36] In fact, the deed had only been developed in 1844, as part of Adam Thom's "negative" strategy. The document was not a deed of grant in fee simple, but of one thousand years peppercorn tenure, based upon a whole series of collateral prohibitions and obligations which amounted to a civic contract with the HBC. The settler agreed not to evade the Company's trading monopoly or trade in furs or sell spiritous liquors. He also agreed to contribute to the expenses of all public establishments and to help with roadworks for up to six days per year. He could not alienate any part of his land without the permission in writing of the Governor and Company. The deed was not valid if not registered in six months, and any violation of its terms abrogated the agreement and rendered the land subject to forfeit. Why this throwback to the Middle Ages did not upset the good liberals at the Colonial Office as much as it did the people of Red River can only be a matter for speculation. Perhaps it was because those who would receive such grants were not really Englishmen. More likely it was because of Isbister's emphasis on Aboriginal policy in the interior.[37]

Enter Herman Merivale

Alexander Isbister did his best to hurry the Colonial Office along, writing a letter on 26 April 1847 whom pointed out the unsettled state of the country.[38] Parliamentary undersecretary Benjamin Hawes replied a week later that the investigation of the voluminous papers "will necessarily make a great demand on his Lordship's time and attention."[39] Isbister replied with a letter, dated 28 May, which finally enclosed the Petition of 977 and a copy of the instructions to the delegates whom he represented.[40]

Although one could not know it from the Blue Book, at this point Herman Merivale entered the picture. Merivale was one of a small group of enormously influential, permanent colonial undersecretaries in the nineteenth century.[41] A nephew of William Wilberforce, he was educated at Harrow and Balliol, becoming Professor of Political Economy at Oxford in 1837 at the tender age of thirty-one. As was usually the case in such academic appointments, Merivale had done precious little to deserve it. As was often the case, he justified the appointment after the fact, producing in 1839 an *Introduction to a Course of Lectures on Colonization and Colonies* which brought him to the notice of James Stephen, his distinguished predecessor at the Colonial Office. Not surprisingly given his classical education, Merivale saw colonization from the perspective of the imperial history of Greece and Rome. One major difference that Merivale perceived between the ancient and modern development of colonization was in regard to their treatment of Aboriginals. The

ancients, with their city-states, did not seek wide-ranging territorial dominance. The Greeks brought their laws and society with them, while modern colonists were from the lower orders seeking to escape society. Hence
the modern settlers were greedy and land hungry, "whose desire it is to
spread themselves as so many individual lords over the soil, the unfortunate beings whom they displace were as constant incitements to savage
cruelty, or to still worse avarice."[42] Moreover, the ancient Natives were
merely barbarians rather than "savages." Dealing with "savages," said
Merivale, required conversion to Christianity and assimilation, princi-
pally through intermarriage between the Natives and the colonizers. That
intermarriage, however, ought not to result from a "corruption of morals,"
and after assimilation, there should be a settling down to a civilized agrar-
ian way of life. Like most of his generation, Merivale associated the progress
of civilization with the progress of agriculture. In many ways Herman
Merivale should have been a major supporter of Alexander Isbister and
his mixed-blood clients. But in practice Merivale was no friend of the
Red River mixed-bloods, chiefly because he saw them, through the eyes
of their critics, as an undesirable mixture of energy and lack of ambition.
The product of the corruption of morals, the Red River mixed-bloods
did not want to settle down and farm. Like the HBC, Merivale did not
view mixed-bloods as acculturated Indians, but rather as a separate and
troublesome group halfway between savagery and civilization.

Merivale's lengthy minute on the dispute was, as was usually the case
in Colonial Office business, based solely on the evidence presented by
the disputing parties to the colonial secretary, plus whatever preconceptions the bureaucrats and politicians brought to the business at hand.
The notion of doing additional independent research was not in great
favour at the Colonal Office, partly because it would be expensive, partly
because it would be time-consuming. After all, Red River was not even
one of Britain's 200-odd official colonies supervised by the Colonial
Office. Moreover, Merivale clearly perceived the attack on Aboriginal
policy to be Isbister's main point—or at least he affected so to understand. Whether he actually had the Petition of 977 to hand is an open
question, but probably he did not. After he had read the material, Merivale
wrote, his impression was "that the answers of the Company show the
accusations to be unfounded:—but that impression is as much derived
from the tone and manner of the accusation and defence as from anything else, and it is, therefore, difficult clearly to explain the grounds of
it."[43] Barry Cooper argues this assessment in class terms, saying that the
tone of the Memorialists "was not the tone of a gentleman; Sir Henry

[sic] Pelly, however, was assuredly a gentleman. And explaining the grounds of gentlemanliness was, of course, very difficult to do clearly."[44]

Doubtless class played its part, but other issues were involved as well. Isbister had gotten well beyond his evidence, and his tendency to blame the Company verged on a fanatical, conspiratorial interpretation. Moreover, Isbister's goal plainly was to destroy the Company's monopoly by indicting its Aboriginal policy. He was not seeking amelioration but major policy change, without actually attacking the Company's charter. Merivale later in his minute suggested that his objection was to the approach often employed by the Aborigines' Protection Society, which he had earlier described elsewhere as unbalanced "fanaticism."[45] Pelly had struck the right tone of beleaguered reasonableness in his response, and Merivale was prepared to assume "that the Company were credible witnesses in their own defence." Nevertheless, some further investigation was probably in order. Merivale's influential minute was not reprinted in the 1849 Blue Book; after all, it was confidential internal business rather than part of the public record.

Mr. Hawes agreed with Mr. Merivale that the charges were essentially groundless but needed to be studied further. On 5 June 1847, Hawes informed Sir John Pelly that Lord Grey, insofar as he could judge statements "resting to a great extent, on mere assertion," was of the opinion "that the charges brought against the Company are for the most part groundless." Nevertheless, further inquiry into "the state and condition of the people under the Government of the Company" was required, and he hoped the Company would co-operate in this process.[46] Nine days later Hawes wrote to Isbister that Grey had decided, on the basis of the evidence before him, that the charges were groundless. Nevertheless, Grey would ask the Governor General of Canada to institute a further inquiry. In the meantime, he was sending Isbister a copy of Pelly's counter-statement. Almost as an afterthought, he noted that Her Majesty had very graciously received the Petition of 977. Isbister responded to this news with a letter dated 21 June 1847, which questioned the authorities employed by Pelly to impugn the Memorial and promised a more detailed refutation.[47] Sir John Pelly wrote to Grey the same day, offering his co-operation and asking for an early decision since "the parties opposed to the Company are promulgating, through the press, statements calculated to mislead the public."[48] Grey responded through Benjamin Hawes by emphasizing that he had not found the report deficient, but required independent corroboration. Further information could be given to the Governor General of Canada.[49]

Isbister Tries Again

One might have thought that Alexander Isbister would have understood that he had lost the game. Lord Grey was not convinced by the attack on the HBC's Aboriginal policy, indeed had found the charges "groundless," and was merely playing matters out by writing to Canada. A moment's reflection might have led Isbister to realize that the Canadian Governor General was in no position to offer much enlightenment, being separated from the West by over one thousand miles. What Lord Elgin was sent in the way of documentation, moreover, did not include either the Petition of 977 or the instructions to the delegates.[50] Isbister was politically naïve, morally self-righteous, and unduly impressed with his own importance. It had never occurred to him, for example, that there was anything significant in the fact that in the entire business over Red River, he never spoke directly with Lord Grey nor received a communication directly from him. In any event, Isbister took the possibility of a Canadian investigation seriously. He responded to Hawes's letter by attempting to influence what the Canadian Governor General found out about the HBC. In July of 1847 he wrote to Alexander Rowand, a fellow mixed-blood who was a physician in Montreal, that he had "literally forced" Grey to take up the case of the mixed-bloods and that Grey had transferred the matter to Canada. He hoped that Rowand could help with the inquiry, since "now is the time or never to overthrow the Company," which did not have the "shadow of a right to the Monopoly of the trade to Hudson's Bay." Rowand was to "fish up some retired servants of the Company who are thick as blackberries in Canada" to advise Lord Elgin. Isbister concluded the letter to Rowand by observing, "Sir Geo. Simpson was over here in the spring. He immediately on his arrival commenced his old despicable trick of endeavouring to *bribe* the Memorialists, Factorships and Traderships were at an enormous discount and according to Sir George there were this year an unusual number of *vacancies which he had always intended to fill with halfbreeds.* Ah! the crafty old vagabond! If I don't flay him before I have done with him my name is not Isbister."[51]

Isbister had sadly mistaken his correspondent. Instead of scouting up evidence to support the mixed-blood case, the Montrealer took the letter to Simpson's secretary, Edward Hopkins. It was recognized, as A. Barclay put it in 1848, as "a precious document and I think a very choice and special mercy."[52] Simpson forwarded the letter to Elgin, and Elgin sent it on to Lord Grey.[53] To make sure this "mercy" got to the Colonial Office, Simpson also shipped the letter to Pelly, who passed it on to Lord Grey with a note that suggested Isbister had been caught with his hands in the proverbial cookie jar.[54] Isbister, who had not been born a "gentleman," totally failed to understand how gentlemen behaved, particularly when their livelihood and property were at stake. One did not hope to flay one's enemy, one simply passed his private correspondence on to those in authority.

In August of 1847, Isbister supplied Earl Grey with a detailed refutation of Mr. Pelly's report. He provided a critique of Pelly's authorities, a series of parallel observations on the report, and copious extracts from a number of writers who had personally observed the conditions of the Natives of Rupert's Land, their experience and credentials indicated in a special table included with the documents. Isbister began his refutation with a general statement, observing that Pelly had seemed very knowledgeable about the Petition of 977 mentioned in the Memorial. This knowledge was explained by a letter of Mr. John McLeod, one of the Memorialists, which was included in the appendix. McLeod's letter, dated 12 April 1847, charged Sir George Simpson and others with attempting to induce him to withdraw his name from the Memorial by signing a document to the effect that if he had read the Memorial before signing it, he would not have put his name to it, since he knew "nothing whatever personally about the matters there stated."[55] Isbister observed that the Company disposed of their lands at 12 shillings 6 pence per acre and allowed private traders to import goods in Company ships at £9 a ton, "which is somewhat more than three times the average freight from London to China." He insisted that the missions to the Indians were entirely supported by the Missionary Society, although the Company was supposed to take steps to introduce civilization and Christianity under their 1821 licence of exclusive trade. He charged Dr. John McLoughlin in the Oregon Territory with working on behalf of the Americans. Through careful textual comparison, he sought to show that Pelly had misused Thomas Simpson's testimony.

Isbister then turned to a set of point-by-point observations on Pelly's report.[56] Isbister had no problem with Pelly's distinction between Native Indians and Native mixed-bloods, but he objected to the conclusion drawn from the distinction, which was "that the half-breeds are, from the circumstance of their mixed parentage, divested of the rights inherent in the aboriginal inhabitants." This, said Isbister, was at variance with usage in Canada and the United States. Red River was the last place where such a policy should be in operation. From the 571 Native families (Indian and half-castes) in the settlement, nearly 1,000 persons had signed the petition, "a large proportion of whom are the Christian Indians attached to the missions of the Church Missionary Society."

Isbister still accepted that this was not the place to discuss the Charter's merits, and quickly passed on to other matters. He insisted that the Hudson's Bay Company's capital of £400,000 was "well known to be fictitious," and that under the Company's licence of 1821 there was express provision for civilization and Christianization of the Indians. He demanded proof for any assertions about the annual expense incurred by the Company in civilizing the Natives. Instead, the Company actually drew profit from the expenditures of the Church Missionary Society. There were schools and churches in Red River, but almost nowhere else in the vast HBC territory. As for agriculture, it worked when it was attempted. The custom-house returns documented an export to Hudson's Bay of 9,075 gallons of spirits, besides which there was a distillery at Red River.

Ignored was Pelly's point that this amount of spirits would provide the Company's own employees (not to mention the soldiers and pensioners) with about two teaspoons of liquor a day. The land deed accompanying the report was a recent development and was now being forced upon the settlers. Isbister pointed out that the HBC traditionally dismissed hostile testimony as coming from discontented former employees. He did not add that there would be few other witnesses except former employees, who could likely be labelled as malcontents. Isbister did try to supply some testimony by non-servants, ransacking the published literature by travellers, which he gathered together in an appendix. These observations noted the many problems experienced by the Indians, but did not directly attempt to associate them with the HBC. Isbister therefore also included answers to a series of questions posed to five retired employees of the HBC by an Orkney merchant in 1847.[57] This evidence was slightly more telling. Four out of five said that the Indians were kept in debt; all agreed that intoxicating liquors were supplied to the Indians; three of five said the Indians could not do what they liked with their furs. But the answers were too brief to be very useful. The documentation that Isbister supplied certainly suggested that the state of the Indians was deplorable, but did not for the most part even attempt—much less succeed—to blame the HBC for these conditions. Moreover, little of this material spoke to the political complaints of the inhabitants of Red River.

One of the most curious features of Isbister's submission of August 1847 was his inclusion of two pages of personal testimonials. Isbister explained that since he had been for a short time employed by the HBC he wanted to provide evidence that he was not "actuated by personal considerations in the present movement." Such an explanation could

William Kennedy Isbister.

account for one brief testimonial, but not for the subsequent letters dealing with Isbister's educational achievements in Great Britain. Their presence can be explained only as a bit of unnecessary preening by Isbister, who was understandably proud of his accomplishments but should have recognized their irrelevance to the question at hand. Isbister also appended a copy of a pamphlet by him, entitled *A Few Words on the Hudson's Bay Company*.[58] As published, this pamphlet had reprinted the petition and the Memorial as evidence of "how far the Company have complied with the terms of their agreement."[59] The pamphlet's text was no more specific than this about the nature of the Red River complaints, however, emphasizing instead the bankruptcy of the Company's Aboriginal policy. As Barry Cooper points out of this entire submission, "there is no evidence that it was noticed by anyone at the Colonial Office besides the archivist," although most of it was duly printed in the 1849 Blue Book.

The Pelly-Isbister Negotiations

What was not printed in the Blue Book was a private minute summarizing the exchange between Isbister and Pelly by Mr. Hawes, written in

early August of 1847.[60] The memo insisted that the Memorial must be
an exaggeration, since it was "unreasonable" that the HBC "would commit
or sanction such enormities as those charged against them by the Memorialists." It agreed that the mixed-bloods did have some Aboriginal
rights, a point that would subsequently become lost. The Memorial
exaggerated, and the Company had probably done no worse with the
Aboriginals than had other traders in other parts of the world. But Pelly's
insistence that the Company had promoted the welfare of the Indians
was going "too far." This minute provides one more bit of evidence that
from the perspective of the Colonial Office, the issue was indeed the
Company's policy and treatment of the Aboriginal people in the interior
of its territory, and not the political problems at Red River.

The Hawes minute renders very curious the events that next transpired. On 1 September 1847, Sir John Pelly wrote to Alexander Isbister,
suggesting a meeting at Hudson's Bay House. The two parties duly met,
and Pelly proposed that the "matter in dispute between the memorialists and the Hudson's Bay Company" be left "to the award of Earl Grey."
Isbister replied in writing to this offer in mid-November, and transmitted "an abstract of the requisition of the petitioners, as embodied in their
instructions and petition," not—he said—as the basis of a future arrangement but "that you may be fully acquainted with the sentiments
and wishes of the people generally."[61] This list, of course, was quite
different from the charges against the Company in the Memorial of
1847. Did Isbister think that the "matter in dispute between the memorialists and the Hudson's Bay Company" was something different than
the complaint of the Memorial? Did Pelly concur in this perception?
Pelly acknowledged the transmission of the list, claiming he did not
understand it.[62] The two men met and Isbister explained the objects in full.
Further discussion occurred in which Isbister explained in detail the
objections of the settlers to the land deed, and commented on the absence
of an independent judiciary. After this explanation, Pelly summarily denied
that he had ever offered to allow Grey to settle the matter.[63]

Attempting to make sense out of this whole episode between Isbister
and Pelly is not easy. Barry Cooper suggests that Pelly backed off because
he had come to realize that the "stakes were clearly too high to be wa-
gered on the decision of one man, no matter how friendly to the Company."[64] Even more likely was that Pelly had somehow or other come to
appreciate that the issues before the Colonial Office for deliberation were
quite different from the "Objects sought by the Petitioners." Pelly had offered to allow Grey to adjudicate the matter of the Company's Aboriginal

policy, expecting easily to win that judgement. If the question were instead political policy within the Red River Settlement, the Company might not do so well. Certainly Pelly had no intention of introducing new issues or allowing Grey to judge anything other than the case the Colonial Office thought it was deciding.

Closing the Books

Isbister continued to press the Colonial Office for action. He inquired about progress on 18 December 1847, and was informed by Mr. Hawes on 2 February 1848 that there had been no word from Canada.[65] By the time of Hawes's letter Sir John Pelly had forwarded Isbister's letter to Alexander Rowand to the Colonial Office, observing that Isbister was not dealing with "slight grievances" that "might be redressed by an individual inquiry, but what he seeks is the *overthrow of the Company.*"[66] This insight should have been evident from Isbister's earlier documentation, and hardly required confirmation from private correspondence. In his letter, Hawes added that "his Lordship is in communication with the Governor of the Hudson's Bay Company, with the view of devising the best mode of instituting an inquiry on the spot into the allegations of the Company." This information must have driven Isbister up the wall. Consulting with the subject of the complaints on how best to inquire into them was hardly likely to produce an independent investigation. But Isbister kept his head, writing to Grey in February 1848 that he was pleased there would be an inquiry on the spot. He then proceeded to warn Grey of "the difficulties against which the commission of enquiry would have to contend," especially the total control which the HBC had over the territory.[67] It was a subtle way of pointing out the unlikelihood of getting justice by consulting the abusers. Isbister then spoiled his effect, however, by forwarding a letter written to him from Quebec by Father Belcourt, which consisted mainly of unsubstantiated charges of persecution against himself, including one that Sir George Simpson had demanded his recall of the Archbishop of Quebec.[68] Hawes fired off an instant response, noting that Isbister was "under a mistake" in assuming that there would be a commission of inquiry.[69]

What Hawes did not write Isbister was that the government, on the advice of Sir John Pelly, had written Lieutenant-Colonel John Crofton, who had commanded the Sixth Regiment of Foot and acted as governor of Assiniboia in 1846 and 1847, to "furnish Her Majesty's Government with an impartial opinion on the question at issue between the Hudson's Bay Company and the Indians on the Red River, so as to enable Her

Majesty's Government to determine whether the complaints against the Company are well founded, and if so, what measures should be taken for affordng the Indians redress."[70] Pelly and the Company knew perfectly well that Crofton was on their side. So did the Colonial Office. Lord Elgin had written in 1847 on debriefing Crofton that his report of the Company's administration was "very favorable."[71]

Crofton responded to the official request for an "impartial opinion" within a week, probably because he had actually been approached about the business considerably earlier. He had been sent an abstract of the charges against the Company, and responded to them in order. We do not have a copy of the abstract, but can deduce it from Crofton's responses. It said little about the political complaints of the settlers, which allowed Crofton to maintain that the government of the HBC was "peculiarly mild and paternal," especially in its Indian regulations. He pointed to the many missions in existence in Red River and elsewhere as refutation of the second charge, completely ignoring Isbister's point that the Company took credit for missionary activity it had not originated nor financed. The missions refuted the charge that the Company kept the Indians in ignorance. Spiritous beverages were never sold to the Indians, who were equally not made hungry by Company policy. There was no extermination of the Indians, who were increasing in numbers. Those who traded in furs knew that they were breaching the law. As for Alexander Simpson, he had a disreputable character at the settlement. Crofton admitted that he knew nothing about the Oregon Territory, but he insisted that there was no local evidence at Red River that "the Hudson's Bay Company permitted lawless deeds."[72] In 1857, protesting that he was only a "simple soldier," Crofton, under fierce cross-examination, confessed that he had not been in the Hudson's Bay Indian territory, and had no personal knowledge on which to base his answers to most of the charges.[73]

The charges on which Crofton gave his judgement are worth contrasting with the "Objects sought by the Petitioners" discussed earlier by Isbister in his meetings with Sir John Pelly. The "official" charges deal almost exclusively with HBC treatment of the Aboriginal peoples in their vast territories. The maintenance of the fur-trading monopoly was merely one charge buried in the midst of many others, and was apparently described solely as a commercial rather than as a political matter. One reason for the differences between the charges and the "Objects" is because the charges were based on the Memorial, while the "Objects" were based on the Petition of 977, which were never properly presented before the Colonial Office. Isbister had, in effect, been hoist with his own petard. His arresting overstatement of the abuse of Aboriginal peoples got the attention of the Colonial Office, but only managed to deflect attention from the legitimate political complaints of the residents of the Red River Settlement. The HBC might well have dodged the bullet of accusations of political tyranny, but such charges were never clearly the main item placed on the agenda. Instead, by legitimately arguing that the complaints about the Aboriginals were misplaced and overdrawn, the Company would manage to escape censure entirely.

Although he did not know that the Crofton report had been submitted, what Isbister was coming to suspect was that his detailed submissions were not having much effect on the process. He wrote asking whether his communication of last summer had been received, and was assured by Herman Merivale, in his only official appearance in the Blue Book, that indeed it had.[74] Isbister then addressed a lengthy letter to Earl Grey, dated 22 March 1848. It provided the documents in the recent exchange which Isbister had with Sir John Pelly. Isbister took this occasion "to recapitulate a few of the most important points to which it was the object of the memorial and petition to draw the attention of Her Majesty's Government." Had he finally twigged to the fact that the Colonial Office was dealing with a quite different case from the one which it ought to have been? In any event, Isbister began his recapitulation with the "chief evil" of the present system of administration, which was "the anti-colonizing spirit manifested by the Hudson's Bay Company." The HBC was not content with a monopoly of the fur trade, he emphasized, but laid claim "equally to all the productions of the country, exercise a species of property in the natives, and an absolute right in the soil, of which they will neither make any beneficial use themselves nor suffer others." Only as his second point did Isbister turn to the effect of the monopoly on the Natives scattered elsewhere in Rupert's Land. The solution the inhabitants sought to these evils was the protection of the British government, either by incorporation into Canada or by establishment of a separate government. Isbister relegated the fur trade to his third point, suggesting that he would be satisfied with "some more effectual provision" for the well-being of the Aboriginals than at present existed, perhaps with the establishment of an Indian department. He enclosed an editorial from the *Morning Herald* which attacked the Company's Charter.

But it was too late to place the issues before the Colonial Office into the political frame in which they should have existed from the outset. On 6 June 1848, Lord Elgin sent his report to Earl Grey.[75] The territory involved was so distant that it was hard for Elgin to investigate. What he found, however, was that the Company's authority was "on the whole very advantageous to the Indians." Ardent spirits were discountenanced, and "if the trade were thrown open, and the Indians left to the mercy of the adventurers who might chance to engage in it, their condition would be greatly deteriorated." Elgin added that he thought it unfortunate that such a vast jurisdiction should be so far removed from British surveillance. He suggested the stationing of a military officer somewhere in the Company's vast territories, who could provide accurate information about the behaviour of the HBC. Grey responded to this suggestion with alacrity, appointing William Bletterman Caldwell as governor of Assiniboia—his salary paid by the Company—and requesting "a candid and detailed report of the state in which you find the settlement you have been selected to preside over."[76] Caldwell was available because he was commander of the pensioners who were dispatched to the colony in 1848.[77]

By this point even Isbister recognized that he had been checkmated. On 17 August 1848 he wrote a petition to the House of Commons which described a number of grievances against the HBC at Red River and noted that the government planned to add new territory on Vancouver Island to the HBC "for the purposes of colonisation." Because the Company was so totally unsympathetic to colonization, Isbister wanted an inquiry into the grievances of the Red River settlers "before any new privileges are confirmed to the Hudson's Bay Company."[78] This petition, of course, opened another whole dispute.

The Colonial Office was not quite finished with Isbister's 1847 Memorial, however. On 13 January 1849, Mr. Hawes requested an opinion on the charges against the HBC from Major John Griffiths, Crofton's successor as commandant of the troops at Fort Garry.[79] In this case an abstract of the principal documents (rather than merely an abstract of the charges) was sent, although it was not included in the Blue Book. This was apparently the same abstract of the principal charges sent Crofton, but on this occasion, one of the documents forwarded was the Petition of 977, for Griffiths commented upon it separately. Griffiths was hardly likely to be sympathetic to the petition, but at least he did consider its contents. He was probably the first person in the entire controversy, apart from Alexander Isbister, to do so. In his "Memorandum upon the Petition of the French 'Half-breeds' of the Red River Settlements, Hudson's Bay Company," Major Griffiths insisted that he had no idea what promises had been made to the people of Red River, or how the monopoly of the HBC could be a problem.[80] Certainly the Scots settlers did not complain about

broken promises—Griffiths had obviously never listened to Donald
Gunn on this subject. The French settlers, mainly "half-breeds," were a
"lawless, roving race," who did not farm and whose focus was on the
buffalo hunt, which was often ultimately followed by a period of starvation. Griffiths saw the petition not as a request for a redress of grievances, but "as an attempt to obtain a participation in the advantages derived by the Company from their vested rights (to which, I imagine, the
Red River settlers have about as much claim as a South Australian colonist), or as an excuse for providing the means for increasing their roving
habits." The settlement had an able Recorder and set of councillors.
None of the councillors were "French halfbreeds," but then, they were
"at present neither from position, habits or character fitted for legisla-
tors." The good major found it quite a novel feature, "the idea of the
settlers at the Red River imagining that the territory of the Hudson's
Bay Company forms a part of their settlement." Both his praise of Recorder Adam Thom and his utter misunderstanding of most of the points
of the petition ought to have disqualified Griffiths. But they did not.
Instead, his reiteration of the standard line on the Métis found a ready
audience at the Colonial Office.

Within less than a week after the reception of Griffith's comments, Benjamin
Hawes wrote Isbister that Earl Grey now had reports from the Major and
from Lieutenant-Colonel Crofton on the charges brought "at different times"
against the Hudson's Bay Company.[81] Neither soldier had any present connection with the Company, and "both may therefore fairly be regarded as
unbiased, as well as fully informed," proclaimed Hawes. Their accounts were
favourable to the Company. Only a powerful case against the Company would
have led Grey to recommend to Parliament any interference with the Company's charter. Not only had that case not been made, wrote Dawes, but the
evidence collected completely negated the allegations. Under the circumstances, Grey could only refer Isbister to the Company, "which, as he is assured, will readily consider any representations which may be made of substantial grievances." The Colonial Office files were, for all intents and purposes, closed for the time being on the Memorial and petition.[82]

As one of Isbister's former teachers commented, Isbister had appeared
in the affair of the Memorial as "an advocate of the civil rights of the
Indians."[83] While this was a perfectly proper role for him to play, it was
one which allowed the Colonial Office to ignore and evade the legitimate political complaints from Red River that had provoked the Memorial in the first place. The result was a vindication of the Hudson's
Bay Company's administration of the Aboriginals, not its treatment of
the people of the Red River Settlement.

ANOTHER LOOK AT THE
BUFFALO HUNT

NE of the most important social and economic institutions of the Red River Métis was the buffalo hunt. Some aspects of the hunt are quite controversial, as we shall see later, but for the most part there is substantial descriptive agreement among both contemporaries and later historians.[1] We have three lengthy descriptive narratives by three contemporary eyewitnesses, resulting from participation in different hunts at three different points in time.[2] Alexander Ross spent much of the summer of 1840 with the main summer hunt; Father Georges Belcourt travelled with the autumn hunt in 1845; and an observer, unnamed in the *Nor'-Wester* but otherwise known to be Viscount William Fitzwilliam Milton, spent some weeks with the summer hunt in 1860. In addition there are a number of briefer descriptions of the hunt in the accounts of virtually every visitor to the region before Confederation. Alexander Ross was quite articulate on the notice shown the hunt by visitors:

> We are now occasionally visited by men of science as well as men of pleasure. The war road of the savage, and the solitary haunt of the bear, have of late been resorted to by the florist, the botanist, and the geologist; nor is it uncommon now-a-days to see Officers of the Guards, Knights, Baronets, and some of the higher nobility of England, and other countries, coursing their steeds over the boundless plains, and enjoying the pleasures of the chase among the half-breeds and savages of the country. Distinction of rank is, of course, out of the question; and, at the close of the adventurous day, all squat down in merry mood together, enjoying the social freedom of equality

round Nature's table, and the novel treat of a fresh buffalo steak served up in the style of the country—that is to say, roasted on a forked stick before the fire.[3]

From Ross's perspective, this romantic picture was designed to retard the "elevation of the savage" in his "progress in civilization."

The Hunt Described

The organized and formal hunt came into existence around 1820, playing an important role in the ethnogenesis of Métis society.[4] Before that time both Indians and mixed-bloods hunted the buffalo on the prairie, but the mixed-bloods did so without large-scale organization. Donald Gunn describes the hunt in his account of the first Red River settlers wintering at Pembina in the winters of 1812-13 and 1813-14.[5] According to him, the settlers had to go out to the hunters' camp and bring back the frozen meat on sledges drawn by themselves. It is clear that even at this early date, the buffalo frequented what came to be the American side of the Red River Valley. Some writers think that the buffalo were more plentiful around the Lower Red River Valley before the arrival of settlers, but others, led by Frank Roe, insist that the buffalo had always been a migratory commodity and that the Lower Red was the outer limit of their range.[6]

The creation of a formal hunt probably had much to do with the establishment of the Buffalo Wool Company in Red River in 1821. This venture, a spectacular failure to find an exportable staple for the colony, was a disaster for a variety of reasons, not least because it transpired that the buffalo wool which the company hoped to weave into cloth was impervious to bleaching; one could have any colour one wanted so long as it was dark brown/black.[7] But if the Buffalo Wool Company impelled the Métis to sophisticate their organization in order to gather the wool, then it had something to show for its existence. As well as the creation of a new market in the Buffalo Wool Company, the presence of hostile Indians in the grazing grounds of the buffalo helps account for the development of an organized community approach to hunting.

As has been noted earlier, there was more than one hunt, involving more than one party of Métis. The big hunt was the summer hunt, which began in June and lasted until August. Although all hunts ultilized many parts of the buffalo through a number of different processes, the summer hunt was chiefly concerned with the production of dried meat and pemmican. In any event, all parts of the buffalo were processed on the spot by the summer hunt. A smaller hunt went out in September and returned to the settlement in late October or early November, eventually driven off the prairies by the arrival of winter. Because the weather was colder, this hunt was able to use the cold to help preserve some of the meat, and did not attempt to process everything on the ground. The meat brought back, in a more or less frozen state, was known as "green meat." The hides were much superior in the autumn, because the buffalo was by that time in the midst of producing his warm, thick coat. Not as many people went on the autumn hunt, partly because it competed with harvest time in the settlement, but more critically, because many of the mixed-bloods, unable to afford to winter in the settlement, had already begun moving to winter quarters and camps where they would survive by hunting.

There were also different parties of Métis involved in each of the hunts. One party was based at Pembina. A second consisted of those who lived on the Red to the north of St. Boniface. A third had its centre in St. François Xavier and was known as the "White Horse Plain brigade." By 1860 it had separated from the other groups and hunted independently, although still in close contact with the main expedition. Through the early years the White Horse Plain group had been led by Cuthbert Grant. Jean-Baptiste Wilkie of Pembina usually led that contingent, and William Hallett was a frequent chief of the main river party. In view of the frequent association of the buffalo hunt with the Francophone mixed-bloods, it is perhaps worth noting that all three of these leaders were "English halfbreeds."

When the parties assembled at the start of the hunt, they held councils that selected their leaders and organized the rules of the hunt. The rules were designed to avoid confusion during the actual hunt and to guarantee safety, especially from marauding parties of Indians who remained a constant danger throughout the buffalo-hunt period. A number of captains or chiefs were chosen—Ross says ten—with two senior captains. Each captain was given ten "soldiers," who were expected to follow orders without hesitation. Their job was to keep the expedition orderly and appropriately protected. Ross observed that the Métis were fond of the number ten, but Milton in 1860 wrote of twelve guides, which suggests that organization was to some extent dependent upon numbers. This quasi-military form of organization was obviously taken over by Louis Riel in the insurgency of 1869-70. Some observers in the 1870s also claimed that the ad hoc judicial process employed to condemn Thomas Scott derived from the buffalo hunt. While this is quite possible, the "rules of the hunt" did not contemplate serious crime such as murder or treason and certainly did not include any form of capital punishment.[8]

Men were also chosen to guide the expedition. They guided on a daily rotating basis, being responsible for raising the flag in the early morning (a signal for breaking camp) and for lowering it at night (the signal for striking a new camp). During the day their authority was primary, although when actually in camp the captains were in charge. All observers were impressed by the intuitive ability of the guides to navigate the seemingly featureless prairies. Viscount Milton wrote, "to avoid marshes, go round lakes, and find a path between precipitous hills, requires a very correct knowledge of the country, and is certainly a very difficult and responsible duty."[9]

The size of these expeditions was substantial. We do not have anything resembling a reliable series of numbers over time, but Alexander Ross wrote of an increase from 540 carts in 1820 to 1,210 carts in 1840, and Milton and Cheadle write of "1500 or 1600" carts in 1862.[10] Father Belcourt in 1845 accompanied the smaller autumn expedition, which he reported consisted of 213 carts and 55 hunters, 300 horses and over 100 oxen. Mr. Flett in 1849 made a census of the summer White Horse Plain brigade and found 603 carts, 700 half-breeds, 200 Indians, 600 horses, 200 oxen, and one cat.[11] The *Nor'-Wester* in 1860 listed the size of the White Horse Plain group as: "154 families, including 210 men able to bear arms (of whom 160 were buffalo 'runners'); and 700 'non-combatants' women and children," accompanied by "642 horses, 50 oxen, 6 cows, 522 dogs, 533 carts, 1 wagon, 232 guns, 10 revolvers, 21,000 bullets and 270 quarts of gunpowder." The newspaper also reported the size of the main hunt, a product of a "close and careful count" as "500 men, 600 women, 680 children, 730 horses, 300 oxen, and 950 carts."[12] The party camped in what contemporaries described as "lodges" or "tents," but we would label "teepees." In addition there were a number of larger lodges for council meetings and gatherings. Each hunter required three to four carts, which, even when stretched out double-file or quadruple-file across the prairie, produced several miles worth of expedition while travelling from one camp-site to the next. The carts often carried firewood on the outward journey. Each hunter was also accompanied by three to four family members, for women and children did much of the work. Not even advanced stages of pregnancy kept women at home during the time of the hunt. The result was a large-sized and not very manoeuvrable moving community, difficult to protect from marauders. Ross thought it "the largest of the kind, perhaps, in the world."[13]

Any expedition generated a good deal of noise and was not likely to go undetected for very long. Each cart was usually drawn by one ox in rawhide harness, with a collar like that for a cart-horse, although some-times horses were employed. The sound of the creaking of the wheels and axles of the carts was legendary; Charles Mair wrote his brother in 1868 that the sound "makes your blood run cold."[14] At night, the bel-lowing of the cattle and the neighing of horses provided a constant back-ground continuo of noise against which performed the virtuoso dogs. Viscount Milton wrote of the dogs that they "seemed to delight in noise, and the bark of one was quite sufficient to get the entire canine popula-tion of the camp yelping in full chorus."[15] Protection for this fairly audi-ble community was thus provided by very detailed precautions. The camp usually broke at daybreak, with the daily guide in front accompa-nied by parties of armed scouts and soldiers. Other scouts rode on the flanks and to the rear of the caravan. Casual firing of the guns was strictly prohibited by the laws of the camp, mainly to avoid alerting the buffalo. When the caravan stopped, either because of alarm, for lunch, or for the night, it wheeled itself into a large two-columned circle with each cart parked wheel-to-wheel to its neighbour. The carts themselves thus con-tained the livestock. Inside the ring the tents were pitched, each beside

The buffalo hunt ("Grandes Chasser") as painted by Henri Julien.

its own carts. Belcourt said that the 1845 autumn hunt was one of sixty lodges, which suggests one for each hunter and his family.

Eventually the expedition would encounter buffalo, usually many miles south of the international boundary. The fact that the Red River hunts operated mainly in the United States had not escaped the notice of the American authorities, who, beginning in the 1840s, had attempted to force the hunters to become American citizens. Contemporary observers argued that the Americans could cripple Red River by strict policing of the boundary, although most Métis were quite prepared to take on American citizenship if required. In any event, often bulls were discovered first, since they grazed on the outer fringes of the larger herd of cows, which provided the preferred meat. The hunters were happy to practise killing the bulls, but it was the cows they were really after.

All observers were singularly impressed with the skillful ways in which the hunters operated. They were able to manoeuvre their horses by leaning from one side to other, leaving their hands free for handling, and especially for reloading the gun. The horse was trained to spring to one side after the kill to avoid stumbling over the fallen animal. Although this was the perfect place for a repeating rifle, most hunters did not use such modern equipment. Instead the hunters wadded down the first shot in their single-shot smoothbore rifles and carried up to four additional balls in their mouths, spitting one into the barrel after pouring in another charge of powder. This was a fairly dangerous procedure. In one notorious incident in 1860, the hunter had put his powder in too soon after the last discharge, and used his mouth over the muzzle to blow the powder home. Suddenly igniting, it severely burnt his mouth and throat, and he died two days later.[16] Observers were equally impressed with how each hunter appeared able to distinguish his own kill; there were remarkably few disputes over the dead animals although they were usually not marked by the individual hunter.

The chase not only tested the skill of the hunter, but also challenged his courage, for the work was highly hazardous. A hunt was seldom completed without at least one serious injury or death. Falls when horses stumbled over rough ground were common. The buffalo, who were alleged to see better sideways than straight ahead, often thrust at the horse and knocked it down. The fallen rider was liable to be trampled, or even tossed and gored by an infuriated animal. The hunter could as easily become caught up in a mindless stampede by the buffalo. Father Belcourt reported one such incident that he had witnessed in 1845:

Having dashed off in pursuit of a numerous herd of cows, they were in full career, in the very midst of the herd, when they arrived suddenly at the brink of a steep, rock-stewn cliff. Over they went, pell-mell—hunters, horses, and buffalo—in such confusion that it is difficult to explain why some were not killed, crushed against the rocks or trampled beneath the hooves of the following horde. Only one man was knocked unconscious, and he soon recovered. . . . The hunters who had been un-horsed jumped quickly back into their saddles with reassuring cries, and took up the chase once more, cracking their whips with a will in an endeavour to make up for lost time.[17]

There was also the danger from stray bullets, for, "from every direction they whistle through the clouds of dust in a most disconcerting manner." Finally, the hunter who was skinning his kill on the open prairie was sometimes exposed to great risk from lurking Sioux. Every hunter had a tale or two of danger to tell around the evening campfire. Alexander Ross was probably correct in his assertion that most of these men were positively drawn by "the mixture of hope and fear—the continual excitement—the very dangers themselves."[18]

After the chase was finished—it consumed no more than an hour or two at the most and was usually limited by the need to reload the guns—the hunters leapt off their horses, removed their coats and rolled up their shirt-sleeves, and began to dress and butcher the kill right on the ground where they lay. The hunter propped up the dead animal on its knees, spreading its hind legs so that the buffalo was supported on its belly. First the small hump was removed, then the hide was slit down the back and taken away. Then the animal was cut up. Father Belcourt identified sixteen different cuts or parts of the animal.[19] The heat from the freshly killed animals was very intense as the hunter laboured. He worked up a considerable thirst which he quenched with water from a small keg or by chewing on various raw parts of the carcass. The hunter worked backwards through his kill, skinning the last animal first.

The carts collected the meat and carried it to the camp, where the women took over the task of processing. The men were responsible for cracking and boiling the bones to extract the marrow, but the females in the party dealt with most of the remainder of the work. "The day of a race is as fatiguing for the hunter as the horse," wrote Alexander Ross, "but the meat once in the camp, he enjoys the very luxury of idleness."[20] The women cut the meat into long strips and hung it upon wooden frames to dry. The choicer bits were then rolled up and packaged into bundles of jerky weighing sixty to seventy pounds each. The remainder were fried to a crisp over a hot fire, then pounded into a powder to which melted fat was added. The mixture was worked with shovels and then packed into raw-hide sacks called "taureaux." Sometimes dried fruits were included in the mixture, which produced the finest "taureaux" or pemmican.[21] According to Father Belcourt, one cow's meat supplied only enough for half a "taureaux" and less than one bundle of jerky. The dried hides supplied parchment after they were dried and scraped on the inside by the women to remove the hair. When the hunt was finished, the carts—each filled with 1,000 to 1,500 pounds of meat—would creak their way back to the Red River. This time, the women and children would walk behind.

The Critics of the Hunt

Although contemporary observers were in general agreement about how the hunt operated, the questions of its implications were more controversial. Much of the debate originated with Sheriff Alexander Ross, whose views of the hunt were generally negative, because the excitement and adventure of the buffalo chase helped prevent the Métis from settling down to a steady agricultural existence which was the basis of civilization. One central feature of Ross's critique was the extent to which the hunt perpetuated the improvidence of the Métis as a people. He maintained that the "plain hunter's life is truly a dog's life—a feast or a famine," and wrote movingly of the starvation experienced by the children in the hunt's camp before the buffalo had been sighted.[22] As part of the pattern, he pointed out that once the buffalo were run, the hunters often left much of the kill on the ground for the wolves, while in camp, the dogs were allowed to gorge themselves. "There is a manifest conflict of want and waste in all their arrangements," Ross maintained, and as "a proof of the most profligate waste of animals," he insisted that on the hunt he observed, 2,500 animals were killed to provide a quantity of pemmican and dried meat that 750 animals could have supplied. Even allowing for the feasting at the campfire, said Ross, most of the food was wasted. "Scarcely one-third in number of the animals killed is turned to account."[23] This behaviour merely perpetuated a Métis "improvidence and want of forethought" inherited from their "savage" ancestors.

This sort of evidence fit well into the arguments of those who sought to document that the profligacy of the hunt was in large part responsible for the disappearance of the buffalo from the plains. The first major writer in this line of argument was William T. Hornaday, whose *The Extermination of the American Bison, With a Sketch of Its Discovery and Life-History* was published in 1887.[24] Hornaday relied almost exclusively on Ross's testimony to support his conclusion that the "Red River settlers, aided, of course, by the Indians of that region, are responsible for the extermination of the bison throughout northeastern Dakota, as far as the Cheyenne River, northern Minnesota, and the whole of what is now the Province of Manitoba."[25] Frank T. Roe in 1935 pointed out the dangers of extrapolating from one expedition to the entire hunt, particularly when Father Belcourt's figures suggested a yield per cow of three and one-half times that stated by Ross.[26] Nevertheless, he observed that "the legend of Red River wastefulness has become so embedded in popular belief that it is apparently considered to be an indispensable feature in any allusion whatever to the Hunt."[27] In other writings, Roe offered a variety of explanations apart from Métis profligacy for the disappearance of the buffalo.[28] Even if the hunt were profligate, the figures presented for wastage before 1870 ought not to have destroyed the buffalo if indeed there were many thousands still grazing the plains.

The question of the range of the buffalo and its supposed narrowing over time under the pressure of hunting has been the subject of considerable debate. Professor Hind talked about two herds of buffalo known to the Red River hunters, one that of the Grand Coteau/Red River, and the other, that of the Saskatchewan. Hind wrote of the westward pressure on the buffalo of the Métis hunt, noting, "the country about the west side of Turtle Mountain in June 1858 was scored with their [Métis] tracks at one of the crossing places on the Little Souris, as if deep parallel ruts had been artificially cut down the hill-sides. These ruts, often one foot deep and sixteen inches broad, would converge from the prairie for many miles to a favourite crossing or drinking place; and they are often seen in regions in which the buffalo is no longer a visitor."[29] Roe, on the other hand, disputed the multiple-herd theory, arguing that the buffalo's appearance had always been irregular.

Beyond the question of Métis profligacy (and its impact on the buffalo population of the region) lurked Alexander Ross's larger socio-economic criticisms of the buffalo hunt. The hunt was not only wasteful but uneconomic and socially disfunctional, maintained Ross. To illustrate the economy of the hunt, Ross calculated at £24,000 the capital outlay required to equip the 1840 expedition he accompanied. Half of this outlay came from credit, Ross insisted, and he described (unfortunately not in detail) a system of truck in Red River in which the Métis were constantly caught in an ever-escalating web of debt:

before they have paid their debts in part, got their supplies in part (for everything they do is by halves), the whole of their provisions, one way or other, is dribbled off. In less than a month, therefore, they have to start on the second trip, as destitute of supplies, as deeply in debt, and as ill provided as at first....The writer is not acquainted with a single instance, during the last twenty-five years, of one of these plain-hunters being able to clear his way or liquidate his expenses, far less to save a shilling by the chase; the absence of a proper system, and the want of a market, render it impossible.[30]

Moreover, the hunt was socially disruptive, argued Ross, for it agitated the remainder of the inhabitants of the settlement both before its departure and after its return. The labour market and prices of provisions in the settlement were controlled by the hunt. The worst feature of all of the hunt, said Ross, was its blithe persistence in the face of its certain termination. "The buffalo, the exciting cause, once extinct, the wandering and savage life of the half-breed, as well as the savage himself, must give place to a more genial and interesting order of things; when here, as in other parts of the world, the husbandman and the plough, the sound of the grindstone, and the church-going bell, will alone be heard."[31] This theme would be constantly reiterated in the settlement, not least by Alexander Ross's son James in the pages of the Nor'-Wester.

In an editorial in the Nor'-Wester in late 1860 entitled "The Plains-Hunting Business," James Ross indicted the hunt "as the business, or regular, ordinary pursuit of a large proportion of the Red River people."[32] The hunt created and strengthened restless habits. It encouraged extravagance, and the editorialist repeated the earlier arguments of Alexander Ross, insisting that six or seven hundred souls on the hunt consumed enough meat "as would suffice for six or seven thousand in Great Britain, France, or Germany." It put every hunter into permanent debt. The hunt led to the neglect of education for the young, who were permitted to wander about the prairie all summer, "like savages." The editorial spelled out its theory of social progress. Hunting represented a "rude or primitive state of society," the first "stage of civilization." The progression was from hunting to pastoral to agricultural and ultimately to industrial. The Nor'-Wester doubted that this progression would occur in Red River, but the first link was clearly present. The hunt suited the "tastes of nature's children." But it was "an outlandish, temporary make-shift, quite unworthy of people pretending to a respectable degree of civilisation."

In Defence of the Hunt

Recent research on the Métis has suggested that the Ross analysis of the economics of the hunt was hardly a complete one. The emphasis has been less directly on the questions of profligacy and the truck system than on the overall economic strategy of the Métis. By the evidence of Ross and virtually every other contemporary observer of the Red River economy, the major problem with agriculture in the settlement was the want of market once the demands of the Hudson's Bay Company had been satisfied. At the same time, it must be added that after the early 1840s the demands of the HBC were substantial, and usually were not met by the farmers of Red River.[33] Ross may have been accurate in his assessment of the future. But the problem may have been less a want of market than a lack of trust for the continued demand of that market and for the HBC which controlled it. Colonel John Ffolliot Crofton told the Select Parliamentary Committee in 1857 that he had attempted to talk the Métis out of the hunt. They answered, "that they did not cultivate their lands for two reasons; one was, that they could not export corn which they might raise beyond that required for their mere subsistence, and that it was better for them to purchase the means of subsistence with the produce of the plains, the pemmican which they made, than to cultivate their lands, for if they grew corn they did not know what to do with it; they could not export it, and they were not allowed to distil it."[34] These arguments were simply not true after 1845. The problem was not in marketing crops, if harvested, but in the uncertainty of being able to harvest them, given the continual natural disasters of the pre-Canadian period.[35] Farming in the early settlement had been chiefly on a subsistence basis. The hunt had offered the possibility of cash payment. Given the circumstances of the time, the hunt was a sensible and inevitable economic choice. The hunt complemented the agricultural economy of the early period, rather than conflicted with it, not least in its supply of food in the many years of bad harvest.

Moreover, it must be remembered that Alexander Ross had written in the 1840s, and was not able to take into account the subsequent behaviour of the Métis in the changing market economy of the region. Despite James Ross's reiteration of his father's earlier arguments in 1860, to generalize from Ross's criticism of the hunt in terms of the post-1840 period would be quite unfortunate.[36] According to one recent argument by Gerhard Ens, the real choice for the Red River Métis, particularly in the post-1840 period, was "increasingly between a kin-based capitalist fur trade, wage labour, and peasant agriculture." Not the least part of the new economic regime was the employment of the carts previously used mainly in the hunt to carry goods between the United States and the settlement. This extensive haulage system, which employed upwards of 2,500 carts per year, would only last until the arrival of the railroad, but it was quite important between 1850 and 1880.

While the Ens argument is theoretically attractive in many respects, it does have some problems, chiefly in its assumption that agriculture in Red River was and would be in the future a peasant—i.e., subsistence—occupation. We know that agriculture could be and would become a capitalistic enterprise after 1870, but more to the point, we know that Red River farmers after 1845 could sell all they could grow and harvest. The consistent failure to supply the market does not suggest the absence of one. If the buffalo hunters saw "peasant" farming as their only agricultural choice, this suggests some preconceptions about agriculture which had nothing to do with the opportunities presented by the market. In the end, it must be remembered that contemporary discussion of the hunt was a moral rather than an economic one. From the Ross perspective, as well as other observers, the hunt was part of the Aboriginal inheritance of the Métis. Agriculture, on the other hand, represented the progress of civilization which the Rosses desired the Red River settlement to attain. But economic reality did not necessarily harmonize with this dichotomy. In embracing the hunt, the Métis may not have been so much recalling their ancestry as behaving like rational Economic Men. The Rosses sought for them something else.

THE QUEEN V. G.O. CORBETT, 1863

"The World hath been often compared to the Theatre; and many grave Writers, as well as the Poets, have considered human Life as a great Drama, resembling, in almost every Particular, those scenical Representations, which *Thespis* is first reported to have invented, and which have been since received with so much Approbation and Delight in all polite Countries. This Thought hath been carried so far, and is become so general, that some Words proper to the Theatre, and which were, at first, metaphorically applied to the World, are now indiscriminately and literally spoken of both: Thus Stage and Scene are by common Use grown as familiar to us, when we speak of Life in general, as when we confine ourselves to dramatic Performances."
—Henry Fielding, *The History of Tom Jones,* book 7, chapter 1

IN February of 1863 a criminal trial took place in the courthouse outside the walls of Upper Fort Garry that would have been the sensation of British North America, perhaps of the entire Empire, had it not been conducted in the remote settlement of Red River. As it was, reports on the event were published as far away as Montreal.[1] The courthouse was a small wooden structure, half devoted to a courtroom, the other half to the gaol. In the gaol, prisoners shared space with liquor confiscated for non-payment of duty. In the courtroom, quarters were cramped. The elevated box that served as the dock for the prisoner was very small. The raised bench for the justices at the back of the room was extremely narrow, and a portly judge could only just squeeze into his place behind the chairs of his colleagues. There was a small table covered with green cloth in the centre of the room, at which sat the clerk of the court with his Bible, his record book, and a jug of cold water. Around the clerk clustered the various "agents" in the case: the prosecutors, the defence counsel, and the interpreters. To the left of the judge were two rows of benches for the jury, who wondered whether they would be paid for their services.[2] Only a small space existed for the accommodation of spectators. "The very imperfect ventilation of the courthouse," noted one contemporary, "has long been a subject of remark."[3] The trial was on five charges of procuring an abortion under 24 & 25 Vict., c. 100.[4] Abortion had become a serious matter in Victorian Britain and its Empire. This was one of a handful of criminal trials in British North America that dealt with it.[5] The accused was neither a professional abortionist nor an advocate of birth control, however, but, according to the testimony in the trial, an abuser who was attempting to escape the consequences of his actions.[6]

Although the Red River Settlement was not officially a colony of Great Britain, it did have a government separate from the Hudson's Bay Company, as well as a fully developed system for the administration of justice. The General Quarterly Court of Assiniboia (as the Red River court was officially called) had been founded in 1835 as the principal court of the settlement. After 1839 its chief officer was the recorder, appointed by the HBC and assisted by unpaid magistrates, including all members of the Council of Assiniboia who sat in magistrates' courts to consider cases involving small sums of money and not concerning threats to life or limb. The General Quarterly Court was the principal civil and criminal court in the territory, although it was forbidden by parliamentary statute from hearing capital cases, which were to be taken to Canada for trial. Despite this prohibition, the court had adjudicated capital cases, and had even sentenced several convicted offenders to execution. The court's jurisdiction extended only fifty miles in all directions from Upper Fort Garry, however.[7]

The legal procedures in the General Quarterly Court were an amalgam of practice in various British jurisdictions. When the court had been created, the HBC had been under no obligation to introduce fully the English common law, and it had not done so. Most of the early recorders had Scottish rather than English legal training, and the procedures of the Scottish courts mixed unacknowledged with those of the common law and English criminal law. Legal practices from eastern Canada were also employed. In 1852, a new legal code consolidated Red River law, adding that the laws of England as of Queen Victoria's accession (20 June 1837) "shall regulate the proceedings of the general court."[8] Cases were heard before a twelve-man jury, which over the years had come usually to mean (in Quebec fashion) six jurors of French background and six of British. In the early days, the recorder had acted as prosecuting attorney, "laying the case before the jury," and while there were occasionally attorneys of sorts for the defence, they had no training. Because Assiniboia was not a Crown colony, there was no right of appeal from the decisions of the Quarterly Court to the Crown, either in Canada or in Great Britain. The abortion trial of 1863 marked a number of differences in court proceedings for Red River. The jury selected comprised more British than French jurymen. There were formal prosecutors, as well as a formal defence, and the judge attempted to apply appropriate English practice rather than the more informal Red River one. The trial was clearly a transitional one, pointing towards a more formal court better integrated into the imperial legal system.

The trial was also an early colonial manifestation of a Victorian phenomenon of relatively recent vintage: the public sex scandal. All kinds of scandals proliferated in the British popular press, beginning in the 1850s. They usually required the public prominence of at least one of the participants, whose career could be threatened and questioned by the exposure of private misdeeds. As William S. Cohen has recently pointed out, the best sex scandals of the Victorian period usually also involved the contravention of other social borders besides mere sexual misconduct. "Even the most licentious scandal rarely arises solely in the wake of a sexual transgression; most cases involve the crossing of rigid class, national, or racial lines, as well as the highly ossified gender divide, which organize Victorian society."[9] Sex was permitted to provide an occasion for the playing out of other sorts of social conflict. In these scandals, whether or not there was actually a trial, the densely plotted narrative involved an accuser making public a terrible secret and an accused (who had to be a prominent public figure) responding with denials; the ultimate model was the judicial one of plaintiff, defendant, and jury.[10] In some cases the reading public, through newspaper reporting, could be the jury. In Red River, a young mixed-blood servant girl accused her master of rape, seduction, and attempted abortion. Almost by definition, the Red River trial exposed the underlying tensions of Red River society, most of which would emerge again in the insurgency led by Louis Riel a few years later.[11] The lines dividing the races, the genders, and social classes were clearly revealed for those who sought them out.

The rape or seduction of a young servant girl by her master was a relatively common occurrence in the nineteenth century.[12] Domestic servants were often at social risk because of what one scholar has called "the peculiar combination of class subordination embedded in a personal relationship."[13] The female servant's position was a particularly anomalous one. Servants worked at home in a feminine occupation, but were not family. The work was physical but the relationships could be intimate. The young maiden sexually exploited by an older man, often her master, was perhaps an even more common literary and mythological theme.[14] While the courtroom inevitably turned the real-life crime into a theatrical drama, it did so in Red River at a time when Victorian melodramatic theatre was evolving into sensationalist fiction.[15] Not surprisingly, the Red River case positively reeked with literary and theatrical allusions, some deliberate and some unintentional. Courtroom scenes allowed writers of melodrama and sensationalist fiction the opportunity "to bring into open conflict the values of the public and private spheres," and had the same effect on the British North American frontier.[16] Although it was an isolated community, the Red River Settlement had a substantial public subscription library, and current Victorian novels were readily available for purchase from the bookshop of Messrs. Ross and Coldwell at Colony Gardens.

The accused defendant was the Reverend Griffith Owen Corbett, a controversial Anglican clergyman and medical practitioner, who was also the chief spokesman for the Protestant Anglophone mixed-bloods in the settlement.[17] Born in 1823 in England, Corbett had come to Montreal in 1851 under the auspices of the Colonial Church and School Society (CCSS), serving as a catechist. For some unknown reason, the Bishop of Montreal refused to ordain him. He came to Rupert's Land in 1852 and founded a new church at Headingley, about twelve miles from the Forks, on the Assiniboine River. Returning to England in 1855, Corbett attended medical lectures at King's College, London, and testified against the Hudson's Bay Company before the Select Committee of the House of Commons investigating the renewal of the Company's licence in 1857. Corbett insisted that the HBC sought to constrain both the Anglican Church and the economic development of the settlement in its own interests, but he could offer little concrete evidence to support his accusations. Edward Ellice, acting in favour of the Company, insisted on formal documentation of the alleged obstructionism and managed to cast into question most of Corbett's charges. One of Corbett's accusations was that the Company had greatly increased the charges for land in his parish, although most involved in acquiring it claimed Aboriginal title.[18] Despite objections in England that he was a troublemaker, he and his wife returned to Headingley in 1857 upon the insistence of Rupert's Land bishop David Anderson, at a stipend of £150 per annum.

Over the next few years, Corbett made himself very popular at Headingley and amongst the Protestant mixed-bloods of the settlement, and simultaneously very unpopular with the ruling elite of the colony. His connection with the CCSS led him to be viewed with suspicion by most of the settlement's other Anglican clergy, who were associated with the low-church Church Missionary Society. His continued attacks on the Hudson's Bay Company made him suspect in official circles. His advocacy of Crown Colony status for Red River, instead of Canadian annexation or continued Hudson's Bay Company rule, met with a warm response from the mixed-blood community.[19] His hostility to Roman Catholicism also found fervent support from many Anglophone mixed-bloods, although it hardly made a friend of Governor MacTavish, accused of selling out Protestantism when he married a Catholic in 1861. Contemporaries were agreed that Corbett's chief constituency was among the poorer and less well-educated mixed-bloods of the settlement.[20]

In 1862 rumours circulated throughout the settlement that Corbett's young mixed-blood servant girl, Maria Thomas, was carrying the minister's child. Corbett attempted to staunch these reports by having the girl swear an oath, which he drafted, denying his sexual involvement with her. This oath was taken on 2 August 1862 before Headingley magistrate John Taylor, the girl's mother, and Reverend and Mrs. Corbett, but the girl refused to swear properly (claiming she passed the Bible over her chin and thus "gave the matter the go-by"). The oath was signed by John Taylor rather than by Maria Thomas. The court would later view it as an oath improperly taken and obtained under duress and coercion. In the autumn of 1862, Corbett's friends circulated along the Assiniboine River a petition of support for him as a clergyman and as a medical practitioner. This was presented to him as a "testimonial" on 5 November, which happened to be Guy Fawkes Day. A number of those who signed it later disowned their signatures, claiming that they had not realized that they were doing more than acknowledging his medical services.[21]

Eventually Maria Thomas's father, a Hudson's Bay Company tripman (a boatman who "tripped" between Red River and Hudson Bay), complained to the Anglican bishop, David Anderson, who sent his archdeacon, James Hunter, to investigate Simon Thomas's charges.[22] While Hunter did conduct an informal investigation, he did so single-handedly in a manner that provided no safeguards for the accused. The archdeacon examined the girl at length at her father's house in Mapleton, and then spoke several times to magistrate John Taylor, who had come down from Headingley. According to the court report at the trial, the archdeacon testified, "I asked him if Mr. C. was innocent or guilty he said guilty—I asked if Mr. C. had confessed it he said yes—I was anxious to know the words Mr. C. had used. J. Taylor told me that Mr. C. had told him at his J. Taylor's house outside where he was winnowing wheat mentioned a letter he Mr. C. had received from the bishop he said no doubt I am to blame but go down and see if she can put it on any one else and tell the girl to keep it quiet and come back as quick as possible. . . ."[23] Corbett was probably wrong when he charged that the Hudson's Bay Company had paid Simon Thomas to complain, but quite correct in his sense that the settlement's establishment was quite happy to pursue the complaint. Even J. J. Hargrave, who was no friend of Corbett, noted that the "result of the Archdeacon's inquest was a conviction, which he did not scruple to state in public, that Mr. Corbett was guilty as libelled."[24] As a result of this investigation, the bishop advised Corbett to flee the country to avoid prosecution. Corbett consulted with his friends in Headingley and re-fused to depart, maintaining that he was innocent, although fearful of not receiving a fair trial.

The subsequent official investigation by magistrates Thomas Sinclair and Thomas Bunn took place in early December 1862 at the bedside of the girl. It followed a meeting of the magistrates and constables at the house of James Fidler in Mapleton on 1 December 1862.[25] Maria's "death-bed deposition"—she was presumed to be dying—was supplemented by evidence from her family, leading the magistrates to issue a warrant that led to Corbett's arrest and confinement in prison at Upper Fort Garry. It is impossible to tell to what extent the presumption that Maria was dying was influenced by contemporary fictional treatments of "magdalen figures," who found their redemption in death, usually fol-lowing emotional deathbed scenes.[26] In any event, Maria Thomas was no Victorian "Angel in the House."[27] She was a mixed-blood girl from a poor family. She had been a behavioural problem at home before being placed by her parents into service with the Corbetts. She had certainly flirted, if nothing more, with the boys. The magistrates had decided to charge Corbett not with "criminal conversation" or "carnal connection" with the girl but with attempting to procure a miscarriage on five sepa-rate occasions, a charge that Judge Black insisted was not bailable.[28] In prison, Corbett read up on the law, discovering—he later wrote—that Blackstone's version was far different from Judge Black's.[29] The mixed-bloods wanted Corbett released on bail. Over 150 mixed-bloods from all over the settlement congregated at the gaol on 6 December. The *Nor'-Wester* denied they had any intention of using violence to release the prisoner. The governor of Assiniboia, A.G. Dallas, met the crowd, allowed Corbett to address them, and then only with difficulty retired from the scene. One mixed-blood commented gratuitously to the governor, "My father bought 14 chains of land from the Company and they pocketed the money, although they never paid the Indians for their lands."[30] According to Samuel Taylor, Corbett at this juncture refused to be forcibly removed from prison; "he prepared to remain in some time longer until the General Court."[31] Corbett was eventually allowed to post bail on 16 December amidst continuing rumours that the HBC had set Corbett up. All this pre-trial manoeuvring contributed substantially to complicating the plot of the courtroom melodrama.

If the Company was pleased to see Corbett in trouble, the clergyman was equally pleased to be able to associate his personal difficulties with the political problems of the day and to wrap himself in the mantle of a champion of "British liberty."[32] Although James Ross, who advocated the Canadian annexation of Red River, had earlier opposed Corbett over the Crown Colony business, he had recently become a political ally. Late in 1862 the Council of Assiniboia had collected nearly 1,200 names to a petition to the British Colonial Office for troops to defend the settlement from marauding Sioux. Corbett and Ross had circulated a counter-petition calling for a Crown Colony in Red River. As co-editor of the *Nor'-Wester*, Ross refused to publish the official petition. In punitive response, the Hudson's Bay Company stripped Ross of his offices as sheriff, governor of the jail, and postmaster. A number of leading officials of the HBC cancelled their subscriptions to the *Nor'-Wester*. An angry Ross and a large number of mixed-bloods were thus quite prepared to believe Corbett's accounts of Company persecution and to defend him in court. For his part, Corbett sent a stirring letter from "Red River Prison" accusing the Company of "an attack upon our social, political, and religious freedom."[33]

The entire settlement chose sides, and even before the trial, a spirit of partisanship sprang up that demonstrates why trials often require a change of venue. Given Red River's isolation, no such change was possible at the time. The accused and his lawyers did their best to speed the legal process by demanding the opening of a special session of the court.

They claimed that a special session had been suggested by the authorities as an alternative to bail. The court understandably insisted on waiting until Maria Thomas, who gave birth to a baby girl in early January, could travel to the courthouse at Fort Garry. Meanwhile, one John Tait, a friend of Corbett, made extravagant statements around the settlement about Archdeacon Hunter, who in turn brought suit for defamation of character. Tait settled out of court in early February 1863 through payment of £100 and a retraction of all his remarks.[34] David Tait, another friend of Corbett, attempted to lay an information against Maria Thomas for perjury, based upon the discrepancies between her earlier oath sworn before John Taylor and her later deposition to the magistrates. This information was not acted upon by the magistrates.

The trial itself began on 19 February 1863, and was literally a nine-day wonder.[35] Recorder John Black was on the bench, supported by a number of his magistrates. Born in Scotland, Black had accompanied Adam Thom to Red River in 1839, entering the service of the HBC and rising to post of chief trader. In 1845 Black married Margaret, daughter of Alexander Christie, governor of Assiniboia. From 1850 to 1852 he served as chief accountant of the Upper Red River District, but Governor Eden Colvile did not like him. After his wife's death in 1854 he went to Scotland and Australia, returning to Red River in 1862 to become recorder and president of the General Quarterly Court of Assiniboia. He apparently had acquired some legal training in Scotland and Australia.[36] This trial was one of his first major tests. According to Hargrave, the people of the settlement protested the hearing by refusing to enter the courthouse until the preliminary formalities were finished.

The trial was covered virtually verbatim (minus only the salacious medical bits) in successive instalments of the local newspaper, the *Nor'-Wester*, with co-editor William Coldwell using his stenographic skills, honed in Toronto police courts, to great effect. This serialization of the report added yet another literary dimension to the trial, for it echoed the way in which most popular fiction was delivered to its audience in the mid-nineteenth century. Why *Nor'-Wester* editor and publisher James Ross, who also served as Corbett's defence attorney, chose to publish a complete transcript of the trial is an interesting question. Joseph James Hargrave wrote in his history of Red River that "the fact that the *Nor'Wester*, as a family magazine, survived the publication of the details of that trial, has always here been considered surprising."[37] The newspaper had, since its inception, covered the activities of the local court in great detail, as did its eastern Canadian models. It is likely that Ross, fearing that the case might go against him in the courtroom, may have sought to appeal to the entire community as jury. The full record was possibly the best way of showing just how complicated the evidence really was, as well as how much of it was unsubstantiated beyond the testimony of the victim. To some extent this appeal to the community may have worked, since Corbett would be quickly broken out of gaol after his conviction. Ross's main motive, however, was probably a potential increase in circulation for his newspaper, which he encouraged by printing the report in serial instalments. The entire case constituted what literary scholars would label a mixed genre (composed chiefly of a combination of court transcriptions, newspaper reports, and melodrama) with an indeterminate plot.[38]

The *Nor'-Wester* editors do not appear to have tampered much with the actual report of the testimony, although it is true that since he was also defence attorney, James Ross had some considerable opportunity in the courtroom to shape the case that would be presented in the newspaper.[39] As well as the newspaper account, another, less complete, court report is still to be found in the records of the Court of Quarterly Sessions at the Manitoba Provincial Archives; it includes all the medical testimony, and confirms that the *Nor'-Wester* reported fairly accurately those parts of the trial where its texts can be verified.[40] For example, the *Nor' Wester* reported the testimony of Lower Fort Garry storekeeper A. J. McLean as follows:

> A. J. M'Lean sworn. Knew Maria Thomas and Mrs. Leask. Recollect their coming together to make purchases in the shop at the Lower Fort, on the 20th June. Mrs. Leask purchased the things and paid the money. She used always to refer to her sister in buying so that witness thought Maria was the real purchaser. Three days afterwards, Maria was in the shop again, with her mother. She purchased about 30s. worth that day; observed that she looked unwell, and her mother said that she had been unwell since she went to Corbett's, and that she spat blood. On the 20th June, she bought goods to the value of 2 pounds 15 shillings 6 pence, and on the 23rd her mother and herself bought to the amount of 1 pound 17 shillings 4 pence.[41]

The court record reports this same testimony as:

> Mr. McLean sworn—I know Maria Thomas and Mrs. Leask came to the Lower Fort on the 20th June. Mrs. Leask was the real purchaser—I did

not know Maria Thomas then—three days after on the 23 June she and her mother came to the Fort and bought property as follows—on the 20th June 2 pounds 15 shillings 6 pence on the 23rd June one pound seventeen shillings four pence (this was read by the Comp'y's sales book) on the 23 the mother told me that she Maria was spitting blood.[42]

The court record did not reproduce the final arguments to the jury of the prosecution or the defence, however, nor did it report the judge's charge to the jury. These may well have been "enhanced" by the newspaper's editors, as Erika Smith has suggested, although there is no evidence on this point.[43]

Beyond these two reports, Joseph James Hargraves was in attendance and has left an eyewitness account, clearly hostile to Corbett but full of the anecdotal details for which he was renowned. Thus the Corbett trial is easily the best documented of the handful of criminal abortion cases

A group photograph at the Headingly Anglican church and school (G.O. Corbett's church) c. 1860s. John Taylor is fifth from the left.

heard in the courts of nineteenth-century British North America/ Canada.[44] Sixty-one witnesses were examined and cross-examined in considerable detail over the nine days of the trial. The defence team included the first qualified legal practitioner ever to appear before a Red River court, although, as we shall see, this attorney's part in the defence was very small and his behaviour eventually damaging to the defendant.

Secondary accounts of the trial, assuming without question that Corbett was guilty as charged, do not take the court proceedings very seriously.[45] The best study describes the evidence against Corbett as "damning."[46] The machinations of the trial itself were really much more fascinating than would appear initially, however. The evidence was quite complex and the case was anything but "open and shut." At first glance this was both a classic "abuse" case in the modern sense and a classic abortion case in the nineteenth-century sense. As we have seen, the victim, Maria Thomas, was young, female, a servant-girl, and a mixed-blood from a poor family of little social standing in the community. The family lived in a one-room house in Mapleton, a mixed-blood community on the Red River near St. Andrew's.[47] Her mother would give most of her testimony in Cree, with James McKay serving as interpreter. Many witnesses referred to the Thomas family by their clan designation, further suggesting that they were often thought of as Aboriginals.[48] The accused was a very popular English-born clergyman and an ersatz medical practitioner who often dealt with pregnancy and the delivery of babies. He was a man of considerable stature, influence, and authority in the community, however much the establishment distrusted him. As was usual in Victorian abortion cases, the prosecution went after both the medical practitioner and the father who obtained his services. In this case, they happened to be the same person. Also typically, the female was not prosecuted. In fairness to Maria, if her story were to be believed, she had never realized in her innocence that Corbett was attempting an abortion upon her.

The star witness had something of a local reputation as a gossipy teller of tales who flirted with the boys. The story she told was certainly quite unlikely, worthy of one of the "sensational" novels fashionable in London in the early 1860s. Thomas insisted that Corbett had drugged her with laudanum and first raped her as a virgin while she was unconscious. The girl maintained that the clergyman had then continued to have sexual intercourse with her on an almost daily basis in the hayloft of the barn, while the two were supposedly feeding the cattle. Mrs. Corbett became increasingly suspicious of Maria, who described in great detail a peephole through which Corbett could spy the movement of his wife or visitors heading towards the barn. She talked of carriage rides which ended with sexual activity in the bushes and of frequent presents of both clothing and money. Although by her own account Maria had initially been raped, she had subsequently entered into the affair more or less willingly, and had accepted the gifts without question. According to her testimony, the Reverend Corbett could not keep his hands off her for nearly a year. "He said he never loved a servant girl as he loved me," she told the court. The girl also described in considerable graphic detail several later occasions in which Corbett had tried to give her medicine which medical testimony associated with abortion, as well as attempts at both manual manipulation and surgical interference. Neither the prosecution nor the defence asked her what she thought Corbett was doing if he were not attempting to bring about an abortion.

One recent commentator has described Maria's story as "straight chronicle, stripped of imaginative glosses."[49] The account may have lacked "imaginative glosses," but in its own way it verged on the sensational, with its narrative of a drugged rape, a peephole, a besotted clergyman who often needed the "creepers" picked out of his hair, and an understandably suspicious wife. Anna Clark has pointed out that in England, when a woman produced her own tale of seduction, "she almost invariably adopted a tone of melodramatic romance." Clark adds: "in fact, this was the only discourse common to working-class and middle-class culture which provided an acceptable explanation for an unmarried mother's plight. . . . The romantic tone of the rhetoric of seduction also contrasted with the reality of women's lives."[50] Whatever the rhetoric, there certainly was also a tone of innocent naïveté in the girl's narrative. She hinted that her mother was willing to negotiate her virginity, while insisting that she thought that she must have sex with Corbett because servants had to obey their masters. If Maria had actually testified as was reported, without extensive prompting from the prosecution, she was clearly a master storyteller. If the editors omitted the prompting questions, then it is hardly the case that they had found the girl's narrative unworthy of altering, as Erika Smith has suggested.[51]

Whether or not it was deliberate, Thomas managed to produce a narrative that fit squarely into the melodramatic traditions of Victorian fiction.[52] Indeed, the plot line of her rape and seduction bore similarities to that in a number of contemporary fictional works, something which may not have been lost on at least some of those involved in the trial, especially Judge Black. Mrs. Gaskell's *Ruth* (1853) was one story of a working-class girl who was seduced by a rich young man and while pregnant was subsequently abandoned by him. Ruth bore a son, and, redeemed in part by him, made a new life. Her old lover returned; she rejected him. The author was not willing to subscribe totally to redemption, however, and ended the book with a conventional death-bed scene. "Why should she die," Charlotte Brontë asked, "why are we to shut up the book weeping?"[53] The story of Marian Erle— indeed, the very description and situation of the girl herself—in Elizabeth Barrett Browning's narrative poem *Aurora Leigh* (1857) had even more distinct parallels to that of Maria Thomas.[54] Browning's poem, claims one critic, was "the fullest and most violent exposition of the 'woman question' in mid-Victorian literature."[55] Marian "was not white nor brown, / But could look either, like a mist that changed / According to being shone on more or less."[56] Marian had been born in a hut on the edge of Malvern Hill and grew up "to no book-learning,—she was ignorant / Of authors."[57] Her mother attempted to sell her to a squire, but she ran away. Eventually an unstable aristocrat fell in love with her, but she refused to marry him and escaped to France. Marian was tricked into a brothel, raped ("So with me, / I was not ever, as you say, seduced, / but simply, murdered"), became pregnant, and bore a son.[58] Her love for the child ultimately allowed her rehabilitation, for Mrs. Browning was more courageous an author than Mrs. Gaskell.

The prosecution, headed by John and Thomas Bunn, two sons of the previous recorder, avoided charges based on the sexual intercourse part of Maria's story, probably less because what Corbett had allegedly done was not regarded as criminal than because there was no real substantiation to be found for it. The rape/seduction tale rested entirely on the girl's testimony. The abortion charges seemed on firmer ground. The medical details involved appeared beyond the inventive powers of an ill-educated young woman, and there were other eyewitnesses (admittedly all members of the girl's own family) to several of the attempts. Despite the maintenance of the distinction of the actions of carnal connection (or rape or seduction) and abortion, the Crown nevertheless saw the two sets of actions as a single package, as doubtless did most of the onlookers. The prosecution, confirmed by the charge of the judge, simultaneously emphasized that it was not bringing carnal connection charges, but that the girl's tale of the sexual intercourse provided the context for the attempted abortions. There was no inherent reason why the two matters had to be connected, however.

Because the formal charges were attempted abortion rather than either rape or seduction, it is difficult to compare the treatment of this case by the court to others of the nineteenth century. Karen Dubinksy found no associated rapes among the abortion cases in the Ontario court records she examined.[59] No other case appears to survive in which the abortionist was also responsible for the pregnancy. If the charge had been only rape or seduction, the record on cases of this sort was ambivalent. On the one hand, the girl might not have been expected to be heard because she was a lowly servant. On the other hand, since the person she was accusing was prominent and unpopular with the authorities, her charges would probably have brought some action. In any event, the likelihood is that Corbett would have gotten off on rape/seduction or carnal connection charges in most jurisdictions, both because he was a male being judged by an all-male jury and because the defence was able to raise some questions about the girl's sexual past and previous conduct.[60]

The defence team consisted of James Ross, part owner of the *Nor'-Wester,* and Frank Hunt, an experienced lawyer recently arrived in the settlement from Chicago.[61] Hunt was a neighbor of Corbett, and had agreed to act for the clergyman at the time of the first letter from the bishop. Hunt and Ross had agreed in advance that Ross would handle the cross-examination of prosecution witnesses. Hunt was then to open the defence case and examine defence witnesses. As the prosecution case unfolded, Hunt was seen to distance himself physically further every day from his client. By the last day of the hearing of prosecution witnesses, he was sitting in a corner with his feet on the stove, silently whistling to himself.[62] He disappeared from the courtroom at this point, claiming illness. James Ross had to take over the entire case for the defence at short notice.

Why the defence allowed the prosecution to collapse the rape/seduction and the abortions into a single, seamless narrative is not clear from the surviving documentation. A modern defence attorney would certainly have insisted that testimony and evidence on the rape/seduction ought to have been separated from that on the abortion attempts and would probably have blocked its appearance completely. James Ross was not a very experienced defence attorney, of course, although he had achieved one acquittal on a murder charge in 1860 and was not a complete neophyte. It is more likely that Ross thought that the girl's rape/seduction account was more easily countered than her abortion narrative, and inherently less likely to be believed. If one part of the narrative could be shaken, it would all fall to the ground. The defence obviously sought to impeach Thomas's character and testimony, frequently contrasting her "incredible" story with Reverend Corbett's standing in the community as both a clergyman and a medical practitioner. Ross succeeded in showing a number of inconsistencies in the girl's testimony, but was unable to break her nerve on the witness stand. The judge in his summation to the jury made much of the point that the girl had withstood a gruelling two-day cross-examination without collapse. J.J. Hargrave (who was no friend of Corbett) agreed. "The nature of the evidence she gave was such as to give an air of strong probability to the truth of her tale," he wrote. "Her descriptions of conversations with the prisoner, and of draughts and potions administered by him, were invested with overwhelming force, as coming from an ignorant girl, while the cunningly devised series of questions, put with the object of entrapping her, only confirmed the truth of her story by precluding all possibility of her having been prompted in her replies."[63]

The defence tried to explain away the graphic evidence of the abortions by insisting that the girl had access to Corbett's medical books. But it never produced any tomes that provided the information required, nor any evidence that Maria would have any inclination or ability to make use of such material. A more promising line of argument might have been to argue that everything Maria described was part of the folk-medicine of the community. Contrary to the implications of the testimony of the male doctors, who sought to control medical practice and prevent outsiders from competing, nothing Maria described ought to have been arcane knowledge known only to professionals.[64] On this level, the Corbett case could be viewed as another instance of the work by doctors to eliminate the competition of alternate medical practitioners.[65] The line of argument that the girl recounted nothing that was not common knowledge to women in the community could have been explored through the female witnesses the defence called, although it would have required a more flamboyant and confident lawyer than James Ross, one who was prepared to ask embarrassing personal questions. What the Corbett case certainly demonstrates is how difficult it is to arrive at an understanding of the prevalence of abortion in the nineteenth century. The medical men pretended to know very little about it, and the women were never asked what they knew.

James Ross had also attempted to introduce as evidence the "oath" Thomas had earlier taken before magistrate John Taylor that declared

James Ross, co-editor of the *Nor'-Wester,* and defence counsel for Corbett, with his wife, Margaret, c.1860s.

that Corbett had not had sexual intercourse with her. Judge Black dismissed this oath as improperly administered. Perhaps it was. But Ross complained bitterly that such a ruling ignored the principles of the court on which it had always conducted its business—"on precedents in this Settlement, disregarding rules and giving prominence rather to the attainment of substantial justice than rigid form."[66] The reference to "substantial justice" reminded Judge Black that he had earlier written to the *Nor'-Wester,* "so long as the ends of substantial justice are really attained among us, we ought not too eagerly to desire the introduction of subtle refinements and ingenious technicalities."[67] John Taylor had previously taken many oaths in this manner. Ross returned to this matter in his lengthy address to the jury, commenting, "we must not lightly and without notice, take up and censure a magistrate because he happens to do things in the old fashioned way of the place." Judge Black's regularization of the law, Ross argued, cut against the veracity of the oath, whatever its form. Ross handled the oath business well, as the foreman of the jury observed when he commented that despite the judge's ruling on the oath, "we cannot altogether throw it from our minds, for we believe the girl must have understood she was on her oath in as legal a manner as she was a little while ago in the box."

On the other hand, the inexperience of the defence showed when Ross allowed archdeacon James Hunter to describe in detail the "confession" made by Corbett, which John Taylor had allegedly heard privately and related to the archdeacon during his investigation. This hearsay evidence should have been thrown out of court. Curiously enough, much of Oliver Gowler's evidence was dismissed because it consisted of what he had heard from the same John Taylor (about one John Favel's admissions of criminal connection with Maria). Taylor himself insisted that Archdeacon Hunter had "teased him" very hard about what Corbett had said. "He questioned me in every way. I never got such a teasing in my life." According to Taylor, "I said that Corbett said he was to be blamed or to blame." But, he emphasized, when Corbett later received the message from the bishop to flee, "he affirmed his innocence of the charge."[68] He also insisted that his statement that Corbett had sent him to find another young man who might have been the father was his own invention, designed to end the archdeacon's insistent hectoring.

James Ross offered a counter-narrative to that of the girl. He tried to paint a picture of an entire family who were not to be trusted, who had engaged in collusion against his client. But what he managed mainly to communicate was a general class bias against the poor and marginal members of the mixed-blood community which he—as a "respectable" mixed-blood—shared with the remainder of the settlement's elite. Indeed, most of those involved with Maria Thomas and this case, apart from the Corbetts and other members of the clergy, were clearly part of the "less respectable" mixed-blood community in the settlement for which Corbett had provided leadership. Ross inevitably attempted to characterize the girl as a "prostitute." This was relatively standard defence practice in rape/seduction cases, and not entirely out of keeping with the image the presiding judge preferred of Maria as a "magdalen" figure. For Victorians there were precious few gradations among "fallen women."[69]

The role of Corbett's wife Abigail in the trial proceedings was a fascinating and ambivalent one. As wife, Abigail did not testify in her husband's trial. We get two, contrasting second-hand views of her. One comes from Maria Thomas, who sees Abigail as a somewhat menacing figure who became increasingly suspicious of what was going on with her husband. From Maria's perspective, Abigail was a lurking and disapproving presence, part of the aura of suspicion and tension around the Corbett home. In his speech to the jury, however, James Ross tried to present Abigail as the "Angel in the House," contrasted implicitly with the magdalen figure of Maria. His chief aim was to suggest that Mrs. Corbett's feminine worthiness deserved better than the unthinking acceptance of the girl's unsubstantiated charges against Reverend Corbett. Ross also queried whether Mrs. Corbett would have kept the girl if she had suspected anything of what the girl claimed. "I need not speak of Mrs. Corbett's character, or paint her noble, pure feelings. We see it in her very face, we notice it in her conversations, in her manner, her every movement: she is a refined, honest, pure-hearted noble Englishwoman."[70]

The prosecution called a series of witnesses in an attempt to confirm parts—any part—of the girl's story of her torrid affair with Corbett. The result was a good deal of contradictory testimony which, on the whole, cast more suspicion on the witness's account than it did on Reverend Corbett's behaviour. Thomas claimed Corbett had given her a French merino dress as a present, but some witnesses insisted she had the dress before she entered Corbett's service, while others testified that she had told them it was a present from her mother. Even the judge in his charge to the jury had to admit that the merino dress remained a puzzle. There was some evidence advanced that the money given to Maria by Corbett had been intended to pay her family for building materials they were to supply, but there was also a suggestion that the orders for building materials had been extracted from Corbett as part of the price of her sexual violation. Whether there was actually any evidence of the hole in the barn wall that Corbett had allegedly used as an early-warning device was quite doubtful. One witness insisted that he had later uncovered the "bung hole" filled with mud, but half of Headingley was prepared to deny this under oath. Maria had been seen at one point emerging from the bushes near Headingley village with a male, but none of a series of prosecution witnesses could actually say that the male was Corbett. James Ross pointed out to the jury how ludicrous the scene being painted by the girl really was. "Fancy the picture—a clear open prairie where they could be seen from several miles away, a dozen of houses a few hundred yards off—about 2 o'clock in the day, people passing and repassing. Under such circumstances can you believe this girl, when she says Mr. Corbett, the clergyman of the Parish, took her away some distance from the public road into *bushes,* and there *lay* with her!"

For its part, the defence brought witnesses (mainly female) to demonstrate that the girl was mendacious, but most of their examples of falsehoods were not very telling. Instead of labelling her a "liar," a word both the defence witnesses and the defence used all too frequently, James Ross would have been better advised to describe Maria's behaviour as one of living in a romanticized adolescent world of imagination and fantasy. Thomas Gardner, for example, testified that Maria had told him the previous autumn that the Sioux were about to attack and that Mrs. Corbett "was at Rev. Mr. Chapman's raving mad, because the Indians had taken one of her children and the servant maid. The people in the Upper Fort were, Maria said, boring holes in the wall of the Fort to fire through at the Indians; and that all the ministers and Magistrates and 20 riders were after the Sioux to try and get Mrs. Corbett's child back."[71] A series of young men testified that they had themselves engaged in various bundlings and even sexual intercourse with Thomas. One was already a father with six children. According to Hargrave, "the list of Mr. Corbett's witnesses included few names of respectability," although as has already been noted, this merely reflected the status of most of those involved in the business. This hostile testimony was totally compromised, however, when one of these witnesses claiming intercourse with the girl—Joseph Sayer—returned to the witness box and insisted that he had been paid by Corbett to perjure himself (by the girl's own account, she and Sayer had lain together clothed in bed on several occasions). James Ross disastrously allowed the defence's case to close on this extremely damaging note.

In his charge to the jury, Judge Black not only glossed over the contradictions in the Thomas story, but over the evidence of the girl's vivid imagination. Black did his best to bring the narrative back under control by providing what amounted to a concluding authorial synthesis. But because this was real life and not a novel, tidy resolutions kept eluding him. From the prosecution's perspective, either the girl was believable as a witness or she was not. The judge chose to believe her totally, and thus brushed aside considerable contradictory evidence that she had often lived in a world of fantasy and had flirted consistently with the boys. He dismissed the most damaging of the defence witnesses as people of no standing in the community and paid perjurers. The judge made much of Corbett's efforts to "find a father for the child," never once allowing that an innocent man was as likely to respond in this way as a guilty one. In Black's version of the story, Maria was unquestionably a "magdalen figure." He told the jury, "To the unfortunate woman herself, the consequences of this prosecution cannot alas! . . . affect her very much. By some one or other, she has already been deprived of all that makes female character valuable— her virtue; and probably there is now nothing on earth that concerns her but preparations for death."[72] Nevertheless, Judge Black's charge was a powerful indictment of Griffith Owen Corbett. Black was treated much more generously in this case by the defence than he would be a few years later, when he faced an experienced trial lawyer in his court.[73]

Corbett himself did not testify. James Ross tried to suggest in his speech to the jury that his client had been prevented by the court from appearing on his own behalf. As a result of the clergyman's non-appearance, what we know of Corbett's response to the girl's accusations comes from his "confessions," those recounted as hearsay by witnesses at the trial and one in his own words afterwards. Corbett never commented directly on the abortion charges, but he consistently maintained his innocence of paternity. In even the most damning admissions, the language was equivocal. In them, Corbett insisted that he was responsible or "to blame," which could have meant that he had allowed the girl too many liberties rather than that he had engaged in sexual intercourse with her. The abortion attempts were a different matter. Corbett never explicitly denied them, and indeed never really discussed them at any point. It is possible that he attempted to induce a miscarriage because he knew he would be accused of being the father or because he felt sorry for the girl. It is also possible that he was protecting someone. If this were the case, the logical candidate was a young protegé whose connection to Corbett was most mysterious.

From a historian's perspective it is not so necessary that Maria Thomas's story be true from beginning to end as it was to contemporaries.

At this distance it is difficult to see through to the "truth" buried in the discourse. James Ross was able to catch out Maria on some embellishments, but he could not shake her on the main story. Even the detailed trial reports do not help. They do not reproduce the apparently obvious aura of perjury that Judge Black insisted emanated from all the young men who claimed to have slept with Maria Thomas. Nor do they communicate the untrammelled credibility of Maria, which the judge maintained she had demonstrated under vigorous cross-examination.

One of the curiosities of trials in Red River was that because the settlement was not an official British colony, there was no means of appealing a decision of the Court of Quarterly Session. After the jury found him guilty, Corbett had demanded an appeal, but was quite properly denied. Had appeal been possible, the decision might well have been overturned, however. There are enough inconsistencies in the written evidence, carefully read, to raise considerable doubts about the complete veracity of the Thomas story of the sexual affair, although James Ross had made a number of serious tactical errors. On the other hand, only the paternity question relied solely on Maria's evidence. The question remained: if Corbett had not actually engaged in sex with the girl, why had he tried to bring about an abortion? Since the prosecution accepted the related package of paternity and abortion, it never needed to explore this question, and the defence was obviously in no position to do so, since it was not admitting either responsibility.

The jury found Corbett guilty as charged, but recommended mercy. The recommendation may have been because of the political controversy hanging over the trial, but equally likely because the jury was not thoroughly convinced that Corbett was the father of the child. Corbett was sentenced to six months in prison. A band of his supporters, claiming that his health had broken down under incarceration, soon broke him out of the gaol and refused to allow him to be returned there. The court, faced with the possibility of open civil war if it chose to enforce its sentence, allowed him to remain free. Instead, Judge Black read to a subsequent grand jury excerpts from a private letter written by Corbett from jail to his bishop. The excerpts seemed to confirm the clergyman's guilt. But in a subsequent letter to the *Nor'-Wester,* Corbett insisted that the excerpts read had been taken out of context. The clergyman admitted that his mental state had led him to write a confused letter, but maintained he had not intended to admit to any responsibility beyond allowing the girl too many liberties. He excoriated Judge Black (and by implication the bishop) for reading from a private letter, although his high-minded position was somewhat weakened by the fact that he was himself a fugitive from justice at the time of writing. Was justice done in the case of *The Queen* v. *G.O. Corbett*? Griffith Owen Corbett was almost certainly guilty as charged of attempting to procure an abortion. The full story behind those charges was very possibly not the one advanced by the prosecution, however, or the one frequently recounted in other histories of the case. The doubts raised by the defence, even more than the high politics of the case, probably led the jury to the recommendation of mercy and the judge to the light sentence.

The Corbett case was a real-life melodrama rather than a purely fictional one. Consequently, as we have seen, its narrative lacked proper authorial control and kept threatening to get out of hand. Most significantly, the trial did not provide a neat resolution or closure for any of its major participants. Corbett was again broken out of prison by his supporters, and never served out his sentence. He went back to England, eventually becoming rehabilitated and gaining another parish there. Later reports suggest that he had more trouble with sexual abuses many years later.[74] He lived until 1909. Mrs. Corbett and her daughters remained in the Red River Settlement and did not accompany Corbett back home; she eventually moved to Swan Lake and resided there until 1918.[75] Maria Thomas died in Mapleton in 1867. James Ross sold his share of the *Nor'-Wester* in 1863 and moved to Toronto to work as a journalist. He returned to Red River in 1869, by which time he was drinking heavily. He died in 1871 of an alcohol-related illness. Judge Black's incompetence was thoroughly exposed by a clever American defence attorney in a murder trial in 1868; he was nevertheless selected as one of the provisional government's negotiators with Canada in 1870.

The Corbett affair had obviously compromised the maintenance of law and order in Red River. It also compromised the authority of the Church of England, not only in the sense that one of its clergymen had been involved in scandal, but in its equivocal response to the entire business. It had allowed its own quite casual and legally improper investigation of the charges to become part of the prosecution case, and even more damagingly, had actually encouraged Corbett to become a fugitive from justice rather than expose himself (and his Church) to public obloquy. Perhaps even more significantly, the case revealed for public view the many tensions that existed in the settlement at mid-century. The population was obviously badly divided along religious, racial, class, and gender lines. If Red River had ever been a place of utopian harmony, as some of its residents had liked to believe, it clearly was no longer.

THE RED RIVER FAMINE OF 1868

HE Red River Settlement was notorious for the floods that occurred in the nineteenth century. Flooding was not the only natural hazard suffered by the early settlers of Red River. The climate of the region provided a variety of trials sufficient to test the endurance of any people. Severe winter cold, often combined with heavy snowpacks, was so common an occurrence that few residents of Red River regarded it as unusual. Blizzards, complete with whiteout conditions in which the unwary easily became lost on the open prairie and died of hypothermia, occurred fairly often.[1] Grass fires on the open prairie were equally common, and equally dangerous. House fires were endemic in a community that built with and heated for months on end with wood.[2] Thunderstorms, with heavy rain, hailstones, and high winds, occurred regularly in the summer.[3] Epidemics were not unknown; an influenza known as the "bloody flux" visited the settlement in 1846, killing 321, or one-sixteenth of the entire population.[4] Every visitor commented on the summer bugs, especially the mosquitoes, and the *Nor'-Wester* provided its readership with a long catalogue of the insects that afflicted the settlement.[5] The chief enemy of the notorious Wolseley Expedition of 1870 proved to be not Louis Riel's Métis, but the dreaded "mozzie," which was impervious to all the measures taken by the army to protect against it.

Perhaps the most serious type of natural disaster in Red River besides flooding was, ironically enough, also connected with water. Unlike flooding, which resulted from too much water, drought and accompanying insect infestation resulted from too little. The Red River

Valley was highly susceptible to great variations in annual precipitation. Protracted periods of too-little moisture were as serious as periods of over-abundance, particularly since they were frequently accompanied by hot weather and the appearance of the ubiquitous grasshopper.

The Western Grasshopper

The western grasshopper (Orthoptera: Acrididae) and Rocky Mountain Locust (Melanoplus spretus) are closely related to those insects which were the scourge of Biblical times, continually eating up the crops. There are and have been a number of Manitoba varieties of grasshoppers, not carefully distinguished in the historical evidence. We do not even today really have a very good picture of the dynamics of grasshopper infestation in the province. It has been difficult to forecast grasshopper outbreaks or to check them before they become acute. The solitary grasshopper, which is the classic Manitoba variety, creates little danger; swarms of grasshoppers invading fields and devouring all before them are unquestionably a major disaster. Manitoba grasshoppers are not by nature swarmers, but occasionally do reach a volume of numbers where they can generate mass outbreaks. Scientists have learned that grasshopper invasions tend initially to be local in nature, but can develop a general momentum over the course of time.[6]

Whether grasshopper or locust, these creatures could put the finishing touches on seasons of heat and drought, which encouraged the hatching of their eggs, by eating whatever plants managed to survive the dry conditions. Red River governor Alexander Macdonell was known as the "grasshopper governor," not because he governed during the years of their infestation—although he did so—but because of his voracious appetite for any assets that passed within his grasp.

Grasshoppers were mentioned by Captain Jonathan Carver in 1768, perhaps the first recorded reference to these insects on the western plains.[7] Alexander Henry the younger reported from what is now Pembina in 1808 that "swarms of grasshoppers have destroyed the greater part of the vegetables in my kitchen garden, onions, cabbages, melons, cucumbers, carrots, parsnips, and beets. They had also attacked the potatoes and corn, but these were strong enough at the root to sprout again."[8] The swarms came about mid-June from the south. Grasshoppers first threatened the Red River Colony from 1818 to 1820. Curiously enough, given Lord Selkirk's known scientific interests, there had been no one sent to the settlement capable of providing a careful entomological account of the infestation. Former mercenary soldier Captain Frederick Matthey insisted that in 1818 the locusts had "dug the earth to eat the stems of the potatoes under ground. In some places they were two and three inches thick on the ground."[9] The grasshoppers laid their eggs in the fields in September, and several years of dry, hot weather provided ideal breeding conditions. According to Captain Matthey, the young first appeared in May, "coming out of the ground like froth out of the bunghole of a cask of fermenting fluid." The 1820 crop was totally consumed, and the settlement had to send to the United States for seed for 1821. The visitor Nicholas Garry reported in 1821 that "the Grasshoppers have again visited the Colony, but in fewer Numbers, and their Devastations were not general, the Crop having suffered but little." Infestations were spotty. Garry later observed at Mr. Laidlaw's Hay Farm "dreadful Devastation, whole Beds of Potatoes eaten without a Vestige remaining, fine Fields of Wheat destroyed and the whole having a most desolate melancholy Appearance."[10]

Although there were sporadic returns of the grasshopper after 1821—in 1857 and 1858, for example—crops were not seriously affected until the dry years from 1864 to 1874.[11] North Dakota had infestations in 1853, 1854, 1856, and 1857, and again sporadically in the 1860s. "Dry, dry," wrote one observer at Lower Fort Garry, "the weather was never seen, people Say, so long without rain, it thunders often and yet no rain, sometimes it is very hot, but it gets very rainlike sometimes but it clears off and there is no rain."[12] Whether the dry weather was actually responsible for the infestations has never been clear. An alternate theory is that the locusts flourished only when the prairie sod was broken, either by wandering bison or the plough, which enabled the insects to lay their eggs.[13] According to the Nor'-Wester, the insects caused little problem between 1821 and 1864, since they were confined to small localized areas. In the latter year "they made their appearance from the south-west in clouds,— they quickly overspread the Settlement, but did little damage, as the crops were too nearly ripe to be affected by them."[14] In 1868, however, the young emerged from their nests in the spring to destroy totally the freshly planted crops in the fields. The Nor'-Wester described the invasion: "The front rank pressed forward, urged on by millions at the rear; and thus the march was kept up until every green thing was destroyed. Their line of march was always in one direction, and nothing but a house, a wall, or a river impeded their progress. At the base of a wall it was astonishing to see the accumulations of insect life during the march of this devouring scourge. They were heaped up in such immense numbers that altho' but half grown, they were piled upon one another, sometimes to the depth of a foot."[15] According to other accounts, the dead bodies of the insects were piled up four feet high around the walls of

Upper Fort Garry.[16] The bodies were burned in huge bonfires to eliminate the stink of their decay.

Further Disasters in 1868

As if the grasshopper scourge were not enough, on 3 July 1868, the settlement experienced another disaster in the form of a bout of unusual (although not entirely unique) weather.[17] The weather had been extremely hot for days, with a good deal of heat lightning. About 2 A.M., a monster thunderstorm began, waking the residents with the crash of the thunder. The sky was absolutely black, broken only by the lightning which lit the heavens with "perpetual brilliant flashes."[18] Then the deluge began. Joseph Hargrave, who described the incident, does not record hail, although hail often accompanies storms of this nature. What Hargrave did note was the sudden appearance of a heavy wind, which lasted for about an hour.[19] The wind caused heavy damage to property and some loss of life. The building most damaged was the incompleted Church of the Holy Trinity, the unadorned timbers of which were summarily deposited on the ground by the strength of the wind. Peter Mathieson, a carpenter working on the structure, who was sleeping nearby, was killed. The spire of St. Andrew's Church was blown into the roof of the building. The *Nor'-Wester* office was nearly destroyed; it was saved only because the winds hit the building diagonally rather than head on. Many roofs were blown off, countless trees uprooted, and much fencing was carried away. The *Nor'-Wester* described the storm (which it labelled both a "hurricane" and a "tornado") as "the most serious ever witnessed in this country."

The rain of 3 July was both too late and too heavy. Much of it ran off without really soaking the ground. The settlement tried to clear up from the disaster, but by August of 1868, it was clear that an even greater disaster had come. This crisis was a combination of short-term and long-term ecological factors. Not only were there no crops, but the years of drought had completely devastated the wild vegetation on the prairie. The buffalo disappeared, as did rabbits and other game. While the total absence of game animals was probably to be associated with the drought, the disappearance of the buffalo may well have been part of a long-term trend which observers had been warning about for years.[20] A warming of the lakes was probably responsible for the simultaneous failure of the fisheries. The steamer *International* had not been able to run regularly since 1865, because of the low volume of water in the Red River. The *Nor'-Wester* claimed that "within the whole Colony not one bushel of any kind of grain will be harvested," and there would be precious few potatoes, either.[21]

The *Nor'-Wester* invited comments on the impending crisis from the leading clergymen in the settlement, and published their replies in its issue of 11 August. Roman Catholic bishop Taché confirmed that there would be no crops, and opined that "the combined plagues of this year" were "the worst yet experienced as far as food is concerned." Anglican archdeacon John McLean concurred that there would be "a fearful amount of suffering from want among the poorer settlers during the coming winter, unless some steps are taken to make provision for them." Presbyterian John Black added that the buffalo hunt had also failed. Methodist George Young called for a public meeting "to appoint a committee from among the experienced and prominent and influential members of this community, whose duty it will be to present the case before a charitable public in the distance as fully as may be deemed advisable, and also to receive and distribute any contributions that may be sent." Although none of the clergymen made reference to the fact, all were well aware of the prospect, reported in the *Nor'-Wester* throughout its summer issues, that the settlement and the entire Northwest would shortly be transferred to Canada.

The Relief Programme Begins

The Council of Assiniboia voted all the funds it had available for relief in early August of 1868.[22] Sixteen hundred pounds sterling was to be spent immediately: £600 on seed wheat, £500 on flour, and £500 on twine, hooks, and ammunition to encourage the settlers to try fishing. The *Nor'-Wester* newspaper appealed for aid to eastern Canada, and local religious leaders wrote to newspapers in the east of Canada and the United States asking for help. A retired pensioner named Michael Power wrote a letter to the *Times* in London, outlining the disaster. The governor of the Hudson's Bay Company in England, the Earl of Kimberley, added his voice in the newspaper as well.[23] A letter from F. E. Kew, "Agent in England for the Red River traders," also appeared in the *Times*.[24] The *Nor'-Wester* was soon able to report on a meeting held in Ingersoll Hall in St. Paul "to take measures to aid the sufferers of the Red River country," although it admitted it "was not very fully attended."[25] Norman Kittson of Pembina reported that up to 5,000 inhabitants of Red River would starve over the winter. The governor of Minnesota, who was in attendance, himself offered resolutions calling for assistance. Those present raised $1,137.75. The St. Paul Chamber of Commerce was soon soliciting aid "from the commercial and other organizations, from the churches, all benevolent associations, and from individual citizens of this State and elsewhere, for the people of the Red River Settlement."[26] The American committee (consisting of H.H. Sibley, R.

Blakeley, R.N. McLaren, N. W. Kittson, and James J. Hill) thought that up to 5,000 people would have to be provided with food over the winter. Ten thousand barrels of flour would be required. These supplies would cost 75 cents per 100 pounds to transport to Red River before winter, and more thereafter. The appeal soon spread beyond Minnesota. In Milwaukee, Wisconsin, for example, $1,000 in contributions was raised at the Chamber of Commerce, and a local railroad executive offered to carry all supplies contributed to St. Paul without cost.[27]

The realization of the probability of the transfer to Canada added some little public consciousness in the East of the existence of Red River, although the principal of the university at Kingston, Ontario, who had actively collected money for the settlement, reported, "I could have collected the money quite as easily, and the givers would have given it quite as intelligently, had the sufferers been in Central Abbyssinia."[28] Nonetheless, Canadian newspapers did their best to publicize the need, and their efforts were thoroughly reported in the Nor'-Wester. No reader of Red River's newspaper could have any doubt of Canada's ambitions for the settlement. The Essex Record, for example, noted that those who preferred "to limit their charity to those of their own faith" would find a resident clergyman in Red River "happy to receive and properly disburse any contributions."[29] The paper added that Nova Scotia fishermen had been assisted in 1867, "and we are sure the Assiniboians are not a whit less deserving than they." The Canadian Free Press of London began its appeal by describing the inhabitants of Red River as "our fellow-colonists, that are soon to be." It added, "we are seeking to embrace this brave but distant people in our political system; to make them part and parcel of ourselves. Should we not then be the first to spring forward to their assistance?"[30] The Kingston British Whig managed to support the appeal and criticize the victims at the same time. It wrote: "the history of this Red River Settlement shows the great inconvenience of going far ahead of civilization with an isolated settlement. When population overflows, filling up a region of country by degrees, there is always help near, but when a small band of settlers go away far from all others—if they have no market for it—and if they suffer from scarcity there is no help near.[31] The Toronto Globe soon reported that $195 had been collected in London, "with but a small part of the city canvassed."[32]

The Nor'-Wester reported at length on the meeting held in Mechanics' Hall, Hamilton, held by proclamation of the mayor upon the request of many of the leading merchants of the city. In his opening remarks, the mayor regretted that the attendance had not been larger, and several speakers echoed these sentiments. But an ecumenical collection of clergy spoke eloquently on behalf of the Red River settlers. Wesleyan minister John Potts thought that sympathy was required both because of "our common humanity" and because of the "prospective political position" of the sufferers at Red River. "They desire to cast their lot in with us and become part of the Dominion of Canada; they have asked, and they wish to be one with us."[33] He moved a resolution to that effect. In seconding that motion, Dr. Maclean observed that "the Red River country was not only a great necessity to Canada, but to the teeming millions of Europe. There were vast tracts of prairie, on the Assinniboine [sic] and Saskatchewan rivers capable of maintaining millions of settlers, and it would not do to allow the pioneers of these settlements to be driven out now for want of support in their affliction." The London newspaper had argued that the Dominion government should assist as well, and indeed, the Canadian government at Ottawa also contributed money to the relief effort. Moreover, as the *Nor'-Wester* reported in early October, the Canadian government had decided "to expend a considerable sum in the construction of Fort Garry and the opening up of the road to Red River."[34] The man appointed as superintendent of the road was to be John Snow, who announced that he would need many carts to haul in his supplies from Georgetown, at the head of the American railroad.[35]

The Red River Co-Operative Relief Committee

As the Reverend George Young had suggested in his newspaper letter of 11 August, the "Red River Co-operative Relief Committee" was organized in the settlement to administer the incoming relief fund. It was to consist of all the settlement's clergy, plus a lay delegate from each parish, and a number of local leaders. Subcommittees were also to be formed in each parish, composed of the local clergyman, the delegate, and four others. Their job was to identify those in need of relief and to guard "against any who would be included to impose upon this charity so kindly extended from abroad."[36] Local agricultural censuses taken in a number of parishes survive, covering the years immediately before 1868. While not covering the entire colony, they do suggest that Francophones and Anglophones had moved closer together in terms of agricultural activity. The difference between the two communities in terms of agricultural output in the years immediately preceding the famine was small.[37] The general committee quickly organized an executive to do most of the business. The minutes of this subcommittee still survive in the Provincial Archives of Manitoba.[38] It was chaired by William

McTavish, the governor of the Hudson's Bay Company, and included most of the clergymen of Red River, both Protestant and Catholic, as well as the local newspaper editor and several public-spirited merchants. Most of these gentlemen had been named individually by eastern bodies as local custodians of funds remitted to Red River. In theory, a lay delegate from each parish was also a member of the committee. The first meeting of the executive was held at the courthouse near Upper Fort Garry on Monday, 19 October 1868, when the committee agreed to meet every Wednesday afternoon at 3 P.M. at the same location. It did so until at least late January of 1869, when the minutes cease.

The chief function of the executive committee was to receive and distribute relief in the form of foodstuffs. At its second meeting, the committee deferred a request from the Ladies' Bazaar requesting that a portion of the relief funds be given to clothe the poor in the settlement, and never did respond to the request.[39] Most contributions came as money, often gold shipped west to St. Paul, Minnesota, which could be used to purchase food in the United States. The food, chiefly in the form of 196-pound barrels of flour, had to be imported into the settlement. The committee chartered over 100 Red River carts at 14 shillings per 100 pounds from Fort Abercrombie. Later, 100 sleds were hired to transport the supplies to the colony. A detailed procedure was worked out for the parish subcommittees, organized by denomination, to report on cases of destitution. A printed form was drawn up to be sent to each parish delegate, "reporting the number in each case, and stating the age, also any male members in any family able to work who can leave home."[40] The famine was relatively nondiscriminatory in its effect, striking at Francophones and Anglophones, Protestants and Catholics alike. At one point more than 2,500 people, about 20 percent of the population of Red River, were receiving aid, and most of the colony was on short rations. The committee noted that food assistance was limited to two pounds of flour per victim per week, and acknowledged that much of the money contributed was spent on transport.[41]

The amount of money put at the disposal of the committee was more considerable than the inhabitants had expected when the appeals for funds had been placed. According to Joseph Hargrave, by winter of 1868-69, more than £3,000 came from Britain, $3,600 from Canada, and over £900 from the United States. The final tally would be over £9,000. The *Nor'-Wester* in November 1868 estimated that the relief fund had already collected $26,000: $10,000 in England, $8,000 in the U.S., $5,000 from the Dominion government; and $3,000 from Canadian subscriptions. As Hargrave noted in his history of Red River, "the isolation of the colony had almost forbidden its inhabitants to believe in the possibility of a living interest being taken in its affairs by the busy people dwelling in the great outside world."[42]

The Controversy over Relief

At the same time, the famine and the relief effort produced considerable controversy. Many criticized the Hudson's Bay Company for not doing enough to help the victims. The government of Canada attempted to integrate famine relief into its preparations for assuming control of the West, when it announced that it would built a road from Thunder Bay to the settlement in order to provide employment for the destitute residents of Red River. Canada did not bother to consult with the local authorities before it sent the head of the roadbuilding crew, John Snow, into the settlement. Moreover, as Joseph Hargrave complained later, the amount of relief produced by the road building was relatively small. John Snow never employed more than forty people, and he sold the workers their provisions at very high prices.[43] There was much resentment that the Canadian government money pledged to famine relief was never paid, a fact noted in the pages of the minutes of the relief committee.

While some in Red River were suspicious of Canada's assistance, many rumours within and without the settlement circulated that the crisis had been greatly exaggerated. The first sign of this critique was reported in the settlement by the *Nor'-Wester*, which reprinted a story from the *Saint Paul Pioneer* on the subject of the famine. The American newspaper noted the market prices of foodstuffs from the *Nor'-Wester* in its early September numbers, claiming that they were only 30 to 40 percent higher than normal. These prices "were far under famine prices and do not indicate a condition of terrible distress." The *Pioneer* continued, "we are inclined to think that the famine alarm exceeded in its proportions the depredations of the grasshoppers; or, at least, that the speculators were led to import largely, and that the price of provisions had not increased to the extent that might be expected." There were no more poor and no more suffering in Red River than usual. The *Pioneer* did admit that prices were controlled.[44] The *Nor'-Wester* had emphasized on 14 November 1868 that "our readers must not judge the amount of supply by the amount of dollars subscribed in the East. Because of the lateness of the season, the newspaper continued, much of the cost would be expended upon transporting emergency relief to the settlement.[45]

"U.S." wrote from Portage la Prairie to respond to complaints, apparently within the settlement. He argued that it was mistaken policy to insist that sufferers had to be "perfectly destitute" before they could be assisted. Settlers should be aided to live through the winter without having to sacrifice their stock. He also answered the criticism that no one was actually starving, pointing out that it would be nearly a year before another harvest could be reaped. "The noble charities of our neighbors, should not be *misused* or *misdirected*," "U. S." concluded, "but there should be no cold, cramping, mean spirit exercised in its distribution."[46] The *Nor'-Wester* used the letter to insist that every case of real distress would be relieved "without any reference to race, religion, or previous circumstance." It was not necessary to be totally destitute to receive relief. The newspaper added that nearly a year's supply of food was needed before the settlement could return to normal.

The *Nor'-Wester* acknowledged the misrepresentation critique in its issue of 21 November.[47] When he had first published reports from Saint Paul that the famine had been exaggerated, wrote editor Walter Bown, he had been threatened with violence. Bown offered substantiation of these reports. He noted that General Sibley had written Bishop Machray to say that the reason American subscriptions were less than expected was the rumour that the crisis had been overstated. The Milwaukee Chamber of Commerce had reported to the Saint Paul Chamber of Commerce that an item originating in Saint Paul had appeared in the local press to the effect that sufficient assistance had already been given to the Red River residents to prevent them from suffering.[48] The *Nor'-Wester* and the local organizers of the relief efforts did their best to counter the rumours, and the controversy apparently died down, at least in its original form. The relief committee in the settlement certainly continued to receive contributions and dispense aid through the winter of 1868-69.

But "relief" was never entirely free from controversy. "Philanthropist" took a slightly different tack in a letter to the editor of the *Nor'-Wester* from Winnipeg dated 20 November 1868.[49] This correspondent insisted that the suffering in Red River was real enough, but that those who had contributed to relieve it expected the victims to be experiencing real distress and starvation. He feared that many who were not really needy would receive the charity. He complained that the saloons in the settlement appeared to be flourishing. Moreover, many "able-bodied" men, he insisted, refused to work "except for unreasonably high wages, evidently calculating on getting from the relief supply."[50] Although it is quite possible that the remarks of "Philanthropist" were directed at the Métis, especially the buffalo hunters, the *Nor'-Wester* was careful not to engage in racial comments of any kind in its discussions of the famine. Nonetheless, echoes of these sorts of racial remarks kept emerging.

In the Quebec newspaper *Nouveau Monde* of 1 February 1869, a letter to the editor appeared from a "Métis" who signed himself "L.R."[51] The letter answered one from recent arrival Charles Mair that had appeared in several Ontario newspapers. Mair had suggested that the only reason famine assistance had been necessary was because of "halfbreed" indolence. "L.R." insisted that famine aid had been given to people of "all colours." He went on, "there are some half-breeds who do not ask for charity, as there are some English, some Germans, and some Scots, who receive it every week." "L.R." continued, "it was not, of course, enough for these gentlemen to come to mock the distress of our country by making unfortunate people driven by hunger, work dirt cheap. They had also to spread falsehoods among the outside world, to lead people to believe that the relief sent to R.R. was not needed." He concluded, "in other circumstances than those in which we are, I should not have taken note of the falsehoods of this letter. We are accustomed to see strangers arrive every year who come to look us up and down, and who then print in the news-papers or in big books their reflections more or less queer on us and our country; but after the bad times which have befallen on us, driven as we are to have recourse to public charity, I have thought that it was my duty to protest against falsehoods which could give the impression elsewhere that there was no need of relief in Red River." "L.R.," of course, was Louis Riel, and this was his first known appearance in print. His response, probably reflecting that of many of the settlement's Métis, suggests a sensitivity both to racial stereotyping and to condescending outsiders. Within a year Riel would be leading the Métis in resistance against the Canadian government.

The Executive Relief Committee's final task was to distribute seed in the spring of 1869. Those whose crops had failed the previous year, of course, had no seed for the next year's planting. The controversies of the previous winter had obviously had their effect. The committee's rules for the distribution of seed were quite careful to ascertain that only the "needy" were included among the recipients, who had to sign a declaration "that I cannot without great disadvantage supply myself otherwise." The committee also worried about misappropriation of its seed, insisting that recipients attest that they would sow the seed themselves. Quantities were strictly limited according to the number in a family, with five bushels the maximum limit of free distribution, "which shall be given only to those in circumstances of actual poverty." Others would have to purchase the seed at "fair value" or on condition of making returns after harvest.[52] There would be no free rides in the settlement in 1869.

Despite the suffering, the *Nor'-Wester* saw in the famine some advantage.[53] It claimed that the fields needed resting, and perhaps more arguably, that the grasshoppers had destroyed noxious weeds as well as the crops. Moreover, said the newspaper, the farmers of Red River would in future sow more widely. As for the buffalo hunters, they "will see that the cultivation of the ground is far likelier to supply their wants than the uncertain chase." And finally, the people of Red River had learned that "their brethren abroad have a regard for their welfare." Perhaps, although the buffalo hunters had probably been more influenced in any change of lifestyle by the absence of animals than by the harvest of 1868. The concern of outsiders for Red River was a two-edged sword, influenced as much by imperialism as charity.

Conclusion

Given the chronology of events in Red River in the late 1860s, it is tempting to posit some sort of relationship between the famine and the subsequent Métis uprising in the settlement. What part the famine may have played in the insurrection can never be demonstrated conclusively. Given the extent of the aid supplied by the relief committee, it is clear that thousands of people in Red River were on short rations over the winter of 1868-69. The famine may have led the buffalo hunters to realize that the dire predictions made for years about the future of the herds was coming true. The shift from the buffalo hunt to sedentary agriculture would have been more clearly accelerated had not other events intervened in 1869-70. Indeed, the appreciation of the need for agricultural land may have sparked some of the Métis protest. Many Métis, including perhaps Louis Riel, found short-term employment in the transport of relief supplies. Nevertheless, the inhabitants' normal sense of self-worth was undoubtedly considerably shaken by these events beyond their control, as well by the demeaning need for outside assistance and demands for means tests. Much of the population was probably rendered more sensitive to outside interest and involvement in the settlement, and many were rendered suspicious of Canadian largesse. The French-speaking Métis may have been particularly sensitized. At the same time, the relief activities had demonstrated that—in a crisis—the divided religious and racial communities of the settlement could be brought together to pull for the common good. That fact at least augered well for the future.

Less promising would be the ensuing harvests after the politics were finished. Despite the *Nor'-Wester*'s confidence that the insect invasion had come historically only once every fifty years, the grasshoppers were back in 1875 and 1876, causing so much damage that the federal government loaned farmers thousands of dollars to buy seed, backed by mortgages on their homesteads. On the other hand, this later relief programme, unlike the one in 1868, was never conceived as charity but as business.[54] It was not necessary to show gratitude to moneylenders in the same way as to charity-givers.

JOHN CHRISTIAN SCHULTZ AND THE FOUNDING OF MANITOBA

(written with the assistance of Wendy Owen)

———◦•((•))•◦———

T HE historical period covering the founding of Manitoba
encompasses a number of enigmatic figures and personali-
ties, headed—of course—by Louis Riel.[1] But Riel is not the
only individual whose behaviour and actions in 1869-70 are difficult
to fathom. Others who might be placed on any record of "Enigma
Variations" would include Governor William McTavish, who failed to
govern in the autumn of 1869 for reasons never satisfactorily explained,
and Charles A. Boulton, whose reluctance to lead should have disqualified
him from leadership—but did not.[2] The actions of James Ross during
the crisis are most confusing.[3] James McKay stood on the sidelines during the entire affair.[4] Whether John Christian Schultz belongs on such
a list is disputable. It is certainly true that most of his contemporaries
thought that they understood where Schultz stood and could explain
his behaviour. He was seen by many in Red River, including Louis
Riel and Alexander Begg, as the evil genius of the Canadian Party in
the settlement.[5] Whether Schultz lived up to this advance billing is another matter. To a considerable extent he was employed as a convenient
bogeyman by the various contending interests, and has certainly been
demonized by pro-Métis historians ever since.[6] A careful look at Schultz's
activities during the Resistance is thus quite instructive.

The Early Career of J.C. Schultz

John Christian Schultz came to Red River in 1861, initially to help his
half-brother Henry McKenney in his various business ventures. He soon
hung out a shingle as a doctor, although he had no medical degrees.[7]

There was nothing untoward about such behaviour. Schultz had studied medicine back East, and the assumption of undocumentable qualifications was a major reason why men moved to frontiers like Red River. Moreover, the settlement had no standard for medical practice, and the standards even in more settled regions were a good deal more fluid than they are today. Schultz was accepted in the settlement as a medical practitioner. He testified as medical examiner in the murder trial of Paullet Chartrand in 1861, for example. Schultz had received an order for an inquest on the body of the deceased on 16 August. He had conducted a post-mortem examination and determined that death had been caused by the wound. He offered a good deal of technical detail in support of this judgement.[8] He also testified in the 1863 trial of the Reverend Griffiths Owen Corbett. His evidence on this occasion made clear that he had become the chief medical dispenser of drugs in the settlement from his store in the village of Winnipeg.[9] In 1866 he offered free medical treatment for the poor of Red River.[10]

Schultz quickly became the acknowledged leader of the Canadian Party in Red River. There was nothing surprising in this behaviour, either. He was a plausible speaker and a charismatic figure both intellectually and physically. Like many of Red River's most respected men, Schultz was extremely strong physically, and many stories circulated of his great feats of strength. In December of 1869 A.W. Graham described him as "a genial, powerfully built man, over six feet, red hair, sandy complexion."[11]

Like most Canadians in the settlement, Schultz believed that the West was part of Canada's "manifest destiny." As an outsider and one of Red River's most active businessmen, he naturally disliked the Hudson's Bay Company for its cozy assumption of control of government and justice. As sole proprietor of the *Nor'-Wester* from 1865 to 1868, he encouraged a continuation of an editorial policy highly critical of the political, social, and economic status quo in Red River. Were the *Nor'-Wester* under Schultz's proprietorship examined impartially, it might fare well, whatever its editorial position. By comparison with partisan local weekly newspapers elsewhere in British North America at the time—or daily newspapers in Winnipeg today—Schultz's paper comes off very well as interesting and responsible. Its coverage of court trials in Red River, for example, was both thorough and relatively even-handed. The pages of the newspaper under Schultz offer little evidence of serious racial hostility to any group in the settlement.

Despite his fluency in French and his marriage in 1867 according to Roman Catholic rite to Agnes Campbell Farquharson, Schultz was also an active Freemason, founder (in 1864) and Grand Master of Manitoba's first lodge.[12] Freemasonry preached anti-Catholicism in its secret rites and attracted those hostile to the Church to its ranks; its existence also bothered Roman Catholics. As Red River historian Joseph James Hargrave reported of the Masonic founding, "the only section of residents in the settlement which condemned the new project was the Roman Catholic priesthood, from some members of which I was amused to hear a variety of statements, bearing on the association and its objects, which were diverting though quite incredible."[13] By 1867, Schultz had divided public opinion in the settlement. When a petition signed by a number of prominent residents suggested Schultz as a councillor for Assiniboia, there was a counter-petition against the appointment. Bishop Alexandre-Antonin Taché later acknowledged the extent of hostility to Schultz, commenting that his appointment "became an impossibility, as much for the sake of the honour of the Company itself as for the honour of the Council, of which many members would have resigned had men thus disposed been forced upon them as colleagues."[14] Unfortunately, the Council of Assiniboia was the appointed (not elected) governing body of the settlement and not a private club. To refuse membership to as prominent a figure as Schultz, apparently simply because he was an open critic of the Council and the HBC, was politically childish. Co-option to the establishment might well have been a better strategy.

Of all the residents of Red River, Schultz was the most likely candidate for membership in Canada First, a secret fraternity founded in Ottawa in the spring of 1868 by a small number of Canadian expansionist/nationalists.[15] He joined the "apostles" in the spring of 1869 while on a visit to eastern Canada. There was certainly nothing secret about Schultz's advocacy of the Canadian annexation of Red River, about his assumption that Canadian standards of politics, law, and society needed to replace existing ones, or about his hostility to the Hudson's Bay Company. That newcomer Charles Mair would accept Schultz's hospitality—and intellectual leadership—was only to be expected, although all evidence suggests that Mair had far more deeply ingrained racist attitudes than did Schultz.[16] Mair found staying with Schultz preferable to Emmerling's Hotel. It was a comfortable change, he wrote, "from the racket of a motley crowd of half-breeds, playing billiards and drinking, to the quiet and solid comforts of a home." The poet then went on to make slighting remarks about the mixed-blood women of the settlement. Mair's notoriously disparaging remarks about half-breeds ought not to be visited upon his host, however.

John Christian Schultz, c. 1870s.

The Gaolbreak of 1868

Schultz did not make any bones about his willingness to be provocative and combative when his interests were threatened, as evidenced by the gaolbreak orchestrated by his wife early in 1868 when he was imprisoned for debt. The gaolbreak incident offers an excellent illustration of the Schultz style, and its consequences. Although all Red River businessmen spent a good deal of time in court, Schultz's involvement may have been a bit excessive. Initially he was merely a frequent litigant, but he subsequently turned to defiance of the court. In 1865 he had taken Henry McKenney to court over the dissolution of their partnership. As was usual at the time, the court appointed arbitrators to resolve the differences between the partners. But Schultz complained publicly that the court moved too slowly and had "neither the will nor the power to do justice." He refused to retract his statements, and Recorder John Black would not allow Schultz to appear personally in the court until he retracted or apologized.[17] In 1868 Mr. F. E. Kew, a former creditor of the Schultz/McKenney partnership, obtained judgement for an old debt. The sheriff who would have to enforce this judgement was none other than Henry McKenney himself, who did not disqualify himself from the task. Mr. Sheriff McKenney visited Schultz's store to obtain payment of the judgement. When he was refused, the sheriff attempted to seize goods for the amount of the court order. Schultz remonstrated physically—and he was a powerful man. After a struggle with the sheriff's deputies, Schultz was trussed up with rope found in his own store and transported to the local gaol at Upper Fort Garry. The sheriff complained that he had been assaulted in the discharge of his duty. The magistrate (John Black) accepted the charge. Schultz refused to post bail and was committed to gaol until he should stand trial. The whole business was obviously one of those personal feuds which had gotten well out of hand, and it got even more so.

While Schultz was being carted off to gaol, Constable James Mulligan attempted to maintain legal custody of the Schultz store. Mrs. Schultz asked Mulligan to leave, and when he refused, ordered the shop nailed shut with nails and spikes, leaving the constable inside without food, drink, or heat. He was subsequently released, dehydrated but unharmed. As her treatment of Constable Mulligan suggests, Agnes Campbell Farquharson Schultz was a force to be reckoned with in her own right. She proved the point with her subsequent behaviour. At about one o'clock on the following Saturday morning, 18 January 1868, Agnes—who had been allowed to take food to her husband and remain with him—was joined by a party of about fifteen men, who arrived with sleigh bells jingling at the doors of the gaol at Upper Fort Garry. Her husband proudly told the subsequent story himself, in a special edition of his newspaper:

> First, a party at the door to obtain peaceable entrance, then a request from the Doctor to let his wife out of the inner door of the prison, then a rush of the Doctor himself, who grappled with the constables who were barricading the door, then the upsetting of the jailer and the bolts drawn by the Doctor's wife, and then, as the expectant crowd saw the attack on the Doctor within, came the heavy thump of the oaken beam; soon the crashing of breaking timbers, and then the loud hurrah, with maledictions on McKenney, and the escort of the Doctor to his home. It is well to know that no disreputable characters were among the party. When the constables, of which there are said to have been six, with eight "specials," ceased to resist, the victors ceased their efforts, and no violence was used, but the breaking of the door, and the marks of a clenched

fist on one of the special constable's face would not have been there had he not rudely assaulted Mrs. Schultz in her endeavours to draw the bolts.[18]

The fist apparently belonged to Mrs. Schultz.

In many ways, the most important part of this story was its aftermath. On 23 January 1868, the Council of Assiniboia debated the "critical condition of the settlement." It authorized the raising of a body of 100 special constables for the day of the Schultz trial, some of whom could subsequently become part of a permanent force. Settlers were subsequently summoned to a meeting at the courthouse on 10 February, where 300 men were actually sworn in as special constables and paid ten shillings per man for their services. The *Nor'-Wester* complained about the payment of this money and its use to purchase alcoholic beverages. Schultz was away in Canada in April of 1868, when a substantial body of 804 residents of the settlement, including a number of Métis, produced a petition denying that the gaolbreak of Schultz had the approval of the general population of the settlement, as the *Nor'-Wester* had earlier implied. The acting editor of the paper, Walter Bown, initially refused to print the document and demanded protection from the "mob" (fourteen people led by A.G.B. Bannatyne) that entered his office to demand its insertion in the *Nor'-Wester*. Eventually Bown did print a few copies. When several leading Métis took samples of his print job to the post office to have someone familiar with English proofread them, the editor accused them of theft. The result was a suit for defamation of character heard at the May 1868 Quarterly Court. The plaintiffs won a verdict of twenty shillings in damages and costs. Bown refused to pay and was summarily imprisoned. His fine of £5 was eventually paid by a supporter of the Canadian Party.[19] It should be emphasized that this confrontation between the *Nor'-Wester* and the Métis did not directly involve Schultz, who was out of the settlement at the time and unable to communicate with Bown on the matter.

At this same court session, the Schultz case was reheard. At it Herbert L. Sabine, who had been employed by Schultz in 1865, testified that he had witnessed a payment from Schultz to Kew of £275, "the only evidence of the receipt of which was to be the testimony of Mr. Sabine who saw it and heard the verbal agreement between the two men that the affair was to be kept 'quiet,' and the money was to be paid on the debt, but not to be marked on the note."[20] The jury deducted £275 from the debt. Kew subsequently insisted that no such deal had been made, and Governor McTavish personally repaid Kew the amount involved, apparently on the grounds that his approval of a new trial had resulted in a fraud. At this distance it is impossible to ascertain the truth of the matter. McTavish's opinions and actions are irrelevant evidence. He felt politically pressured by the Schultz gaolbreak and was probably responding more from political animosity to Schultz than any hard evidence. Obviously many in the settlement were prepared to think about chicanery and to attribute it to Schultz and Sabine. But there is really no documentable reason to prefer Mr. Kew's version over the Sabine one. Partisan politics often became intimately connected with business and legal issues in the small colonial communities of the nineteenth century. Schultz was definitely a partisan politician.

Schultz and the 1869-70 Uprising

When we discuss John Christian Schultz in the context of the Red River uprising of 1869-70, it is essential that we place the historiography of that event in proper perspective. Increasingly, the history of this period has been viewed by historians either from the perspective of the Métis and of Louis Riel, or from the perspective of Anglophones sympathetic to them, chiefly Alexander Begg.[21] These perspectives are certainly legitimate ones, although their implications are negative for John Christian Schultz. There is no doubt that Schultz was leader of the local opposition to Riel or that the two men cordially hated each other. There is also no doubt that Schultz was disliked by Alexander Begg almost as intensely as Begg disliked James Ross. From either the Riel/Métis or Begg perspectives, Schultz's behaviour in 1869 and 1870 was illegitimate, provocative, and destructive. But such perspectives are totally partisan, however much their proponents would like to portray them as unvarnished or objective "truth." Whether such characterizations of Schultz can be sustained if the rhetorical assumptions underlying his "villainous" activities and motives are discounted, of course, is quite another matter.

There is also a tendency in the recent historiography to forget that the other parties in Red River had their own aspirations, and that those aspirations were not necessarily improper. As usual, historians have allowed those they prefer to be winners to control the interpretation of events. Louis Riel and his provisional government were only players in the struggle, not the inevitable victors, however. From the perspective of the Canadian Party in Red River, it could be argued, John Schultz behaved responsibly and appropriately—even with restraint—at least between July 1869 and September 1870.

In the summer and early autumn of 1869, Schultz kept a low profile, although there were constant rumours about his manoeuvring behind the scenes and complaints that the various Canadian parties in the settlement were much too friendly with him. There were also constant charges that Schultz was behind the Canadian land speculators who were active in the settlement, although little hard evidence was advanced at the time for this assertion.[22] Certainly Schultz was the principal supplier of provisions for the Canadian roadbuilding party, and he established a local store at Oak Point for the purpose.[23] But as the chief merchant in the settlement, there was nothing untoward about such activity. Most of the stories tell us more about the paranoia and hidden conflicts of the settlement than about the machinations of John Schultz. When William Dease, Pascal Breland et al. called a meeting for 29 July "to consider the affairs of the Settlement," Father Noel Ritchot suspected that Schultz's fine hand could be detected in the background, arguing that the notice of the meeting had appeared in the *Nor'-Wester*, the colony's only newspaper.[24] Although Schultz had sold out his interest in the paper to Walter Bown, the settlement persisted in viewing Bown as merely a figurehead. Interestingly, the editorial policy of the paper had become far more strident under Bown's direction, however, suggesting that Bown may well have been his own man. It is possible that Ritchot had other motives for invoking Schultz's name. An internal struggle within the ranks of the Métis was going on for control of any resistance to the Canadian takeover. The chief combatants in the summer of 1869 were the Catholic clergy (represented by Ritchot and Father Georges Dugast, with Louis Riel in the background) and two secular mixed-blood leaders, William Dease and William Hallett, who wanted to invoke Aboriginal rights rather than confessional and cultural rights in the forthcoming struggle against Canada.[25] Associating Schultz and the Canadian Party with the proponents of Aboriginal rights made eminently good political sense, however inaccurate it might be.

Ritchot further insisted that the 29 July meeting's discussion of a Métis seizure of public funds and the creation of an independent government to negotiate with Canada was really an action of the speculators—read Schultz again, one wonders?—who could thereby acquire land from the Indians.[26] The reactions to this whole affair remind us of the role of rumour in the Red River Settlement. When Joseph Howe arrived in the settlement on 9 October on his unofficial fact-finding expedition, he declined an offer of accommodation from John Schultz on the grounds that he wished to remain independent of the Canadian Party.[27] This action of Howe's was doubtless politically astute, but there is no necessary reason to read sinister motives into Schultz's invitation. He was always a hospitable man, particularly to visiting Canadians, and why should he not be? Howe commented at the time that Schultz and his Canadian Party "claimed all the loyalty, all the intelligence and all the respectability, and held that the masses of the people counted for nothing," as well as assuming "all the airs of the superior race."[28] But although such an attitude produced deep suspicions among the Métis, it did not automatically mean that Schultz was an active conspirator against them. Nevertheless, when Walton Hyman, who had recently set up a leather-tanning establishment in St. Norbert on the Rivière Sale, reported to the Council that a body of armed men had barricaded the road in his neighbourhood, rumours spread that he was really a "spy" for John Schultz, who by this time had become the Métis embodiment of Canadian evil.[29]

There could be no doubt that Schultz was seen as an enemy by the Métis, and it was not surprising that his departure from the settlement was one of the Métis demands listed by Walter Bown in a letter to Prime Minister Macdonald on 18 November: "that Dr. Schultz and others shall be sent out the territory forthwith and unless these demands are assented to by Mr. McDougall he shall not be permitted to come within the territory."[30] There is no evidence anywhere in the extensive documents of the period, however, that Schultz was engaged in any conspiratorial activities. The most provocative thing Schultz could be proven to have done was to hoist on Sunday on a flag staff directly in front of his drugstore a British flag with the word "Canada" sewn in the middle of it in white letters.[31] While this action apparently sent the Métis into paroxysms of rage, why should the man supposedly leading the local Canadian Party not be able to fly such a flag? Moreover, Alexander Begg himself admitted that Schultz had dropped the custom when affairs heated up in October of 1869. It is equally unsurprising that when James Ross on 19 November invited A.G.B. Bannatyne and Schultz to his house for the evening—and the two men tried to ascertain where Bannatyne stood—Alexander Begg should see the incident as evidence that "Mr. James Ross is hand in glove with the McDougall Shultz [sic] party irrespective of the claims of the settlers here—a two faced traitor."[32]

When Walter Bown circulated a petition on the morning of 22 November looking to upset Henry McKenney and Hugh O'Lone as Winnipeg delegates to the council meeting between Métis and Anglophones in the settlement, A.G.B. Bannatyne refused to sign "because those engaged in getting it up have been to a very great extent, the cause of all our present troubles." Bannatyne added, it was written "by one who has broken our laws; headed by one who has broken our laws; and handed me by one who has broken our laws."[33] He could have meant nobody else but Schultz. These charges about petitioning may have been true, but political petitioning and political discussion among the English-speaking people of Winnipeg was stirring up trouble only if one believed that everyone should agree with A.G.B. Bannatyne and Alexander Begg. According to notes kept by James Wallace, supposedly a spy for Governor McDougall, Schultz wanted no military threat to the resistance until the Canadians had left the settlement, hardly a very militant position.[34] Schultz continued to be quite unable, however, to persuade anybody in the settlement that Dr. Bown—who was behaving provocatively—was not acting on his behalf.[35] When Louis Riel on 24 November seized all the customs papers of the settlement, Alexander Begg speculated that a provisional government would attempt to collect overdue notes from merchants (headed by Schultz) for customs duties owing.[36] All this rumour tells us is what Begg thought was going on, however. At the meeting held at the Winnipeg engine house on 26 November, Schultz was supposed to have packed the meeting with Canadians "& others who had little interest at stake in the country" and to have wanted anyone to vote who had resided in town for a week. But his group was easily outvoted. Although Schultz had debated with James Ross at this gathering, none of the accounts suggests that he was advocating anything other than support for a Canadian government which had some legitimate claim to the territory.[37]

The first real evidence of unnecessarily provocative behaviour involving John Schultz comes on 27 November, when Louis Riel wrote Schultz a short note of warning. The letter is worth quoting in full. It read, "Sir, Your House is suspected as going to make trouble or be a place of trouble. Mind you, Docteur, and beleive [sic] that I am serious and would be very sorry to be compelled to any energetic action against you."[38] Riel does not accuse Schultz of making trouble in the present tense, but only in the future tense. The warning is not "you have made trouble" but "don't make trouble or I will take energetic action." Riel directed his concern at Schultz's house, of course, because a good deal of the Canadian provisions for the roadbuilding and survey crews, including a supply of pork, were stored in a warehouse connected to Schultz's dwelling. If the Canadians raised a force against the Métis, they would need these supplies. In any event, if Schultz felt threatened by the Métis, he had good reason.

When the exiled lieutenant-governor McDougall issued his proclamation on 1 December—on the mistaken assumption that the transfer had gone ahead as planned—Schultz plastered his house with handwritten copies of the document. Provocative? Perhaps. Also defensive, however, since the Métis who were threatening him might not wish to chance their hand against the authority of the new regime. The Canadian government supplies Schultz was storing quickly became the symbols of Canadian authority around which many of the young Canadians in the settlement rallied. "Guarding the stores" became the alternative way of making a statement of loyalty to Canada rather than joining Colonel Dennis and Charles Boulton, who, under what turned out to be an illegitimate commission from William McDougall, were attempting to recruit forces in the settlement to disperse the rebels. The position of those guarding the stores was a much more defensive one than Dennis's activities.[39]

On 4 December President John Bruce (of the provisional government) visited Schultz to attempt to arrange a truce. The two talked past each other. There was reason for confusion. Bruce wanted to know what was the "sticking point" for Schultz in the Métis list of rights. Schultz replied, "the insulting nature of the last one." Bruce answered, "they had not meant it so and that he [Schultz] must have an incorrect copy."[40] Schultz's reference was undoubtedly to the list of rights that Dr. Bown had obtained in November, which listed Schultz's departure from the settlement as its last demand. Bruce's reference was to the list of rights which had been produced by the Metis on 1 December 1869 in response to a challenge from James Ross.[41] Schultz obviously had not seen this latest listing, which had been circulated since he had been placed under siege. It was intended to rally all Red River residents under the flag of the provisional government, and was quite innocuous. But assuming that the document Bown had forwarded to Ottawa—with its demand for the removal of Schultz from the settlement—was something that the Métis had actually prepared, Schultz had good reason to be suspicious. As with the earlier letter to Schultz from Riel, all the provocation was on the Métis side.

In any event, within the Schultz house A.W. Graham recorded on 5 December that "we would fire on them, but our orders are not to fire the first shot." These orders probably came from John Schultz. Graham added, "we are looking for Col. Dennis up from the stone fort, with reinforcements."[42] It should be added that in the wake of the debacle of the proclamation, everyone involved, but especially Colonel Dennis, was anxious to deflect attention from himself and make others responsible for the ensuing disaster. Schultz was obviously a likely candidate as fall guy. Certainly a number of women and children were present in Schultz's house, as well as men provided only with small arms, which suggests something less than full mobilization. Also interesting is that Schultz does not play a prominent role, much less an aggressive one, in the diaries of those contemporaries—

A. W. Graham, Henry Woodington—actually in the house at the time.

Several other points are worth stressing about the party besieged in the Schultz house. One is that "guarding the stores" was a good deal less extreme and provocative an action for young hotbloods to take than joining Dennis and Boulton. The second is that according to Graham, the house was well-guarded by Métis from 5 December, "apparently to prevent our leaving," which made it hard for the party to evacuate short of surrender.[43] A third is that Charles Boulton was sent on 6 December by Dennis to request Schultz to retire from his buildings, when the Colonel discovered that he could not raise a decent military force.[44] According to Colonel Dennis, who was in Lower Fort Garry, Schultz had rejected this direction as "craven." But Charles Boulton, who actually delivered Dennis's request to the Schultz house, recalled in his memoirs that after a consultation, the party agreed to evacuate the buildings the following day, once arrangements had been made for the departure of the women and children.[45] Before the evacuation could be effected, however, Riel confronted the defenders with cannons and threats, forcing them to surrender. After all is said and done, Schultz's position was a defensive one and Riel had taken the initiative. Schultz got precious little applause for his refusal to begin the civil war. Joseph Howe noted of the loyalists that "with all their professions of loyalty not one of them fired a shot for Canada."[46]

Schultz and his wife spent the next month as guests of Louis Riel inside Upper Fort Garry, actually housed with Mr. J.H. McTavish, the company bookkeeper. According to Martin O'Donnell, Schultz was not transferred into the same building with the other prisoners until around 8 January.[47] Two days later Schultz escaped from the fort, by his own testimony employing a knife and a gimlet to work his way out a window. In leaping to the ground he injured his leg and had to scurry several miles for cover in very cold temperatures. He left behind instructions to provide everyone with rum at his expense. The rum was circulated in pails throughout the prison.[48] No doubt both the escape and the rum provoked Louis Riel a good deal, particularly when the Métis leader was unable to recapture the good doctor. Schultz received shelter at the home of Robert MacBeth and, doubtless, others.[49] Riel was probably annoyed even more when Schultz appeared in Kildonan on 15 February 1870 at the head of several hundred settlers and a small cannon drawn by four oxen. Here he joined up with the "Portage Boys" led by Charles Boulton, and other mixed-bloods from Kildonan. The declared intention of this military action was the liberation of the prisoners at Upper Fort Garry. In this context, it must always be remembered that the prisoners had never acknowledged the legitimacy of the provisional government when they surrendered. From the perspective of Schultz and his colleagues, the prisoners were being held illegally and should be released. It was true that negotiations were underway for their release, but to some extent the existence of those negotiations were the consequence of the show of force at the Stone Fort Lower Fort Garry). The little army had no money and no provisions. Schultz emptied his pockets and found a sovereign, but this would hardly feed the assembled multitudes.[50]

Schultz was temporarily deflected from his attempts to stir the mixed-bloods to action by the shooting of Hugh John Sutherland by an escaping Métis prisoner. He joined another unnamed doctor in treating Sutherland, who was mortally wounded. He then sat in a council of war with, among others, Charles Boulton, Judge John Black, Rev. John Black, and Bishop Machray. A "general council for the force," which consisted of fourteen lesser names, also met with these principal figures.[51] By this time the immediate object of the larger assemblage—the freeing of the prisoners—had been met. Boulton argued for dispersal on the grounds the objective had been realized. Schultz was one of those who insisted on demanding terms from Riel. The text of these demands has not survived, but they were summarized by a correspondent for the *Montreal Witness:* "that all prisoners be liberated at once, and that a guarantee be given that neither escaped prisoners nor any others be taken in future; that all confiscated property be stored; safety for Schultz's life be promised, and that we form a Government of our own, allowing him [Riel] to carry on his without any interference, but letting it be understood we countenanced him in no shape or manner. Also, free of all highways for us through the country."[52] The message finally drafted by Reverend John Black and carried to Riel by Thomas Norquay was considerably less specific.[53] Riel responded by blaming the messenger. The gathering eventually dispersed; some of those present (including Thomas Scott) were soon to be recaptured by Riel. Louis Riel later argued that Scott was one of Schultz's henchmen, but such an accusation misunderstood both Schultz and Scott.[54] Schultz himself went into hiding, and a series of efforts by Riel failed to flush him out. He departed the settlement soon after on snowshoes, accompanied by Joseph Monkman and a team of dogs to carry provisions. The trek across the prairies in late February and early March was no easy one, and its successful completion was a tribute to his stamina.

By early April Schultz was in Ontario, ready to be employed in stirring up the people of the province against the Métis. The initial leadership in whipping up public sentiment against the execution of Thomas Scott was taken by George Denison and William Foster of Canada First, however, and not by Schultz. He was one of those present at the great Toronto rally of 7 April, but he was by all accounts the most conciliatory of the major speakers.[55] He corrected some of Mair's more extreme comments about the Métis, and emphasized that "Nothing was to be gained by looking at the past, it was better to look forward to the future." Some critics have suggested that Schultz was at this point concerned lest he too be prosecuted for his behaviour during the previous winter, but it is hard to see what Schultz had done that was criminal. In any event, although he accompanied the Red River exiles on their railroad journey across small-town Ontario to Ottawa, he was not prominent among the crowd-pleasers along the way. In Ottawa, Schultz joined the other exiles in testifying before the Select Senate Committee on the Northwest.[56] He willingly answered questions, mainly about climate and his journey east. The final question was about his intention to return to Red River. He answered yes, adding, "I feel unwilling to say anything that may involve myself in difficulties, and I hope the Committee will not press me on delicate subjects."

Despite the fears of many, Schultz did not make any loud noises during the debates over the Manitoba Act. Indeed, Charles Mair wrote to the doctor, "I felt annoyed at your recognition of the Manitoba bill without concurrence." Schultz met with British envoy Sir Stafford Northcote on 21 April 1870.[57] Northcote found him "a man of very quiet manners," but with "a rather untrustworthy expression of countenance." In any event, Schultz refused to be drawn by Northcote into any finger-pointing on this occasion. Judge Black subsequently told Northcote that Schultz had already received large amounts of compensation for his losses in Red River, with advances given personally by Sir Francis Hincks, adding that he was to receive a major appointment (the reference was probably to a Senate seat for the new province) as well.[58] Schultz's enemies then and later called the advances a bribe. But Schultz was plainly practising conciliation in the spring of 1870. He had a curious meeting with Father Ritchot in May, arranged at the doctor's insistence by Sir George Cartier, which ended with the two antagonists agreeing that what they had done during the past "exceptional events" was now behind them.[59] Schultz was far more anxious to begin anew than was Ritchot, however. He was obviously concerned about his Red River constituency, writing Cartier "I feel that in justice to the people of Red River in fairness even to myself I must not leave Canada till it is distinctly understood how the loyal portion of the settlers and particularly the English are to be classed in the coming economy."[60]

By the time Schultz returned to Red River in September, his spirit of conciliation had waned considerably. On 6 September he led a band of men into the house of Thomas Spence, editor of the *New Nation*, and personally administered a horsewhipping to that worthy, allegedly because Spence had insulted Mrs. Schultz the previous winter.[61] Perhaps even more important, the band of men with Schultz then proceeded to trash the newspaper's printing press, rendering the newspaper silent until well into October. This was far more the John Schultz the settlement had grown to love—and hate—than the man who had hidden from Louis Riel the previous February.[62] But whatever role Schultz had played in the settlement before 1869 and would play in the new Manitoba after September 1870, in the events leading to its creation he was far less the aggressor than he was usually portrayed. Schultz might well have claimed that his behaviour was consistently misunderstood, from the early days through the Resistance into the Manitoba period. But it certainly does appear that Schultz did his best to stay out of trouble during the forma- tive period of the Resistance. We cannot ever know why this should be the case, although it is quite possible that even he sympathized with the settlement's objections to the way in which the Canadians were taking over Red River.

REPORTING THE RESISTANCE
OF 1869-1870

———————◦•⟨(•)⟩•◦———————

A S the Red River Settlement approached its formal transfer from the Hudson's Bay Company to Canada in 1869, it appeared to the outside world to be a small, isolated, frontier community teetering precariously on the edge between civilization and savagery. Certainly this was the view of the settlement held by the Canadians, who intended to take it over and run it as a colony in tutelage to civilization. In some ways the perception was accurate. Physically, the settlement certainly was isolated—although it was rapidly becoming less so—and it was still on the frontier edge of free land. Travelling to Red River either required a lengthy summer journey by water from Lake Superior, or a lengthy overland sojourn of nearly 400 miles from the end of the railroad in Minnesota. Canadian politicians like Joseph Howe and Charles Tupper in 1869 demonstrated that the settlement could be reached in about a month in the middle of winter, but it was no easy journey. Demographically, Red River was not numerically large. It contained about 13,000 people, including a few hundred Aboriginals and a large population of mixed-bloods, both French-speaking and English-speaking. If one excluded the mixed-bloods, there were probably little more than a thousand "white folk" residing on the banks of the Red and Assiniboine rivers.

But at the same time, appearances were in some senses deceiving. Spiritually and intellectually at least, Red River's elite had long since become an integral part of the outside world.[1] It would have been no idle boosterism to maintain that, for its size and situation, Red River harboured one of Canada's most lively and best-educated intellectual communities. As early as 1860, the settlement had three choral societies.[2] The Institute of Rupert's Land had been organized in 1862 to provide a forum for scientific and humanistic discussion within the community.[3] There was a subscription library which consisted of 2,500 volumes.[4] Most of the leading fiction and non-fiction books of the Victorian era were readily available either in the library or at the bookstore operated by the printers of the local newspaper, the *Nor'-Wester*. Regular perusal of that newspaper ought to have suggested the difficulty of visualizing the place as utterly barbaric.[5] Many residents were highly critical of the newspaper. It certainly was highly partisan, hostile to the Hudson's Bay Company and blatantly enthusiastic about Canadian annexation. And it was the only newspaper in town, at least until late in 1869. But in its pages one could find much attention paid to the cultural amenities, ranging from imperial political philosophy to racial theory to the history of the settlement itself.

For a supposedly isolated and barbaric place, Red River had an astoundingly self-conscious historical vision of itself. By 1869 the settlement had already produced three indigenous historians in the persons of Alexander Ross, Donald Gunn, and an anonymous writer (probably a clergyman) whose work, like Gunn's, was first published in the pages of the *Nor'-Wester*.[6] The settlement also had two younger historians— Alexander Begg and Joseph James Hargrave—waiting in the wings to offer on-the-spot accounts of the major upheaval about to occur. Also in residence was a major Canadian poet in the person of Charles Mair, who may have been a recent immigrant to Red River, but had already published *Dreamland and Other Poems,* a well-regarded book of verse. Mair was also a regular correspondent for Ontario newspapers. Other bright young men were present as well. The leaders of the two mixed-blood communities, Louis Riel and James Ross, were both well-educated, articulate, and bilingual. Riel had recently returned from Quebec, ready to write to that province's newspapers in defence of every slight to his people. James Ross, fresh from years as a Toronto journalist, had only recently returned to his homeland.

Thus the insurgency against Canada, which developed so suddenly and unexpectedly in the autumn of 1869, could be chronicled by a highly literate and historically self-conscious group of residents. For a backcountry revolt, the Red River Resistance was always remarkably erudite, as its chronicles and chroniclers will attest. For an event occurring hundreds of miles from "civilization," moreover, the Resistance was remarkably well-covered in the big-city newspapers of Canada, the United States, and Great Britain. These newspapers, especially the Canadian dailies, occasionally sent their own correspondents to attempt to cover the story in Red River. They also reprinted anything off the American wires that they could find, although the Yankees published mainly second-hand information filtered through Pembina. Under normal circumstances, the Canadian papers would have also copied extensively from the pages of the *Nor'-Wester*, as they had been doing for years. But the Métis led by Louis Riel had been in conflict with the *Nor'-Wester* for some time, and in early December of 1869 Riel actually closed down both this newspaper and a potential rival (the *Pioneer*, to be printed on a new press brought to the settlement in the autumn of 1869).[7] As a result, the bulk of what eastern Canadian readers learned about the events of the resistance came through letters written expressly to the newspapers to inform that audience. Occasionally private correspondence about events in Red River was printed, especially in the pages of the non-metropolitan newspapers. Sometimes single letters found their way into the larger dailies, which copied from one another and from the provincial papers. Among Francophone newspapers, both *Le Nouveau Monde* and the *Courrier de Saint-Hyacinthe* carried letters from Red River, although no French paper had a regular series by a single author over the winter of 1869-70.[8]

Most of the correspondence that filled the pages of the eastern press and informed Canadians of events in the West in 1869-70 came from the pens of a handful of writers based in Red River who supplied regular letters to the newspapers. These letters were usually published under pseudonyms or without any authorial attributions, although at least some of the authors' names were known in the settlement. The three major writers were Charles Mair, Joseph James Hargrave, and Alexander Begg, although Louis Riel supplied several letters as well. These young men were all very close together in age, with Mair at 31 the oldest in 1869. Begg was 30, Hargrave was 29, and Riel 25. Very little of their correspondence to the newspapers has survived as manuscript text, so it is very difficult to tell what editorial changes might have been made to the original versions. In a few cases, it would appear that the eastern editors added running heads which may not have existed in the originals.

The two major newspapers in Anglophone Canada that followed most closely the Red River story were the *Montreal Herald and Daily Commercial Gazette* and the *Toronto Globe*. These two newspapers had quite different editorial policies and reasons for interest in Red River. The

Herald was no friend of the Macdonald government and was quite happy to report on its imperial deficiencies. A newspaper with long-standing connections to the western fur trade, the *Herald* had also been critical of William McDougall (the newly appointed governor of the territory) for years. It carried at least two sets of letters from Red River, one much more extensive than the other, which were often difficult to distinguish from one another. George Brown's *Globe* had a historic interest in westward expansion that went back nearly two decades.[9] Unlike the *Herald,* which was happy with local correspondents, the *Globe* actually sent its own reporter to try to cover the story. He failed. Detained by Louis Riel, he never actually got to remain in Red River. The dispatches he filed were not very insightful. Because the eastern newspapers circulated widely in Red River, in their pages local residents eventually got to read about the events with which they were living on a daily basis. The time between the dates of composition and the dates of publication varied between three weeks and a month, suggesting how long it took to get correspondence from Red River to Canada, even employing the American postal system and railways. Return travel took at least another month. But after the suppression of the *Nor'-Wester* by Riel, and apart from a handful of issues in the early months of 1870 of the *New Nation,* a newspaper blatantly controlled by the provisional government, the eastern newspapers were the major printed source for events in Red River for even its own population.

The Mair Letters

The first series of letters was written before the insurgency actually began. They were six in number, written between 3 November 1868 and 31 August 1869 by Charles Mair, the poet, who had been given a job as paymaster with the Canadian roadbuilding operation that had been sent to Red River in 1868, ostensibly to provide work for the famine-starved residents of the settlement.[10] Born in Lanark County, Upper Canada, he had attended Queen's University with John Schultz but did not graduate.[11] In the spring of 1868 Mair helped organize the secret movement "Canada First."[12] About the same time he published *Dreamland and Other Poems*, an echo of John Keats. Mair subsequently received a patronage appointment from William McDougall as secretary for the Canadian mission to London which was to negotiate the transfer of Rupert's Land to Canada. He was unable to go, and settled instead for a government job on the Canadian roadworks near Red River. He was also named Red River correspondent for several Canadian newspapers, including the *Globe* and the *Montreal Herald*. Mair published his pre-insurgency letters under his own name. Some of the subsequent pseudonymous letters printed by the *Globe* during the uprising were undoubtedly his as well, although they cannot with certainty be attributed to him.

Mair's intention in his early letters was to describe the land and the people of the newly acquired territory for an eastern audience which knew virtually nothing about the West. Like most Canadian poets of the nineteenth century, Mair was skilled in the evocation and description of nature and landscape. It helped that he fell in love with the Canadian prairie, quickly becoming an advocate of large-scale Canadian immigration to the region. Like many Canadians of the time, Mair had little but disdain for the Aboriginal peoples. He got into considerable trouble in the settlement over his racist comments about the mixed-bloods in his published letters. One letter about mixed-blood women earned him a horsewhipping, although in fairness to Mair he had not intended the comment to be published. Another letter with disparaging comments about the industry of the "half-breeds" earned him a sharp, printed rebuke from "L.R." (Louis Riel). Mair's early correspondence, as well as containing some fine descriptive writing about the prairies, was characterized by an exaggerated faith in the future of the country when once settled by the proper sort of people.

Mair married a niece of John Christian Schultz and was one of the most active of the pro-Canadian party in Red River in 1869-70. He was part of the group that surrendered to Louis Riel at John Schultz's house in December 1869, but he escaped a month later. He went first to Portage la Prairie, then joined the "Portage Boys" in their march to Kildonan in February 1870. But he was not with the Portage party when it was arrested by Riel on 17 February outside the gates of Upper Fort Garry. Instead, Mair headed south to St. Paul, eventually travelling east with Donald A. Smith. He appeared at a number of rallies in Ontario in 1870 designed to stir up hostility to Louis Riel and the provisional government, and he testified before the Senate subcommittee in April 1870 on the origins of the Resistance. He eventually received $1,910 compensation for lost property and $66 for his imprisonment. Once Manitoba joined Confederation, Mair kept a store at Portage la Prairie until 1883, and then was made an officer of the Governor General's Body Guards in 1885. Under pressure from his friends, he sought Canadian topics for his writing, and in 1886 he published *Tecumseh,* a verse-drama highly regarded at the time. Once well-regarded as a Canadian poet, his reputation

Joseph James Hargrave, whose letters on the Resistance in the *Montreal Herald* appeared under the name "Red River."

has slipped into eclipse, at least partly because of the rawness of his Canadian nationalism.[13]

The "Red River" Letters of Joseph James Hargrave

The early descriptive letters of Charles Mair from Red River were quickly succeeded in September 1869 by a correspondence in the *Montreal Herald* labelled "Red River Settlement, British North America." The anonymous author of this series of fifteen letters written between 18 September 1869 and 29 January 1870[14] was Joseph James Hargrave, the private secretary of Governor William McTavish of the Hudson's Bay Company. The oldest son of Chief Trader James Hargrave and Letitia Mactavish Hargrave, young "Beppo," as he was called, grew up amongst the Scottish fur-trade aristocracy in the settlement before being sent to Scotland to be educated.[15] He returned to Red River in 1861 to enter HBC employment. It is not clear whether Hargrave had already drafted the manuscript which would be published as *Red River* (1871) at the time he began his *Herald* correspondence, but it would appear likely. The volume published in 1871 dealt with the history of the decade of the 1860s, and Hargrave's declared intention to provide an appendix to this work covering the Resistance of 1869-70—presumably to be based on his *Herald* letters—suggests that he saw the material he had produced as part of a single whole.[16] It also seems likely that Hargrave, like his fellow correspondent Alexander Begg, kept a detailed diary or journal at the time of the Resistance to serve as the basis of his account. If so, it unfortunately has not survived.

Hargrave's reputation as a historian has always been an uneasy one. A few scholars have recognized his work, but almost nobody takes it very seriously, perhaps because of its microcosmic approach and its seemingly gossipy (almost bitchy) nature. The only contemporary review of *Red River,* in the *Canadian Monthly and National Review,* complained: "events which happen out of the ordinary dull and monotonous routine of life in such a place, no matter how trivial in themselves, or how unimportant to the outside world, have acquired in the mind of the author, solely by reason of their rarity, an historic dignity."[17] Hargrave certainly had a fine eye for the detail of scandal, and was obviously often much entranced by the shenanigans in the small community he had chosen to chronicle. He also intuitively sensed that gossip and scandal flourished best at the public and private margins of society, and were thus symptomatic of the underlying tensions of society.[18] Far from being a myopic local historian, Hargrave is thus one of the unacknowledged forerunners of modern Canadian social history.

Underneath the amusing surface of *Red River,* Hargrave did have some definite theses about what had been going on in Red River. These were carried over (or anticipated) in his letters to the *Herald* in 1869-70. In letter 9, for example, dated 13 November 1869 and published on 4 December, Hargrave insisted:

> Regarding the advisability of removing the responsibility of government from the Company it can hardly be a matter of doubt that the time has fully arrived for such a step. The action of the Government here for some years past has been grossly misrepresented to the Canadian public through interested agencies, the nature of some of which I may have occasion hereafter to explain. It has certainly been an administration ruled by expediency, inasmuch as men accused and found guilty of criminal offences have been permitted to remain at large after having been rescued from prison by the illegal violence of their adherents—but the spirit of government has been pure, and its administration more lenient. It wanted, however, the element of strength to be found only in a material force to uphold the law.

For Hargrave, it was the breakdown of the system of justice and the failure to be able to maintain order, thoroughly documented by him in *Red River,* which had led to the resistance. Many historians of early Manitoba have adopted this viewpoint without acknowledging its source. The HBC needed to be replaced with a more formal government, either British or Canadian, but not Métis, insisted Hargrave. In his 1869-70 correspondence, however, Hargrave was neither a slavish supporter of the HBC nor a particular friend of the Canadian Party.

Beyond the political analysis of Red River lay Hargrave's understanding of the microcosm's dynamic, something not likely to be appreciated by contemporary historians in Ontario or by their national history successors. Others in Red River saw the prevalence of local scandal as little more than evidence of the backwardness of the settlement. William Ross wrote his brother James in 1856, for example: "You know the fact that Red River is half a century behind the age—no stirring events to give life and vigour to our debilitated life. . . . Just for the reasons above given and because we in Red River live for ourselves and care for no one else—nothing but the little tattle of scandal in every one's mouth—of this we have plenty."[19] But for Hargrave, rumour and scandal were what the place was all about, as he continually demonstrated in all his writing, including his Resistance correspondence. *Red River* would have been immeasurably strengthened by the inclusion of Hargrave's epistolery accounts of the origins of the uprising of 1869-70, which emphasized the gossip and scandal surrounding the events.

Hargrave began his correspondence to the *Herald* with a letter dated 18 September 1869.[20] This letter was plainly intended as the introduction to a correspondence describing Red River beyond the "general features of the country and its people," which the author insisted were "pretty widely known." The ambition appears little different from that of Charles Mair, although Hargrave perhaps gave his readers more credit for knowledge of the region than did the Canadian poet. As the chapters in his subsequent book demonstrated, Hargrave's strength was in providing insider detail. Gradually, however, the stirring events within the settlement began to overtake the author's background detail. At the end of the letter dated 22 October, Hargrave dropped his description to take up a brief narrative of the events literally swirling all around him. The letter dated 30 October 1869 also began as description and ended as narrative. By the letter of 6 November, Hargrave had fully shifted his attention to the disturbances. He lived in bachelor's quarters in Upper Fort Garry, as one of his subsequent letters made clear. Particularly after the occupation of the fort by Riel's Métis in early November, Hargrave was literally right in the middle of the action. His detailed account of Riel's seizure of the land records and accounts of the settlement in November offered one example of what was undoubtedly first-hand intelligence. Hargrave was also clearly present at the meeting held at the Winnipeg Fire Engine House on 26 November at which Louis Riel spoke. The report of the subsequent discussion demonstrated Hargrave's eye for telling detail, as did his revelation that when, after the meeting, he had ridiculed the notion that those in attendance had been armed, he was answered by each of three friends who pulled out a revolver from under his coat.

One major problem with Hargrave's correspondence is distinguishing it from other letters—by "Nor'West," by "Nor-Wester," by "Rivière Rouge"—also published in the *Herald*. These other letters are also by residents in the settlement, probably mainly Canadians. They are often not particularly insightful, and more to the point, they typically are not part of an ongoing series, although there were several letters from "Nor-Wester" to the Montreal newspaper. Hargrave did not sign his earlier letters, and occasionally the *Herald* would run the letters of more than one correspondent together, as it did on 7 January 1870. Hargrave himself eventually recognized the problem, and in his letter published 29 January 1870 wrote, "I beg to conclude by saying that, as I see the fact of my having adopted no specific signature to my letters seems likely to end in committing me, through mistake, to the opinions of fellow correspondents, from which in reality I might dissent, I shall adopt for distinction's sake in any future communications to your Journal the signature RED RIVER." Unfortunately, Hargrave was nearly at the end of his correspondence when he took this step.

Joseph James Hargrave's overall perspective was that of a Hudson's Bay Company official, which led him to a continual ambivalence towards the uprising in Red River. Hargrave was no particular friend of the Métis led by Louis Riel, but he fully acknowledged that Canadian policy toward the settlement had been badly misguided from the beginning. Not only had the Canadians failed to communicate with the local officials of the Hudson's Bay Company, but "successively arriving officials seemed altogether unaccredited to those of the old order of things, and attached themselves to a party, which, while professing itself peculiarly representative of Canada, had always openly gloried in throwing difficulties in the way of the old administration. This party, what influence soever it may have in Canada, never possessed any in Red River."[21] Hargrave saw the subsequent issuance by Governor MacDougall of a premature proclamation of the Canadian takeover and the actions of Colonel John Dennis attempting to stir up opposition to the insurgents in the settlement as further evidence of Canadian irresponsibility. In a letter dated 22 January 1870, Hargrave attempted to correct some of the misstatements he had read in the Canadian newspapers. He insisted that Colonel Dennis had not behaved with lack of courage; instead, "having once commenced hostilities, he persevered with determination and rashness which covered him with failure and obloquy." He also maintained that were Canada to withdraw from Rupert's Land, its inhabitants would not "be consigned to the state of political serfdom, from which they have so lately been emancipated." The recent events denied such a result, Hargrave wrote, for "no such thing as political subjection has ever been known in Rupert's Land."[22] He did not think that the Hudson's Bay Company wanted to continue in control of the settlement, and at this point insisted that events appeared to be drifting toward ultimate American annexation, a conclusion that would "prove fatal to the great project of confederation of British American Provinces."

Hargrave's Red River letters ended abruptly with one dated 29 January 1870.[23] In this epistle he advocated a "Canadian Pacific Railway" and blamed the present "troubles" on "the shameful neglect of the Colonial Office." He left the parties in Red River in the midst of constructing a bill of rights, writing, "at present there appears to be no obstacle in the way of an ultimate solution of the difficulty." He warned that the real question was how much plunder would be taken from the HBC storehouses. The sudden termination of his correspondence means we are deprived of Hargrave's accounts of the stirring events of February and early March 1870, including the arrest of the "Portage Boys" and the subsequent execution of Thomas Scott. There is no evidence to suggest that Hargrave became disenchanted with the behaviour of the provisional government. He indicated in a letter of 8 February 1870 to Sir Curtis Lampson that his original intention had been a series of descriptive articles. We are equally ignorant of why Hargrave published *Red River* in 1871 without including the material on the Resistance, or why he published nothing more after that book. It is possible that the lukewarm reception to *Red River*—according to Isaac Cowie, Hargrave lost £600 by its publication—discouraged him from further activity.[24] The surviving Hargrave papers contain a brief, thirty-one-page fragment of a history of the fur trade, headed in another hand "Story begun by Joseph Hargrave 1878," but its sketchy and incomplete nature suggests that Hargrave had lost whatever incentives had earlier motivated his writing. He may have been another one-book author, of which Canada has had many.

Present at the raising of the British flag at Upper Fort Garry by Colonel Wolseley's troops in August of 1870, Joseph Hargrave was one of those who raised his voice in the singing of "God Save the Queen." After the dust had settled from the "restoration," and certainly after the appearance of his book on Red River in 1871, Hargrave settled into a comfortable niche in the HBC. He was not rapidly promoted, however, serving for a total of fifteen years as a clerk before being appointed a temporary cashier in 1877 and in 1878 a chief trader in the Red River District. He was transferred to Edmonton in 1884, retiring there in 1889. His later correspondence frequently offered the usual complaints of the petty bureaucrat who had reached a plateau, including low wages. In 1878 Hargrave was appointed secretary of an association founded to improve working conditions in the Company, and he helped negotiate improvements with Donald A. Smith. Not surprisingly, in the Winnipeg boom of the 1880s he was an active investor, probably losing heavily when the bubble burst. In any case, he retired only after receiving an inheritance which enabled him to live comfortably. In its obituary, the

Manitoba Free Press commented on a paralysis in later years "which eventually disabled him completely and hastened his death."[25] If this motor disease was one of the hereditary ones which became progressively more severe, it may help account for the cessation of his historical activities. In any event, he removed to Montreal in 1890 and joined kinfolk in Edinburgh in 1893, residing at 7 Atholl Crescent. He died unmarried.

Joseph James Hargrave deserves to be better known as a historian than is now the case. He was not among the early historians of Red River who saw the settlement as "moribund."[26] He saw a far more complex dynamic. He was certainly a "participant historian" in the nineteenth-century sense of the term.[27] Hargrave's reputation (or rather, lack of it) has certainly been influenced by his microcosmic regional approach, but also for the fact that his historical writing on the Red River Resistance has never been properly recognized or made available to the public. A revision of the Resistance letters, added to his 1871 book on Red River, would certainly have given that book a sense of direction and purpose it appeared to lack when it was first published. Not even those historians—like W. L. Morton—who knew that Hargrave had written a series of letters for the *Montreal Herald*, have appreciated how extensive that correspondence really was.

The "Justitia" Letters of Alexander Begg

The other principal Red River correspondent to the eastern newspapers was Alexander Begg. Like both Mair and Hargrave, Begg was a relative newcomer to Red River. He had been born in Quebec City in 1839, his parents having immigrated there from Scotland. After local education at St. John's, Quebec, Begg went off to school at Aberdeen before entering the world of commerce. In 1867 he came to Red River as agent for several firms based in Hamilton, Ontario, and a year later he became a partner of A.G.B. Bannatyne, who operated a general store (and the local post office) in the centre of the village of Winnipeg. Begg's connection with the post office meant that he, like Joseph James Hargrave, had a particularly useful vantage point from which to learn about the ongoing events of 1869-70. While much of Hargrave's information came from his residential position at Upper Fort Garry, much of Begg's intelligence came from the local post office, where residents doubtless chatted as they picked up and posted their mail. There was no mail delivery in Red River in 1869-70. Those wanting their mail had to pick it up at Begg's store. In the stirring days of the insurgency, fact, rumour, and speculation alike circulated at the post-office wicket.

While we may suspect that Joseph James Hargrave probably kept a regular diary or journal, we know that Alexander Begg did. It was edited and published by W. L. Morton in 1956. As well as making detailed entries in his journal, Begg also wrote—between 10 November 1869 and 26 February 1870—a series of ten lengthy letters under the *nom de plume* of "Justitia," which were sent off and were published in the *Toronto Globe*. W. L. Morton knew of "Justitia" and even reprinted several of his letters, and he suspected that "Justitia" was indeed Alexander Begg.[28] Indeed, the proof of this identification itself was in the pages of the Morton edition, for a verbatim version of the first "Justitia" letter served as the "Preface" to Begg's manuscript journal. In some ways the *Globe* was a curious choice of outlet for Begg to have made. It was a strong booster of Canadian expansionism, a phenomenon about which Begg harboured deep suspicions. But Joseph James Hargrave and others were already publishing in the *Montreal Herald,* and Begg doubtless preferred not to bury his reports amongst many others. Moreover, from Begg's perspective, his letters could provide a useful corrective to the *Globe's* usual editorial policy on Red River and the West. Even more curious than Begg's choice of the *Globe* is that newspaper's willingness to publish his correspondence. From his first letter, dated 10 November 1869, Begg set out to be revisionistic. He intended to lecture Canada and Canadians about Red River and their mistakes about it. By the time he picked up his pen in November of 1869, it was clear to Alexander Begg and every other thoughtful person in Red River that the Métis would resist the annexation of Red River by Canada.

Joseph James Hargrave had already sent eight letters to the *Montreal Herald* by the time that Begg wrote his first "Justitia" one, but Hargrave had not set out to write about the Resistance and only gradually discovered that his account of it was assuming so much space in his correspondence. Begg clearly intended to focus on the insurgency. He began his first letter by emphasizing, "that which has been foretold for some time past in the settlement has taken place." A long gestation period of discontent had eventually produced open resistance by the "French half-breeds." Begg proceeded to excoriate the Canadian government, the Canadian Party in the settlement, and the *Nor'-Wester* newspaper on which the *Globe* had often relied for information about Red River, for their collective failure to take the people of Red River, especially its mixed-blood population, sufficiently seriously. Rhetorically Begg asked, "would it not have been wiser policy for them [the Canadians] to have sent authorized Agents to this country as soon as the transfer of territory was agreed upon, for the purpose of feeling the pulse of the settlers, find out their ideas on the change proposed, and opening out, as far as possible, the views of the Canadian Government towards them?" With these sentiments most of the population of the settlement, with the possible exception of the more extreme members of the Canadian Party, would probably have concurred. It is likely that even the editorial people at the *Globe* would have admitted privately that, at least with hindsight, Canada had not approached Red River very sensibly.

From the outset, "Justitia" made clear that he was no particular friend of Canada. What was less apparent in the opening letter was the extent of his sympathies for the Métis people of the settlement. In his first epistle, Begg did not much distinguish the parties or classes of Red River. He had identified the Resistance as coming from the French-speaking Métis, but most of his discussion revolved around the many errors of Canada, some of which had involved working within the settlement with what Begg (joining Hargrave) insisted was a totally discredited Canadian Party. Begg's readers could have been forgiven for thinking after reading his first letter that the opposition to Canada, whoever was leading it, was pretty general in the settlement. In some senses, this doubtless was Begg's belief. He could not know, at the outset, how totally the events of the next few months would come to divide Red River. Begg's general attitude, at least until March of 1870, was that all those who did not support Riel and his colleagues were part of the problem. The small but active Canadian opposition was only the most objectionable of the local obstructionist forces. The English-speaking residents, mostly mixed-bloods, who sat on their hands, were also obstacles. As for the Americans, Begg suspected their motives but had to admit that they generally backed the insurgency.

Like Hargrave, Alexander Begg relied heavily on local "rumours" for his analysis of events. Hargrave's rumours originated mainly in Upper Fort Garry, the headquarters of the Métis and the Hudson's Bay Company; they tended to reflect mainly accurate intelligence. From his vantage point at the post office, Begg had access to a much wider range of gossip and speculation, which he reported in both his journal and his correspondence (but especially the former) without much discrimination. At what point the Canadians came to suspect that Begg was "Justitia" is not clear—some certainly had made the connection by the time of the Wolseley "invasion"—but Begg had always made far less effort than Hargrave to be fair to those with whom he did not agree. Begg cordially detested both John Schultz, the ostensible leader of the

Canadian Party, and James Ross, the leading English-speaking mixed-blood in the settlement. He also had considerable admiration for Louis Riel. These prejudices certainly helped colour his narrative.

Alexander Begg has left us three different versions of events in 1869-70. He doubtless began with entries in his journal, then wrote up the journal entries for his "Justitia" letters, and finally, employed both sources to compose his 1871 history, *The Creation of Manitoba.* There is substantial overlap between the three versions, but they are by no means identical. Take, for example, the account of the raising of the new provisional government's flag on 10 December 1869. In his journal, Begg recorded:

> The French to-day hoisted the Provisional Government flag as below [the sketch was left blank] and fired off a volley of small arms and salutes from the cannon at Fort Garry—the guard at Dr. Schultz house returned the salute. After several vollies had been fired at the Fort and the band of St. Boniface under the leadership of Father Dugast had played several tunes there—a party with the band proceeded to the town and serenaded Genl. Malmoras the American Consul. Three cheers were given for the Provisional Government—three for the leaders and three for the band—followed by three groans for Mulligan—late chief of police now a prisoner at Fort Garry. Mr. Riel addressed the French at Fort Garry and in the course of his speech hoped his men were all loyal to the Queen.[29]

"Justitia" reported this event as follows:

> The Friday last, the 10th inst., the French went through the ceremony of hoisting the flag of their Provisional Government. About four o'clock in the afternoon, a number of armed men assembled in the Court yard of Fort Garry, and were addressed by Mr. Riel, who called upon them to support the new flag until their rights, as free born subjects of Queen Victoria, were respected. The idea of this movement is simply another step towards the grand scheme of a Provisional Government—and emblem, as it were, of its actual existence. After Mr. Riel's address, the flag (the design of which is the *fleur de lis* and *shamrock* combined) was hoisted, and a salute fired by the men in the Fort, at the same time the brass bands from St. Boniface, struck up some lively tunes; again and again the salutes were fired, until at least they thought they had wasted powder enough. The bands accompanied by a guard then proceeded to the town and serenaded its citizens. The shamrock on the flag looks significant; but on inquiry I find that it is merely a compliment to Mr. O'Donoghue, an Irishman, who has greatly assisted Mr. Riel in the present undertaking.

This, at all events, is the only version of the matter I have heard. I sincerely hope there is no deeper meaning to the emblem. I am sure there is not as far as the general body of the French are concerned."[30]

Begg's 1871 book records:

On the 10th December, the French provisional flag was hoisted for the first time at Fort Garry, amidst the shouts of the men assembled to witness it. The flag consisted of a white ground, on which was worked a representation of the *fleur de lis* and *shamrock* combined, the latter being in honour, it was said, of W. B. O'Donohue, a young man who, having thrown off the soutane, left the college of St. Boniface, where he had been studying for the priesthood, and joined the insurgents. He was an Irishman by birth, having lived, however, for some time in the city of New York, and was suspected of possessing strong Fenian proclivities. He afterwards became a leading spirit in the insurrection, and we will often have occasion to speak of him in connection with some of the most important actions of the insurgents. As the flag was hoisted on the pole, a volley was fired in its honor, and the band from the College of St. Boniface being present played several tunes, the French in the meantime cheering lustily; after which Riel made a speech to the crowd.[31]

The shamrock is not mentioned in the journal entry; it is explained away by "Justitia" for his Canadian readers; and it is treated with more suspicion in 1871 through an expanded description of W.B. O'Donoghue.[32]

Of the three versions of the flag hoisting, the "Justitia" one offers the most background description and detail. This is generally true of Begg's three accounts. "Justitia's" letter of 2 December, which describes the anatomy of the settlement in some detail, has no counterpart in either the journal or the history. The letter of 17 December 1869 contained thumbnail descriptions and character sketches of the Métis leaders— Louis Riel, John Bruce, W.B. O'Donoghue, and Father Ritchot—which appear nowhere else in Begg's writing. Of Riel, "Justitia" wrote, "his utterance is rapid and energetic, and his remarks at times are very sarcastic. . . . Riel by his energy and perseverance, has, you may say, conducted the whole of this movement; and, if he does not now overstep the mark, he will doubtless bring his people out safely yet." Begg presented the Métis leaders not as rebels or troublemakers, but as individuals concerned with the Métis community. The letter of 11 January 1870 opens with a wonderful description of a Métis wedding celebration that establishes Begg's credentials as a social commentator, like Hargrave with a sense of humour. The tongue-in-cheek mode is carried forward in this letter with a description of a meeting with the Sioux at the end of December 1869 in which the Aboriginals are all given a charge with a galvanic battery. The "Justitia" correspondence demonstrates that Begg was a far more compelling writer than he appeared in either *The Creation of Manitoba* or his novel *Dot-it-Down*.

Unfortunately, Begg stopped writing his letters to the *Globe* on 26 February 1870—or at least, no more were published after this one. Since Begg's next letter would have probably dealt with the Scott execution, one suspects the *Globe* would have printed it whatever was its interpretation of that event. We must therefore presume that Begg stopped writing. It is certainly tempting in his case to associate the Scott death with the cessation of the correspondence. There is no doubt that Begg's journal—and his 1871 history—become far less sympathetic to the provisional government of Louis Riel after 4 March 1870 and the death of Thomas Scott. In his history, Begg wrote that "Riel, who professed to be working for the good of his country, had in one day brought a curse upon it—a dreadful blot on the name of his countrymen, and a lasting disgrace upon himself."[33] His journal makes clear Begg's utter shock at the execution of Scott. Since Begg's correspondence had consistently attempted to defend the uprising to eastern Canada, he may well have dropped his pen at the point when he felt his support could no longer be sustained.

Like the careers of his fellow correspondents Mair, Hargrave, and even Louis Riel, that of Alexander Begg after 1870 was distinctly anti-climactic.[34] Along with other Riel supporters, he was distinctly unpopular with the Canadians who "occupied" Manitoba in the autumn of 1870. He found it expedient to be absent from the settlement during much of this time. According to one local newspaper, opinion was divided "as to wether [sic] he should be tarred and feathered . . . or whether he should be ridden on a rail" for the "Justitia" letters, "which have earned him the title of Renegade Canadian."[35] Begg weathered the storm, and became increasingly involved in writing, both historical and fictional. He was the author of what was arguably the province's first novel, a thinly disguised satire of the pre-Resistance period published in the same year (1871) as his history of the Resistance, *The Creation of Manitoba*. He was appointed Queen's Printer in 1877. Two years later, in 1879, with journalist Walter Nursey, he published *Ten Years in Winnipeg*. He wrote at least one more novel, which was not well-received. Begg also composed a highly nostalgic volume of reminiscences in 1884 entitled *Seventeen Years in the Canadian North-West,* in which he commented that the pre-Resistance Red River Settlement was one offering as close an approach "to perfect freedom" as he had ever seen or known.[36] From 1884 to 1888 Begg served as immigration agent for the Canadian Pacific Railway in London. He then moved to British Columbia, where he resumed his writing, producing his *History of the North-West* (three volumes) in 1894 and becoming confused with another Alexander Begg who also wrote western history. Despite substantial subsequent literary and historical output, Begg never achieved the same level of mastery of his prose and his material that had characterized his hastily written "Justitia" letters.

With the cessation of correspondence by both Hargrave and Begg, eastern Canadian newspapers and their readers no longer had access to coherent and continuous eyewitness accounts of the course of the insurgency. Nor did they have access after early March to the *New Nation,* which Louis Riel closed down. Affairs in Red River no longer received sympathetic and knowledgeable treatment After the capture of the "Portage boys," recounted in detail in his last letter by "Justitia," eastern newspapers' accounts of the Resistance tended to lack both authority and focus. Reliance on the "wire"—telegraphic accounts from St. Paul recounting the information reaching Minnesota from Red River—was joined to solitary letters on particular points and then to the reprinting of the tales of the returning Canadians, which began appearing in Canada in early April. Not only the death of Thomas Scott but the relative absence of reliable alternative information enabled the Canada Firsters to capture control of the media in Ontario.[37] A Métis perspective on events in Red River was almost totally lost in eastern Canada, with unfortunate results for Riel and his people. Virtually no opposition to the Wolseley Expedition was voiced in eastern Canada, and the rebel leaders ended up fleeing from the military in August 1870.

Why Shoot Thomas Scott?
A Study in Historical Evidence

———◦─◦((◦))◦─◦———

O N 4 March 1870, a young Canadian named Thomas Scott was marched outside the walls of Upper Fort Garry, Red River Settlement, and shot by a firing squad. This execution was a pivotal—perhaps *the* pivotal—event in the Métis resistance to Canadian annexation led by Louis Riel.[1] It is one of the most frequently recounted and analyzed incidents in Canadian history.[2] Riel biographer George Stanley has commented that no act of Riel's "is harder to explain."[3] Obviously, all who have written about Riel must come to some sort of terms with the Scott execution. Thus a variety of authors, most of them highly partisan in one way or another, have attempted to explain why Thomas Scott was shot. In the end, about all the commentators can agree upon is that the Scott execution was a mistake, which cost Riel and the Métis heavily.

Thomas Scott was born in Clandeboye, northern Ireland, around 1842.[4] He had immigrated to Ontario in the early 1860s, and came west to Red River in the summer of 1869. While briefly working on the east-west road construction being supervised by John Snow, he led a worker revolt against Snow for which he was found guilty of aggravated assault. He subsequently appeared in the village of Winnipeg as one of a number of Canadians barricaded in the home of Dr. John Schultz. Scott was one of those captured in December by Riel's Métis, and incarcerated in Upper Fort Garry. In January, along with a number of other prisoners including Schultz, he escaped from captivity and made his way to Portage la Prairie. A month later he accompanied a large party of armed men from Portage to the Red River, apparently hoping to free—by force if necessary—those prisoners still being held captive by Riel. He was part of a large gathering which assembled at Kildonan in February, and which dispersed when the prisoners were let go by the Métis. Unfortunately, he marched with a number of his colleagues past Upper Fort Garry on the return to Portage, was again captured, and was again incarcerated in Upper Fort Garry. Two weeks later he was tried by a Métis court martial and sentenced to be shot. The sentence was carried out.[5]

Scott's trial was an affair not conducted according to the commonly accepted rules of justice prevalent in eastern Canada.[6] The proceedings simply do not themselves explain why Scott was executed. As we shall see, some analysts and observers have tried to explain the trial as following the procedures of justice employed in the Métis buffalo hunt. Others have labelled the trial as a "court martial." Whatever the model, the earliest detailed account of the proceedings formed part of the sworn testimony at the trial of Ambroise Lépine in 1874 for the murder of Scott.[7] The witness was Joseph Nolin, who had served as Riel's private secretary and was present at the trial in that capacity. According to Nolin, Scott was not present for much of the proceedings, which were conducted in French, a language not understood by the defendant. Riel was the chief (although not sole) prosecution witness, and it was he who subsequently summarized the proceedings to Scott in English. Scott was offered an opportunity to respond to the charges, although not to examine the witnesses. The charges themselves were not entirely clear. According to Nolin, "Scott was accused of having rebelled against the Provisional Government and having struck the captain of the guard." The charge of rebellion against the provisional government probably at least in part related to an oath not to oppose the government which Riel had insisted the December prisoners take before releasing them. Scott had taken no such oath, however, for he had escaped in January. The rebellion charge could also be brought because Scott had taken up arms against the provisional government, but while Riel would subsequently label Scott's behaviour as "treason," the question of who was behaving treasonably in 1870 was never entirely clear. Striking a prison guard was a more serious and less ambiguous offence, but hardly one deserving a death penalty. As more than one commentator has observed, the trial of Scott hardly provides the grounds for his execution. The reasons for his death must be sought elsewhere.

A number of explanations for the execution of Thomas Scott have been advanced. Some of these explanations originated with Louis Riel himself, although in many cases they have been elaborated upon by others. Riel's explanations fall essentially into two categories. One set of explanations focusses on Scott's behaviour as the central point. They are based on details of the character and actions of Thomas Scott himself, mainly designed to demonstrate that he deserved to die. Another set treats Scott as a mere pawn in a larger political game, concerned chiefly with establishing the credibility of both Riel and his uprising. Beyond these factors, later historians and biographers have offered further motives for Scott's death. All these explanations deserve careful and detailed analysis, for several reasons. One is that many of them involve information which was not available to Riel's tribunal in early March 1870, and thus cannot really be used to answer the question about why Scott was put to death. One obvious certainty in this historical reconstruction of the Scott affair is that we cannot read back into 1870 more than those involved in it actually knew. As we shall see, some of the explanations depend on a picture of Scott's character and behaviour which cannot be sustained by the available evidence.

Considerable first-hand evidence survives for the trial and execution of Thomas Scott. While some Riel scholars have obviously given great thought to the nuances of the record, others have been quite undiscerning in their use of first-hand material. None of the authorities have ever offered any detailed assessment of the documentation upon which they have relied. When examined closely, a number of problems arise in connection with this evidence. In the first place, the material that is closest in time to the event is not necessarily by eyewitnesses. Only Donald Smith produces an unalloyed eyewitness account chronologically close to the event.[8] Other chronologically close but not eyewitness accounts are by Alexander Begg (who presumably had some sort of access to the fort which made his rumours "reliable"); the account published in the *New Nation,* which was probably written by editor Henry Robinson from Riel's information; the clerical-sounding account in the *Courrier de St. Hyacinthe,* which could be written by any of the priests surrounding the Métis; a letter from Bishop Taché to Joseph Howe dated 11 March; and the newspaper reports of Allan and Coombes, who were fellow-prisoners with Scott in December but not in February.[9] As for the eyewitness accounts themselves, they kept emerging for over sixty years, getting further and further from the event itself and becoming increasingly contaminated by additional information and new developments in the Riel controversy.[10] The court reports of the Lépine trial in 1874, although they provide relatively early testimony given under oath, do not form an important part of the arsenal of any Riel biographer. In theory, the various accounts of Riel himself should provide explanations of some authority. But Riel "testified" in the Scott business on a number of occasions before his death, and his accounts are not only somewhat different in emphasis over time, but increasingly seek to blacken Scott's character.[11] As Neil Allan Ronaghan has pointed out in his unpublished study of the post-1870 period in Manitoba, "the researcher must regard everything written about Scott after April of 1870 with caution, and everything written after 1885 with suspicion."[12] The major explanations can be easily enumerated:

1. One of the principal explanations offered for the shooting of Thomas Scott was that he was an unruly prisoner who aggravated his captors in both word and deed. Scott was accused by his captors of employing obscene language against them, of threatening both Riel and his guards, and on at least one occasion becoming involved in a physical altercation with his guards, which led to an attempt to beat him up in the courtyard of the fort. Leaving aside the question of whether such obstreperous behaviour deserved the death penalty, several other observations must be made about these charges against Scott. In the first place, many people held prisoner against their will react negatively against their captors, particularly when— as in Scott's case—the captive believes that he is being held unjustly. Like most Canadians, Scott regarded the Métis as rebels. Moreover, he and his fellow-prisoners had done nothing to deserve imprisonment simply for marching too close to the gates of Upper Fort Garry. At least some of the charges of violence relate to actions of Scott before he was imprisoned. In the second place, in captivity Scott was apparently suffering from diarrhea, an ailment which would both upset him in general and make him especially unhappy at confinement in a room without toilet facilities.[13] Finally, there is the matter of Scott's attitude toward his captors. In the hands of a number of later commentators, Scott becomes a racist and religious bigot, shouting "racial attacks" upon the Métis.[14] There is no contemporary evidence for any of this characterization, however. In none of the testimony by Riel or by contemporary witnesses is there any suggestion of the use of racial or religious slurs. Scott may have used obscenity, but the recorded examples of it— "son of a bitch," "goddamned"—are quite innocent of other implications. Scott clearly thought his captors were rebels and "cowards," but that is a different matter.[15] Riel told Donald Smith that Scott had "laughed at and despised the French Half-breeds, believing that they would not dare take the life of anyone," but this remark does not necessarily have racial implications. In 1883, Riel told a reporter from the *Winnipeg Daily Sun* that when Riel had pleaded with Scott to behave at the fort, Scott had replied, "You owe me respect; I am loyal and you are rebels."[16]

2. A few hours before his execution, according to the Reverend George

Young in 1897, Thomas Scott was told that "he was a very bad man and must die."[17] Louis Riel explained to Donald Smith on the morning of the execution that, apart from his prison insubordination, Scott had been "ringleader in a rising against Snow, who had charge of a party employed by the Canadian Government during the preceding summer in road making," and that he had been part of a group searching for Riel as the Portage boys had marched through Winnipeg on their way to Kildonan. Furthermore, Scott had admitted in a personal interview with Riel, "we intended to keep you as a hostage for the safety of the prisoners." One remark made by Smith in his report to the Canadian government has been constantly misinterpreted. Smith did not write that Scott was a bad person. What he actually wrote was that he had told Riel, "if, as he [Riel] represented, Scott was a rash thoughtless man, whom none could desire to have anything to do with, no evil need be apprehended from his example."[18]

The Snow incident presumably spoke to Scott's violent temper, and it was a charge Riel repeated several times. It does not seem to impinge on the Métis directly, however, and is a most ambiguous business at best. It is true that Scott led a three-day strike against Snow, which concluded with a march to Snow's office to demand pay for both the time the work party had worked and the time they had been on strike. The strikers threatened to "duck" Snow and he paid up, subsequently having warrants issued against four of the men for aggravated assault. The court record only indicates that Scott and one colleague were found guilty and fined.[19] Alexander Begg, in his journal, suggests that the case had been badly handled by the defence, and if better presented, might have resulted in four acquittals. Begg also adds that Scott was overheard commenting before leaving the courtroom that "it was a pity they had not ducked Snow when they were at it as they had not got their money's worth."[20] This remark has been constantly repeated by later commentators, although what it demonstrates beyond Scott's pawky sense of humour is not at all clear. On the other hand, some of what has been written about the Snow incident cannot be well-documented at all. Scott is first accused by Louis Riel of threatening Snow with a pistol in 1874, and the strikers were not looking for payment for their travel time. As for the later attempted capture of Riel, it speaks for itself in the context of events.

Many later authors have liked to describe Thomas Scott as a constant drunk and a barroom brawler. Little evidence survives that Scott was a drinker, and most of the characterizations of this sort are based on a misreading of the record. A large part of the supposed evidence for Scott's drinking is in testimony by one of his fellow prisoners in the Lépine trial that Scott was on one occasion "apparently half drunk" in Upper Fort Garry. Both George Stanley and Maggie Siggins repeat this description to Scott's disadvantage.[21] Apart from the fact that Stanley attributes the evidence to the wrong prisoner—William Chambers instead of Alexander Murray—it is clear from Murray's statement that he was referring to Alfred Scott, who was visiting Fort Garry with Hugh McKenny and Bob O'Lone for municipal-electioneering purposes.[22] How often Thomas Scott has been confused both by contemporaries and by later historians with Alfred Scott—a bartender at O'Lone's saloon, a notorious drinker and general bad actor—is not at all clear.

In later years, Riel would add other charges to the earlier ones he had advanced against Scott. The Canadian was later alleged to have been personally responsible for the abuse of Norbert Parisien at Kildonan in February of 1870, attaching a belt around the neck of the unfortunate Parisien and dragging him behind a horse for a quarter of a mile. Scott had also, according to Riel, been involved in disorder and riotous living in Pointe de Chênes while working for Snow on the road construction there.[23] There is no pre-execution evidence for either of these accusations, however, and the Parisien business would doubtless not have been known to Riel in 1870, since no other Métis besides Parisien were present at Kildonan. Had Riel been aware of the Parisien incident at the time of Scott's trial, he would presumably have mentioned it and perhaps even used it as part of the indictment against Scott.

3. In an 1883 newspaper interview, Riel labelled Thomas Scott "about the fourth man in influence and prominence" among Métis opponents, behind only John Schultz, John Dennis, and Charles Arkoll Boulton. Schultz and Dennis had been beyond the reach of the provisional government in 1870, Riel admitted. "They were more guilty, too," thought Riel, "although Scott was guilty enough."[24] This interview was the first time that Riel had articulated any precise assessment of the leadership importance of Scott, although he may well have held such a view as early as 1870 and often coupled Scott and Schultz in the same sentence. The account in the *New Nation* described Scott as being "at the head of the party of Portage people, who, on their way to Kildonan, called at Coutu's house and searched it for the President, with the intention of shooting him." Riel's explanation of Scott's sentence to Donald Smith spoke of his bad influence on the prisoners, and especially his efforts to persuade them not to have anything to do with those who had visited them to solicit their votes. Any view of Thomas Scott as an influential Canadian leader was incorrect, however. None of the

dastardly acts that Scott was accused of doing—except perhaps in the Snow business before the uprising—required or suggested a real leadership role. None of his Anglo-Canadian colleagues ever claimed that Scott was anything other than a foot soldier in 1869-70, and witnesses at the Lépine trial insisted under cross-examination that he was not a leader of the Portage party. Scott may occasionally have come to the fore on particular occasions because he was taller, or louder, or less intimidated, but he was not part of the inner circles of the Canadian party. George Stanley insists that Scott was the leader among the prisoners captured in February 1870, especially after Charles Boulton lost the respect of his men.[25] Even in this limited capacity, Scott's role as a leader is hard to document, however. There is certainly no contemporary evidence outside that of his accusers to support the arguments of several of Riel's later biographers that Scott was a trusted henchman of John Christian Schultz. Scott was at Schultz's house, but so were most of the Canadians in the settlement. During the first captivity he was incarcerated in a different building from Schultz, and although the two escaped on the same night, the escapes were quite independent of one another. On the other hand, it is possible that Scott's unruly behaviour in captivity may have, as Riel told Donald Smith in 1870, served as a bad example to other prisoners; their accounts would deny this interpretation, however. In this sense mainly was Scott a documentable "leader."

4. As has been noted, Louis Riel on a number of occasions after 1870 wrote essays in explanation of his role in the trial and execution of Scott. One theme that runs through these exculpatory pieces is Riel's insistence that he was under considerable pressure by the Métis guards—which he found difficult to resist—to try to execute the Canadian. Donald Smith vaguely suggests this claim in his report of 1870, although it does not appear in the account of the execution in the *New Nation*. But we have precious little evidence of what Riel was thinking in 1870, although this argument becomes so insistent in Riel's subsequent accounts of the incident that it has to be taken seriously. Riel could have simply ignored this pressure from his guards, of course, but it was doubtless difficult to do so in the context of the times. On more than one occasion since December of 1869, Riel had threatened to shoot a prisoner and had backed down at the last minute. What Riel did say to Donald Smith, his last words on the Scott affair on the morning of the execution, was: "I have done three good things since I have commenced. I have spared Boulton's life at your instance, and I do not regret it, for he is a fine fellow; I pardoned Gaddy, and he showed his gratitude by escaping out of the bastion—but I do not grudge him his

miserable life; and now I shall shoot Scott."[26] The strong suggestion here, as in Riel's subsequent accounts, is that Riel's credibility was on the line over Scott, and that he could not afford to override the wishes of the guards. This insistence by Riel on the need for credibility as a factor in Scott's death carried over in a number of directions.

5. Riel needed credibility not only with his own followers, but with the population of Red River as well. From his perspective, his attempts to bring and keep the Anglophone mixed-bloods on board the resistance movement had been greatly hampered by the two armed responses of the Canadians, first at Schultz's house and secondly at Kildonan. An example was necessary, the letter from Fort Garry to the *Courrier de St. Hyacinthe* insisted, to "prevent a great loss of life." Riel returned to this point in several of his subsequent attempts at explanation. He and Ambroise Lépine offered an elaborate version of this argument in their letter to Lieutenant-Governor Morris on 3 January 1873. Here the two men insisted that the Indians were threatening and even conspiring with the Portage prisoners, so that "in a word to secure the triumph of peace and order which is was our duty to establish throughout the settlement, we had recourse to the full authority of Government." Riel and Lépine added that they sought to disarm, rather than fight "the lawless strangers who were making war against us," but implied that it was the death of Scott which enabled them to succeed "in establishing quiet."[27] It is impossible to assess this claim, of course. The jury at Ambroise Lépine's murder trial in 1874 was not impressed with it as a political justification for Scott's death, and later scholarship is about equally divided over the question of whether the pacification of the community had already been accomplished or followed on the death of Scott.

6. Beyond the need to satisfy the guards and pacify the community, of course, was the need of the provisional government to be able to negotiate with the Canadian government. Riel emphasized this point in his discussions with Donald Smith before the execution. Smith argued that killing Scott would stain the insurrection with blood and might make accommodation with Canada impossible, to which Riel exclaimed, "we must make Canada respect us."[28] In 1872 he wrote a memorandum to L.R. Masson which insisted, "we wanted to be sure that our attitude was taken seriously."[29] He and Lépine further elaborated their thinking in their letter to Morris in 1873. The provisional government had already decided to send a delegation to Ottawa to negotiate with Canada, they wrote, "when we found ourselves confronted by a new conspiracy to prevent the delegates from leaving, to excite the masses in Ottawa against us and to prevent us

from coming to an understanding with the Canadian government."[30]
The Métis leadership was probably quite accurate in its perception that
Ottawa would not negotiate any deal with a government that was not in
total control of the local situation. Several leading Riel scholars have
maintained that this consideration was the real reason for Scott's execution. George Stanley wrote, "if it was necessary to spill the blood of a
malcontent, one who had not only refused to co-operate with the other
settlers, but had even appealed to force in an effort to disrupt the arrangements the provisional government was making to obtain concessions from Canada, then that blood would be spilled. It was as simple as
that."[31] Stanley's next sentence admitted it was not all that simple, however, for the biographer went on to maintain that the insecurity felt by
Riel and the Métis required some act to impress. Thomas Flanagan has
written that Riel "seems to have felt that an act of capital punishment
would demonstrate the authority of the provisional government" and
show that it "possessed the sovereign authority of a state."[32]

The foregoing six factors are those advanced by Riel himself, at one
point or another before his death, to explain why he allowed Thomas Scott
to be shot. Not all of the factors are given equal prominence in all of Riel's
many attempts at explanation, but some combination of them reflects his
own analysis of the reasons for the act of violence. As we have seen, the
factors divide basically into two categories. The first set focusses on Scott's
own personality and behaviour, seeing him as the principal agent of his
demise. The second set concentrates on political issues of credibility, in
which Scott becomes little more than a pawn in the larger game. Riel's
own argument seems to have been that there was a nice coincidence of
factors. The insurrection required Scott's death, but because of his own
behaviour, he deserved what he got. Not all Riel scholars are agreed on
which of Riel's own explanations was the most accurate, or even on whether
the factors he advanced exhaust the possibilities. Lurking out there in the
literature are a number of other possible explanations for the death of
Thomas Scott that also need to be explored.

7. One of the most persistent of the alternate explanations is that there
was some kind of long-standing personal animosity between Scott and
Riel. Two quite separate sorts of stories are told. The first originated shortly
after Scott's death, partly among his fellow prisoners returning to Canada.
One of the first Canadian reports of Scott's death noted: "Mr Scott, we are
told, was a quiet and inoffensive, but at the same time, very powerful and
determined man. Before his arrest, Riel stopped him on some road he was
going and Mr. Scott with a strong arm thrust him aside and told him to

mind his own business."[33] Further elaboration was soon provided by William Allan and Joseph Coombes, who told the *Toronto Globe* on 15 April 1870 that when Scott had been taken prisoner by the Métis in 1869, " 'Aha!' says the sneaking Louis to Scott, 'you are just the man I was looking for,' and with deep malice gleaming from his treacherous and sinister eyes, he ordered his men to seize him. Scott was a man of great stature, six feet two inches in height, of goodly symmetry, and of an ardent and rather impetuous nature, freely expressing his opinions. The act of the despot was prompted by the pettiest motives of personal revenge. Scott had always treated him with marked contempt. Once in the town of Winnipeg, he [Scott] got into an altercation with him [Riel], in a saloon, and threw him by the neck into the street."[34] It is hard to know what to make of this particular version of the story. The earlier one merely involved a random encounter. The confrontation reported by Allan and Coombes would have occurred between early October, when Scott left John Snow's employ, and early December, when he was taken prisoner. This was a period when Riel, hardly a drinking man at the best of times, would have been unlikely to spend much time in Winnipeg saloons. Moreover, according to Allan and Coombes, Riel was constantly consuming alcoholic beverages, which is most unlikely. But Allan and Coombes were imprisoned for seven weeks with Scott, and their testimony cannot be totally ignored.

The other version of the Riel-Scott hostility involved rivalry over a woman whom both loved. This tale first makes its appearance in 1885, in a "dime novel" written by Toronto journalist Joseph Edmund Collins entitled *The Story of Louis Riel the Rebel Chief.* The book makes no pretensions to historical accuracy.[35] In it, a Métisse named Marie was supposedly rescued from a flood by the brave Scott, who subsequently protects her from Riel and his clumsy courtship of her. After Scott is condemned to death, Riel attempts to get him to reveal the whereabouts of Marie. Scott refuses, of course, and Riel turns on him. " 'She shall be mine!' he hissed, 'when your corpose lies mouldering in a dishonored traitor's grave.' "[36] There is no other substantiation or contemporary evidence for any part of this story, but it has been repeated without comment by several Riel biographers and more than once vehemently denied by them. These accounts all speak to the sense that the official explanations are somehow insufficient to account for the tragedy.

8. Given Riel's later emotional instabilities, one might have expected more speculation on his state of mind in 1870 than is present in the literature. Riel is known to have suffered a bout of some sort of disability—a

"brain fever"—at the end of February 1870. His mother was called in, apparently to nurse him. Most authors do not mention this incident at all, and most of those who do simply present it as part of the background chronology of events. Charlebois writes that brain fever "was the old medical term for encephalitis, inflammation of the subtance of the brain. In these days before antibiotics this could have easily devleoped into an abscess in the brain. Its origin was probably a tuberculous infection in Riel's lungs."[37] Such a diagnosis, if correct, removes Riel's illness from the category of nervous disorder. Only Edwin Kreutzweiser, in a neglected little book, *The Red River Insurrection: Its Causes and Events,* allows himself to speculate at any length on the insanity question. He suggests that Riel's later madness, which he characterizes as megalomania, involved "an obsession of greatness and brooks no opposition or frustration. When contradicted or opposed he becomes irritable or even violent." The death of Scott may have been, therefore, writes Kreutzweiser, "an outburst of insanity."[38] It is possible that the question of instability lies obliquely behind the insistence of some writers, most notably George Stanley, that Riel's decision to execute Scott was no outburst, but "a deliberate act of policy."[39] But while many authors lament the folly of shooting Scott, almost none regard it as evidence of madness.

9. The question of the model of the buffalo hunt for Scott's trial has already been mentioned. Several of Riel's contemporary defenders and some of the later authorities raise the matter of buffalo-hunt justice. It may well be that hunt justice explains the form that Scott's trial took, although not its outcome. Several points must be made about such Métis justice. One is that hunt justice normally involved "one of our own," who spoke the language, was familiar with the customs, and was known to those participating. If it was a model, it was a bad one to use for a defendant unfamiliar with either French or Métis practices. Moreover, there is absolutely no contemporary evidence that hunt justice was ever employed in a capital case, for which its summary practices were obviously unsuited.[40] If Riel had felt that he, Scott, and the Métis had found themselves inextricably caught up in hunt justice, the simple solution was to call off the execution.

10. One of the most common themes of writing on the Riel/Scott confrontation is one that sees Scott as a classic example of the Protestant Anglophone oppressor, both actually and symbolically. Scott, the Protestant Orangeman, becomes a racial and religious bigot. The three most extreme examples of this tendency are in A.B. Morice's *A Critical History of the Red River Insurrection,* Dr. Peter Charlebois in his *The Life of Louis Riel in Pictures,* and Maggie Siggins's recent biography of Louis Riel. Morice

describes Scott as "an Ontarian of no very good repute," and later as "the rabid Orangeman," who may have "had a streak of insanity in his makeup." Morice defends himself from charges of having earlier "blackened" the character of Scott by insisting that "we had scarcely said of the poor man anything that had not already been published by contemporary authors," adding, "in any court of justice, all that is known for and against the accused is not only admitted but even deemed necessary to arrive at the proper decision."[41] Charlebois observes that Scott was "a volatile and ignorant young man, unable to analyze the Orange Order's precepts, puffed up with pretensions of loyalty, and all too ready to believe in the superiority of Ulstermen as fighting men." He adds that Scott was "killed every bit as much by his childhood environment, the vicious bigotry against Catholics and the French and Métis nurtured by the Orange Order of that era, as by the Métis firing-squad."[42] Siggins describes Scott as the "quintessential Orangeman," adding that "he was foul-mouthed, bigoted and outrageously abusive in his never-ending heckling of the 'damned depraved half-breed.'"[43] Almost all Riel authorities refer to Scott's membership in the Orange Order, and most tie it to his treatment of the Métis.

The only problem in associating Scott's behaviour and subsequent execution with his Orangeism is that there is no contemporary evidence that anyone in Red River before or immediately after his death knew that Scott was a member of the Orange Order. His Orange Lodge membership is quickly established in the Ontario press in the journalistic reports of his death, aided and abetted by the activities of the Canada First movement which helped orchestrate a province-wide reaction to the execution. But none of the earlier Red River accounts of his death mention the Orange Lodge. Begg's journal merely describes Scott as "one of the prisoners"; Smith's report characterizes him only as a prisoner; the *New Nation* account has Scott as one "who came here from Canada last summer"; the letter from Taché to Howe notes Scott as a prisoner "who was brought from Canada with Mr. Snow"; and the *Courrier de St. Hyacinthe* story makes him "an Upper Canadian" who claimed that he did not belong to any religion. None of Riel's earliest explanations of his actions refer to Scott as an Orangeman, and no contemporary testimony (including Riel's) offers any evidence of such membership or examples of racial or religious slurs spoken by him. Among the documents left behind after his death there was no certificate of membership in the Orange Order. All the attributions to Orangeism (and to racial and religious bigotry) are based on what was written about Scott after his death rather than on what was known to Louis Riel, the Métis, or Red River. Contemporary stories about bad blood between Riel and Scott refer to drinking, not to bigotry. Whatever was behind the execution of Scott, neither Orange Lodge membership nor extreme Protestantism appear to be involved.

An argument could well be made—although it has not ever been advanced in the literature—that had Scott been well known to be a member of the Orange Lodge, it might have helped save his life. The overwhelming impression one has of Thomas Scott in Red River was of a transient Canadian newcomer—Riel in 1874 described him as one of a party of "strangers"—who was not regarded as being very important by anybody. Scott appeared to be, quite apart from his faults, one of life's expendables. There was no reason for Louis Riel or anyone in the settlement to suspect that his death, whether just or unjust, would set off a furor in central Canada. In the end, his expendability seems to have been one of the chief factors behind Scott's execution.

NOTES

ABBREVIATIONS

Hudson Bay Company Archives (HBCA); Transactions of the Historical and Scientific Society of Manitoba (HSSM); Provincial Archives of Manitoba (PAM); Selkirk Papers National Archives of Canada (SPNAC).

THOMAS SCOTT'S BODY

[1] See "Why Shoot Thomas Scott?" in this volume and my "Thomas Scott and the Daughter of Time," *Prairie Forum*, 23:2 (1998): 145-70.

[2] Most of our evidence for Scott's execution comes from sworn testimony given at the trial of Ambroise Lépine for Scott's murder in 1874. This testimony was published at the time. One version, which appeared initially in eastern Canadian newspapers, subsequently became a book entitled *Preliminary Investigation and Trial of Ambroise D. Lépine for the Murder of Thomas Scott, Being a full report of the proceedings in this case before the Magistrate's Court and the several Courts of Queen's Bench in the Province of Manitoba* (Montreal, 1874). Another version appeared in Winnipeg's *Free Press*. The two sets of reports have much in common. The various participants distributed their set speeches in advance to the press, and the reporters probably often pooled their resources. But the *Free Press* contains some new material not often utilized by historians. In addition to the published accounts, the trial notes of Judge Edmund Burke Wood also survive, in the Provincial Archives of Manitoba. These provide over 160 pages of crabbed judge's notes on the testimony.

[3] Over the years, Young offered a number of accounts of the execution, which was probably the defining moment in his own life. One brief narrative was written on 5 March 1870 to Scott's brother in Toronto and is reprinted in Young's *Manitoba Memories: Leaves from My Life in the Prairie Province, 1868-1884* (Toronto, 1897), p. 140. A second, lengthier version came on 14 October in his testimony in the murder trial of Lépine. Neither of these versions has Scott saying anything in the brief period before his death. The quotations from Scott come from Young's account in *Manitoba Memories*, pp. 136-38.

[4] Testimony of Paul Proulx, 22 October 1874.

[5] Testimony of George Young, 14 October 1874.

[6] J. N. Dingman to *Kingston Whig,* 4 March 1904.

[7] Quoted in Allan Ronaghan, "The Archibald Administration in Manitoba, 1870–1872," (PhD diss., University of Manitoba, 1986), p. 490.

[8] J. N. Dingman to *Kingston Whig,* 4 March 1904.

[9] Quoted in Young, *Manitoba Memories,* pp. 138–39.

[10] This is the spelling of the name in the trial transcript.

[11] Testimony of Modeste Legemonière, 26 October 1874.

[12] Testimony of John Bruce, 17 October 1874.

[13] Testimony of Francis Charette, 19 October 1874.

[14] Testimony of Pierre Gladu, 19 October 1874.

[15] Testimony of Baptiste Charette, 20 October 1874.

[16] Bruce was also one of the first of the insurgents to be "rehabilitated." He was appointed a magistrate by Lieutenant-Governor Adams Archibald in October 1870. Several local newspapers complained about the appointment. The *News-Letter* opined in its issue of 11 October, "Poor Scott! It only needed to have added Riel and O'Donohue's name to the Gazette appointing ex-President Bruce a magistrate to complete the thing." But Bruce was not part of the court-martial party.

[17] Testimony of John Bruce, 17 October 1874.

[18] Testimony of Pierre Gladu, 19 October 1874.

[19] Address of Joseph Royal to the Jury, 23 October 1874.

[20] Address of Chapleau to the Jury, 23 October 1874.

[21] Charge of Judge Wood to the Jury, 24 October 1874.

[22] R.G. MacBeth, *The Romance of Western Canada,* 2nd ed. (Toronto, 1920), pp. 156–57.

[23] W. M. Joyce Papers, PAM, MG3 B23.

[24] J.M. Bumsted, *The Red River Rebellion,* p. 280. Riel had told Donald Smith on the day of Scott's execution, "I have done three good things since I have commenced. I have spared Boulton's life at your instance, and I do not regret it,

for he is a fine fellow; I pardoned Gaddy, and he showed his gratitude by escaping out of the bastion—but I do not grudge him his miserable life; and now I shall shoot Scott." Ibid., p. 164.

[25] Morice, *A Critical History of the Red River Rebellion* (1935), pp. 293-5.

[26] Ibid., p. 294.

[27] "Conversation with Father André and Father McWilliams, 16 November 1885," in Flanagan, ed., *The Collected Writings of Louis Riel/Les Ecrits Complets de Louis Riel: Vol. 3, 1884-1885* (Edmonton, 1985), p. 583.

TRYING TO DESCRIBE THE BUFFALO

[1] Douglas Sprague and Ronald Frye begin their article, "Manitoba's Red River Settlement: Manuscript Sources for Economic and Demographic History," *Archivaria,* 9 (1979-80): 179-193 with the comment that "it is possible that the history of the Red River Settlement is the most thoroughly documented of all proprietary colonies in English colonial experience." The operative word here is "proprietary" in the sense in which the term has been used by early American historians like C.M. Andrews. The reminder that the Red River Settlement fits into a much larger imperial experience which begins in the seventeenth century is a useful one. Because of the way American scholars define "colonial history" as ending with the American Revolution, Red River is not usually conceived to be a part of it. Thus it is not mentioned in Jacob Ernst Cooke, ed., *Encyclopedia of the North American Colonies,* 3 vols. (New York, 1993). This essay could not be published in the *William and Mary Quarterly,* the chief journal of American colonial history, because it deals with material after that journal's cut-off date.

[2] Frits Pannekoek, *A Snug Little Flock: The Social Origins of the Riel Resistance, 1869-70* (Winnipeg, 1991).

[3] Frits Pannekoek, "The Historiography of the Red River Settlement, 1830-68," *Prairie Forum,* 6:1 (1981): 75-85. Why Pannekoek uses the date 1830 in this survey is not clear.

[4] W. L. Morton, *Manitoba: A History* (Toronto, 1957).

[5] James Jackson, *The Centennial History of Manitoba* (Toronto, 1970).

[6] John Perry Pritchett, *The Red River Valley, 1811-1849* (New York, 1941).

[7] "The History of the Red River Settlement," *Nor'-Wester,* 15 June 1861.

[8] Gregg Shilliday, ed., *Manitoba 125—A History,* vol. 1. *Rupert's Land to Riel* (Winnipeg, 1993).

[9] Doug Owram, *Promise of Eden:The Canadian Expansionist Movement and the Idea of the West, 1856-1900* (Toronto, 1980), pp. 192-216.

[10] The term was actually used first used by Donald Gunn in his "History of the Red River, Selkirk Settlement" published in 1869 in the *Nor'-Wester*. It was repeated by H. G. Gunn in a piece entitled "The Selkirk Settlement and Its Relation to North Dakota History," *North Dakota State Historical Society Collections*, 2 (1908), p. 94.

[11] Donald Gunn and Charles Tuttle, *History of Manitoba* (Ottawa, 1880). Gunn's manuscript had earlier been published in 1869 in the pages of the *Nor'-Wester*.

[12] George Bryce, *Manitoba: Its Infancy, Growth and Present Condition* (London, 1882).

[13] Published in Toronto.

[14] R.H. Schofield, *The Story of Manitoba*, 1 (Winnipeg, 1913), p. 138.

[15] Ibid., p. 170.

[16] Margaret McWilliams, *Manitoba Milestones* (Toronto and London, 1928).

[17] Ibid., p. 60.

[18] Morton, *Manitoba: A History*, p. 59.

[19] Ibid., pp. 60-93.

[20] Ibid., p. 93.

[21] Ibid., p. 150.

[22] Lyle Dick, "The Seven Oaks Incident and the Construction of a Historical Tradition, 1816 to 1970," *Journal of the Canadian Historical Association*, n.s.2 (1991): 91-114.

[23] Jackson, *Centennial History*, p. 31.

[24] Ibid., p. 58.

[25] Ibid., p. 88.

[26] I try to dispel this interpretation in my book *The People's Clearance: Highland Emigration to British North America, 1770-1815* (Edinburgh and Winnipeg, 1982).

[27] See W.S. Wallace, "The Literature Relating to the Selkirk Controversy," *Canadian Historical Review*, 13 (1932): 45-50.

[28] Donald Gunn, "History of the Red River, or Selkirk Settlement," *Nor'-Wester,* 21 April 1869.

[29] John S. Galbraith, *The Hudson's Bay Company as an Imperial Factor, 1821-1869* (Toronto, 1957), p. 311.

[30] Rich, *The Fur Trade and the Northwest, to 1857* (Toronto, 1967), p. 270.

[31] Volume 2, 1760-1870 (London, 1959).

[32] A.S. Morton, *A History of the Canadian West to 1870-71; Being a History of Rupert's Land (the Hudson's Bay Company's Territory) and of the North-West Territory (including the Pacific Slope),* 2nd ed., ed. Lewis G. Thomas (Toronto, 1973).

[33] Ibid., p. 860.

[34] Published in Minneapolis in 1965. Other studies include: Donald F. Warner, "Drang Nach Norden: The United States and the Riel Rebellion," *Mississippi Valley Historical Review,* 39 (1953): 693-712, and A. C. Gluek, Jr., "The Riel Rebellion and Canadian-American Relations," *CHR,* 35 (1954): 199-221. One of the few Canadian-based contributions to this theme is Alan Artibise's "The Crucial Decade: Red River at the Outbreak of the American Civil War," *HSSM,* 3rd ser., 23 (1966-7): 57-66.

[35] Hartwell Bowsfield, ed., *The James Wickes Taylor Correspondence, 1859-1870* (Winnipeg, 1968).

[36] David McNab, "The Colonial Office and the Prairies in the Mid-Nineteenth Century," *Prairie Forum,* 3 (1978): 21-38.

[37] The article cited above comes out of McNab's unpublished doctoral thesis, "Herman Merivale and the British Empire, 1806-1874" (Lancaster, 1978), as does a study entitled "Herman Merivale and the Native Question," *Albion,* 9 (1977): 359-384.

[38] Toronto, 1980.

[39] Debra Lindsay, ed., *The Modern Beginnings of Subarctic Ornithology: Correspondence to the Smithsonian Institution 1856-1858* (Winnipeg, 1991); Debra Lindsay, *Science in the Subarctic: Trappers, Traders, and the Smithsonian Institution* (Washington, 1993).

[40] Irene Spry, *The Palliser Expedition: An Account of John Palliser's British North American Exploring Expedition 1857-1860* (Toronto, 1963).

[41] W. L. Morton, *Henry Youle Hind 1823-1908* (Toronto, 1980).

[42] Irene Spry, ed., *The Papers of the Palliser Expedition, 1857-1860* (Toronto, 1968); Henry Youle Hind, *Narrative of the Canadian Exploring Expedition of 1857 and of the Assiniboine and Saskatchewan Exploring Expedition of 1858* (Edmonton, 1971).

[43] Fred Bill,"Early Steamboating on the Red River," *North Dakota Historical Quarterly,* 9:2 (1942); Aileen Garland, "The Nor'Wester and the Men Who Established It," *Transactions Manitoba Historical Society;* Bruce Peel, *Early Printing in the Red River Settlement 1859-1870* (Winnipeg, 1974); Murray Campbell, "The Postal History of Red River, British North America, *THSM,* 1951.

[44] Elaine Mitchell, "Edward Watkin and the Buying-Out of the Hudson's Bay Company," *Canadian Historical Review,* 34 (1953): 219-44.

[45] Alexander Ross, *The Red River Settlement: Its Rise, Progress and Present State* (London, 1856), p. 241.

[46] But see Virginia Berry, *Vistas of Promise: Manitoba 1874-1919* (Winnipeg, 1987).

[47] Ross, *The Red River Settlement.* As its title suggests, Ross intended to write a progressive history.

[48] Ibid., p. 252.

[49] Sylvia Van Kirk, "'What If Mama Is an Indian?' The Cultural Ambivalence of the Alexander Ross Family," in John Foster, ed., *The Developing West* (Toronto, 1983),

[50] "Red River" to *Montreal Herald,* published 21 October 1869.

[51] "Red River" to *Montreal Herald,* published 11 October 1869.

[52] "Justitia" to *Toronto Globe,* published 24 December 1869.

[53] Such as "Louis Riel and the Fenian Raid of 1871," *Canadian Historical Review,* 4 (1923): 132-144; "The Execution of Thomas Scott," *Canadian Historical Review,* 6 (1925): 222.

[54] George F. G. Stanley, *The Birth of Western Canada: A History of the Riel Rebellions* (London, 1936), p. 17.

[55] Ibid., p. 18.

[56] Lyle Dick, "The Seven Oaks Incident and the Construction of a Historical Tradition, 1816 to 1970," *Journal of the Canadian Historical Association,* n.s.2 (1991), p. 106.

[57] The best statement of Morton's debt to Giraud is a piece entitled "The Canadian Metis" in *The Beaver,* September 1950. It is subtitled "An appreciation of Marcel Giraud's magnificent study of the western half-breeds." Morton focusses on the hunters, a powerful group, "drawn so strongly to barbarism." Indeed, in his emphasis on the barbarism of the Métis, Morton passed well beyond the more balanced interpretation that Giraud had offered.

[58] In the 1972 paperback reprint to the Cuthbert Grant volume, Morton acknowledged that he had written most of the key chapters of the book.

[59] The quotations are from Morton's introduction to *London Correspondence Inward from Eden Colvile 1849-1852* (edited by E.E. Rich and published as volume 19 of the Hudson's Bay Record Society, London, 1956), p. lxxxix.

[60] John Foster, "Program for the Red River Mission: The Anglican Clergy 1820-1826," *Social History/Histoire Sociale*, 4 (1969): 49-75; "Missionaries, Mixed-Bloods and the Fur Trade: Four Letters of the Rev. William Cockran, Red River Settlement, 1830-33," *Western Canadian Journal of Anthropology*, 3:1 (1972): 94-125; "Rupert's Land and Red River Settlement, 1820-1870," in L.G. Thomas, ed., *The Prairie West to 1905: A Source Book* (1975); "The Origins of the Mixed Bloods in the Canadian West" in L.H. Thomas, ed., *Essays in Western History* (1976); "The Métis: the people and the term," *Prairie Forum*, 3:1 (1978).

[61] Submitted at Queen's University in 1973.

[62] Published in Winnipeg.

[63] "The Role of Agriculture in an English Speaking Halfbreed Economy: The Case of St. Andrew's Red River," *Native Studies Review*, 4:1-2 (1988), 67-94. See also his *The Road to the Rapids: Nineteenth-Century Church and Society at St. Andrew's Parish, Red River* (Calgary, 2000).

[64] Published in Vancouver in 1980. The articles include: "A Demographic Transition in the Fur Trade Country: Family Sizes and Ferility of Company Officers and Country Wives 1750-1850," *Western Canadian Journal of Anthropology*, 6:1 (1976): 61-71; "Changing Views of Fur Trade Marriage and Domesticity: James Hargrave, His Colleagues, and 'the Sex.'" *Western Canadian Journal of Anthropology*, 6:3 (1976): 92-105; "Ultimate Respectability: Fur Trade Children in the Civilized World," *The Beaver*, Winter 1977: 4-10, and spring 1978: 48-55; "Linguistic Solitudes in the Fur Trade: Some Changing Social Categories and Their Implications," in Carol Judd and Arthur Ray, eds., *Old Trails and New Directions: Papers of the Third North American Fur Trade Conference* (Toronto, 1980), pp. 147-59.

[65] Sylvia Van Kirk, *'Many Tender Ties': Women in Fur-Trade Society in Western Canada, 1670-1870* (Winnipeg, 1980).

[66] Olive Dickason, "From 'One Nation' in the Northeast to 'New Nation' in the Northwest: A Look at the Emergence of the Métis," in Jacqueline Peterson and Jennifer S. H. Brown, eds., *The New Peoples: Being and Becoming Métis in North America* (Winnipeg, 1985), pp. 15-36; Irene Spry, "The Métis and Mixed-Bloods of Rupert's Land before 1870," in ibid., 95-118; Spry, "The 'Private Adventurers' of Rupert's Land," in John Foster, ed., *Developing West*, pp. 49-70.

[67] See Dick's "The Seven Oaks Incident" and his "Historical Writing on 'Seven Oaks': The Assertion of Anglo-Canadian Cultural Dominance in the West," in

Robert Coutts and Richard Stuart, eds., *The Forks and the Battle of Seven Oaks in Manitoba History* (Winnipeg, 1994), pp. 65-70.

[68] Peterson and Brown, eds., *The New Peoples*.

[69] Barry Cooper, *Alexander Kennedy Isbister: A Respectable Critic of the Honourable Company* (Ottawa, 1988).

[70] Published in Toronto in 1984.

[71] Brian Gallagher, "The Whig Interpretation of the History of Red River," (M.A. diss., University of British Columbia, 1986). Gallagher subsequently published his arguments as "A Re-examination of Race, Class and Society in Red River," *Native Studies Review*, 4:1-2 (1988): 25-66.

[72] For example, D. Bruce Sealey, *The Metis, Canada's Forgotten People* (Winnipeg, 1975); Emile Pelletier, *A Social History of the Manitoba Metis* (Winnipeg, 1977); A. S. Lussier and D. Bruce Sealey, eds., *The Other Natives = The-Les Metis* (Winnipeg, 3 vols., 1978-80); A. S. Lussier, ed., *Louis Riel & The Metis: Riel Mini-Conference Papers* (Winnipeg, 1979).

[73] Winnipeg, 1975.

[74] See Brad Milne, "The Historiography of Métis Land Dispersal, 1870-1890," *Manitoba History* (1995), 30-41.

[75] D.N. Sprague and R. P. Frye, comps., *The Genealogy of the First Métis Nation*, with introduction by D. N. Sprague (Winnipeg, 1983).

[76] The key journal articles are: P.R. Mailhot and D.N. Sprague, "Persistent Settlers: The Dispersal and Resettlement of the Red River Métis, 1870-1885," *Canadian Ethnic Studies*, 17 (1985): 1-30; D.N. Sprague, "Government Lawlessness in the Administration of Manitoba Land Claims, 1870-1887," *Manitoba Law Journal*, 10 (1980): 415-441; D.N. Sprague, "The Manitoba Land Question 1870-1882," *Journal of Canadian Studies*, 15 (1980): 74-84; Gerhard Ens, "Métis Lands in Manitoba 1870-1887," *Manitoba History*, no. 5 (1983): 1-22; Nicole St-Onge, "The Dissolution of a Métis Community: Pointe à Grouette, 1860-1885, *Studies in Political Economy* 18 (1985): 149-172; Gerhard Ens, "Dispossession or Adaptation? Migration and Persistence of the Red River Métis, 1835-1890," *Canadian Historical Association* (1988): 120-144; D.N. Sprague, "Dispossession vs. Accommodation in Plaintiff vs. Defendant Accounts of Métis Dispersal from Manitoba, 1870-1881," *Prairie Forum*, 16 (1992): 137-156; Nicole St. Onge, "Variations in Red River: The Traders and Freemen Metis of Saint-Laurent, Manitoba," *Canadian Ethnic Studies*, 24:2 (1992): 2-21.

[77] Gerhard Ens, "Métis Agriculture in Red River During the Transition from Peasant Society to Industrial Capitalism: The Example of St. François Xavier 1835 to 1870," in R.C. MacLeod, ed., *Swords and Ploughshares: War and Agriculture in Western Canada* (Edmonton, 1993), pp. 239-62.

[78] Published by University of Toronto Press.

[79] See Frank J. Tough, "Aboriginal Rights Versus the Deed of Surrender: The Legal Rights of Native Peoples and Canada's Acquisition of the Hudson's Bay Company Territory," *Prairie Forum*, 17:2 (1992): 225-250, which does not deal specifically with the Red River situation or cite any secondary literature on Red River's Aboriginal titles.

[80] Consult, for example, T.C.B. Boon, "St. Peter's Dynevor: The Original Indian Settlement of Western Canada," *Transactions HSSM*, 3rd ser., 9 (1954): 16-32; Robert Coutts, "Anglican Missionaries as Agents of Acculturation: The Church Missionary Society at St. Andrew's, Red River, 1830-1870," in Barry Ferguson, ed., *The Anglican Church and the World of Western Canada 1820-1970* (Regina, 1991), pp. 50-60; Frits Pannekoek, "Protestant Agricultural Zions for the Western Indian," *Journal of the Canadian Church Historical Society*, 12:3 (September 1970). One of the few non-missionary-oriented works is Albert Thompson's *Chief Peguis and his Descendants* (Winnipeg, 1973).

[81] See my *Floods of the Centuries: A History of Flood Disasters in the Red River Valley, 1776-1997* (Winnipeg, 1997).

[82] Roy St. George Stubbs, *Four Recorders of Rupert's Land* (Winnipeg, 1967); Katherine Bindon, "Hudson's Bay Company Law: Adam Thom and the Institution of Order in Rupert's Land, 1839-1854," in David Flaherty, ed., *Essays in the History of Canadian Law* (Toronto, 1981); Dale and Lee Gibson, *Substantial Justice: Law and Lawyers in Manitoba, 1670-1970* (Winnipeg, 1970); Sylvia Van Kirk, "The Reputation of a Lady," *Manitoba History*, no. 11 (1986), 4-11.

[83] Alexander Begg, *History of the North-West*, 1 (Toronto, 1894), p. 370.

[84] Frank Larned Hunt, "Britain's One Utopia," HSSM, 61 (1902): 2-3.

[85] Morton, ed., *Begg's Red River Journal*, pp. 151-62.

[86] See, for example, Frank Peake, "John Smithurst and the Ordination Controversy: Reflections on Red River Society in the 1840s," in Barry Ferguson, ed., *The Anglican Church and the World of Western Canada 1820-1970* (Regina, 1991), pp. 71-82.

[87] James Michael Reardon, *George Anthony Belcourt, Pioneer Catholic Missionary to the Northwest 1803-1874: His Life and Times* (St. Paul, 1955); Frits Pannekoek, "The Rev. Griffiths Owen Corbett and the Red River Civil War of 1869-70," *Canadian Historical Review*, 57:2 (1976): 133-50.

[88] See my "The Queen v. G.O. Corbett," in this volume.

[89] Philippe Mailhot, "Ritchot's Resistance: Abbé Noel Joseph Ritchot and the Creation and Transformation of Manitoba" (PhD diss., University of Manitoba, 1986).

[90] Frits Pannekoek, "Some Comments on the Social Origin of the Riel Protest of 1869," HSSM, 3rd ser., no. 34 (1977-8): 39-48.

[91] The 1987 reprint was published in Winnipeg by Peguis Publishers.

[92] Dennis King, *The Grey Nuns and the Red River Settlement* (Agincourt, 1980); Estelle Mitchell, *The Grey Nuns of Montreal at the Red River, 1844-1984* (Montreal, 1987); Diane Michelle Boyd, "The Rise and Development of Female Catholic Education in the Nineteenth-Century Red River Region: The Case of Catherine Mulaire (M.A. diss., University of Manitoba, 1999). There is also a collection of letters from the nun who had been Louis Riel's sister: Mary V. Jordan, ed., *De ta soeur, Sara Riel* (Saint-Boniface, 1980). See also Donald Chaput, "The 'Misses Nolin' of Red River," *The Beaver* (Winter 1975): 14-17.

[93] *The Canadian Journal of Native Studies,* 3:1 (1983): 40-46; Van Kirk, "The Reputation of a Lady"; Erica Smith, "'Gentlemen, This is no ordinary Trial,' Sexual Narratives in the Trial of the Reverend Corbett, Red River 1863," in Jennifer Brown and Elizabeth Vibert, eds., *Reading Beyond Words: Contexts for Native History* (Peterborough, ON, 1996), pp. 364-80.

[94] Gerald Friesen, *The Canadian Prairies: A History* (Toronto, 1984) p. 113.

[95] Wendy Owen and J. M. Bumsted, "The Victorian Family in Historical Perspective: The Ross Family of Red River and the Jarvis Family of Prince Edward Island," *Manitoba History,* 13 (1987): 12-18.

ANOTHER LOOK AT THE FOUNDER: LORD SELKIRK AS POLITICAL ECONOMIST

[1] What was printed in Selkirk's lifetime was collected and published in *The Collected Writings of Lord Selkirk,* 2 vols. (Winnipeg, 1984 and 1988), edited by J. M. Bumsted. There is at least another publishable volume of papers loosely based on the subject of political economy scattered in the Selkirk papers.

[2] V. A. Eyles, "The Evolution of a Chemist: Sir James Hall, Bt.," *Annals of Science,* 9 (1963): 153-182.

[3] Journal of Sir James Hall of Dunglass, 1791, National Library of Scotland.

[4] See Rosalind Mitchison, *Agricultural Sir John: The Life of Sir John Sinclair of Ulbster, 1754-1835* (London, 1962), pp. 137-58.

[5] Lord Daer to [Sir John Sinclair], 28 January 1798, SRO RH4/49/2.

[6] *Annals of Agriculture,* 26, p. 435.

[7] Istvan Hont and Michael Ignatieff, "Needs and Justice in the *Wealth of Nations: An Introductory Essay,"* in Hont and Ignatieff, eds., *Wealth and Virtue: The Shaping of Political Economy in the Scottish Enlightenment* (Cambridge, 1983), pp. 13-26.

[8] [Thomas Malthus], *An Essay on the Principle of Population, as it Affects the Future Improvement of Society, with Remarks on the Speculations of Mr. Godwin, M. Condorcet, and Other Writers* (London, 1798).

[9] This was published as Essay 3 of his *Essays, political, economical, and philosophical* (London, 1796).

[10] See my *People's Clearance,* 83-107.

[11] Selkirk ignored a warning from Dugald Stewart of the dangers of his involvement. See Dugald Stewart to Selkirk, 1802, Selkirk Papers, National Archives of Canada, 13903-6.

[12] Patrick C.T. White, ed., *Lord Selkirk's Diary 1803-1804: A Journal of his Travels to British North America and the Northeastern United States* (Toronto, Champlain Society, 1958).

[13] Ibid.

[14] "Diary of Nicholas Garry," *Transactions of the Royal Society of Canada,* 2nd ser. (1900), p. 136.

[15] A.E.D. MacKenzie, *Baldoon: Lord Selkirk's Settlement in Upper Canada* (London, ON, 1978).

[16] The best discussion of the development question remains A.J. Youngson, *After the Forty-Five: The Economic Impact on the Scottish Highlands* (Edinburgh, 1973).

[17] The Earl of Selkirk, *Observations on the Present State of the Highlands of Scotland, with a View of the Causes and Probable Consequences of Emigration* (Edinburgh, 1805).

[18] *Critical Review,* 3rd ser., 5 (1805): 366-78.

[19] *Scots Magazine,* 67 (1805): 609-16.

[20] *Farmer's Magazine,* 5 (1805): 483-90.

[21] *Edinburgh Review,* 7 (1805): 186-202.

[22] Francis Horner to Sir James Mackintosh, 25 September 1805, in Leonard Horner, ed., *Memoirs and Correspondence of Francis Horner, M.P.,* 1 (London, 1843), pp. 312-13.

[23] Robert Brown, *Strictures and Remarks on the Earl of Selkirk's Observations on the*

Present State of the Highlands of Scotland (Edinburgh, 1806)); *Eight Letters on the Subject of the Earl of Selkirk's Pamphlet on Highland Emigration, As They Lately Appeared under the Signature of AMICUS in One of the Edinburgh Newspapers* (Edinburgh, 1806); *Remarks on the Earl of Selkirk's Observations on the Present State of the Highlands* (Edinburgh, 1806).

[24] *Monthly Review,* 5 (1806): 411-419; *Critical Review,* 3rd ser., 8 (1806): 374-378; *Farmer's Magazine,* 6 (1806): 241-248.

[25] Alan Swingewood, "Origins of sociology: the case of the Scottish Enlightenment," *British Journal of Sociology,* XXI (1970): 168-80.

[26] *A Letter to the Peers of Scotland by the Earl of Selkirk,* reprinted in Bumsted, ed., *Collected Writings,* 1: 241-58.

[27] Sir John Fortescue, *The County Lieutenancies and the Army 1803-1814* (London, 1906).

[28] Reprinted in Bumsted, ed., *Collected Writings,* 1: 260-87.

[29] John Robertson, "The Improving Citizen: Militia Debates and Political Thought in the Scottish Enlightenment," (D.Phil. diss., University of Oxford), 1980.

[30] See, for example, Andrew Fletcher, "A Discourse of Government with Relation to Militias," in D. Daiches, ed., *Selected Political Writings and Speeches* (Edinburgh, 1976).

[31] Adam Smith, *Wealth of Nations,* 5, i.f.50-3.

[32] Reprinted in Bumsted, ed., *Collected Writings,* 1: 289-357.

[33] As Sir John Wedderburn noted in a reprint of this piece (Edinburgh, 1860).

[34] Reprinted in Bumsted, ed., *Collected Writings,* 1: 358-66.

[35] White, ed., *Lord Selkirk's Diary,* esp.

[36] Bumsted, ed., *Collected Writings,* 2: 46-108.

[37] *Quarterly Review,* 16, no. 31 (October 1816): 129-44.

[38] See *Collected Writings,* 2: 110-273. For a discussion of these narratives in the context of their time, see my *Fur Trade Wars: The Founding of Western Canada* (Winnipeg, 1999), pp. 252-7.

THE SWISS AND RED RIVER, 1819-1826

[1] See [N.R.Wyss], *Reise eines Schweizers nach dem roten Fluss in Nord-Amerika,einziger Aufenthalt, und rueckkehr ins Vaterland. [Journey of a Swiss to the Red River in North America, the stay there, and return to the homeland]* (Bern, 1825); August Chetlain, *The Red River Colony* (Chicago, 1893); E.H. Bovay, *Le Canada et les Suisses 1604-1974* (Fribourg, 1974), especially pp. 41-58.

[2] Winthrop Pickard Bell, *The "Foreign Protestants" and the Settlement of Nova Scotia: The History of a Piece of Arrested British Colonial Policy in the Eighteenth Century* (Toronto, 1961).

[3] Colvile to de May, 14 December 1819, SPNAC, 6598-05.

[4] De May to Colvile, 20 December 1819, SPNAC, 6606-8.

[5] De May to Colvile, 25 December 1819, SPNAC, 6615.

[6] De May to Colvile, Bern, 13 January 1820, SPNAC, 6642-52.

[7] Colvile to de May, 28 January 1820, SPNAC, 6669-72.

[8] Colvile to de May, 10 February 1820, SPNAC, 6702-6404.

[9] De May to Colvile, 16 February 1820, SPNAC, 6705-6713.

[10] Ibid.

[11] Colvile to de May, 6 March 1820, SPNAC, 6761-63.

[12] Colvile to de May, 10 June 1820, SPNAC, 6901-3.

[13] De May to Colvile, 22 March, 27 March 1820, SPNAC, 6766-77, 6782-87.

[14] Colvile to de May, 4 April 1820, SPNAC, 6802-5.

[15] Colvile to de May, 28 April 1820, SPNAC, 6837-38.

[16] De May to Colvile, 29 April 1820, SPNAC, 6839-44.

[17] The date in the text is 24 May 1820. R. de May d'Uzistorf, Capitaine au Service britannique, et Agent plenipotentiare de Comte de Selkirk, *Prospectus d'un Plan d'Envoyer Des Colons à la Colonie de la Rivière-Rouge dans l'Amérique Septentrionale.* In German it was titled *Kurze und wahre Uebersicht aller der Vortheile, welche ein Anseidler in der Kolonie des Rothen-Flusses, in Nordamerika gelegen, zu erwarten und zu geniessen hat.*

[18] See, for example, the complaints of Donald Gunn (one of the early Scots settlers) in his *History of Manitoba* (1880).

[19] Colvile to de May, 21 July 1820, SPNAC, 6928-69. De May subsequently explained the enclosure promise as a translation problem in the English version which Colvile had prepared in London. "Unmarchen" in German, wrote de May, simply meant fixing legal boundaries by border stones, and not actual fencing. De May to Colvile, 2 August 1820, SPNAC, 6937-39.

[20] De May to Colvile, 13 July 1820, SPNAC, 6925-7.

[21] Reprinted in George F.G.Stanley, ed., "Documents relating to the Swiss Immigration to Red River in 1821," *Canadian Historical Review*, 22:1 (1941): 42-50.

[22] De May to Colvile, 22 August 1820, SPNAC, 6959-62.

[23] Colvile to de May, 1 September 1820, SPNAC, 6975.

[24] De May to Colvile, 13 November 1820, SPNAC, 7017-21.

[25] Colvile to de May, 16 November 1820, SPNAC, 7022-23.

[26] De May to Colvile, 29 November 1820, SPNAC, 7027-34.

[27] Colvile to de May, 8 December 1820, SPNAC, 7034-35.

[28] Covile to F. Riser, 19 January 1821, SPNAC, 7054.

[29] Colvile to de May, 19 January 1821, SPNAC, 7055-57.

[30] De May to Colvile, 1 February 1821, SPNAC, 7067-80.

[31] Colvile to de May, 16 February 1821, SPNAC, 7085-87.

[32] Colvile to Alexander Macdonell, 24 February 1821, SPNAC, 7093-95.

[33] De May to Colvile, 21 March 1821, SPNAC, 7118-20.

[34] De May to Colvile, 23 March 1821, SPNAC, 7121-28.

[35] Colvile to de May, 30 March, 1821, SPNAC, 7147-48; Colvile to de May, 6 April 1821, SPNAC, 7149-50.

[36] Colvile to de May, 6 April 1821, SPNAC, 7150-53.

[37] Ibid.

[38] De May to Colvile, 2 April 1821, SPNAC, 7180-84.

[39] De May to Colvile, 6 April 1821, SPNAC, 7190-96.

[40] De May to Colvile, 18 April 1821, SPNAC, 7216-26.

[41] A. L. Prevost, Swiss Consul, to Colvile, 4 April 1821, SPNAC, 7185-86; Colvile to Prevost, 6 April 1821, SPNAC, 7187-88.

[42] De May to Colvile, 12 April 1821, SPNAC, 7203-13.

[43] De May to Colvile, 18 April 1821, SPNAC, 7216-26.

[44] De May to Colvile, 14 May 1821, SPNAC, 7253-58.

[45] William Todd to Colvile, 25 May 1821, SPNAC, 6242-43.

[46] Quoted in Alvin M. Josephy, Jr., *The Artist Was a Young Man: The Life Story of Peter Rindisbacher* (Fort Worth, 1970), pp. 13-14.

[47] 1825 account. The encounters with ice were visually recorded in sketches and watercolours by Peter Rindisbacher on the journey, which is generally well-illustrated by the young artist.

[48] Simpson to Colvile, 5 September 1821, SPNAC, 7381-96.

[49] "Reminiscences of Mrs. Ann Adams, 1821-1829," *Minnesota Historical Collections,* 6.

[50] Alexander Macdonell to Colvile, York Factory, 12 September 1821, SPNAC, 7413-26.

[51] Alexander Macdonell to Colvile, 13 November 1821, SPNAC, 7440.

[52] For a listing, see Stanley, ed., *Documents*, pp. 47-58.

[53] Colvile to de May, 23 April 1822, SPNAC, 7583-84.

[54] Simpson to Colvile, 20 May 1822, SPNAC, 7587-7627.

[55] SPNAC, 7571.

[56] SPNAC, 7570.

[57] Colvile to de May, 7 December 1821, SPNAC, 7481-82.

[58] Colvile to D'Orsonnens, 20 December 1821, SPNAC, 7483-84.

[59] De May to Colvile, 20 December 1821, SPNAC, 7486-92.

[60] Colvile to de May, 4 January 1822, SPNAC, 7523-25; de May to Colvile, 22 January 1822, SPNAC, 7546-48; Colvile to de May, 1 February 1822, SPNAC, 7526; de May to Colvile, 2 February 1822, SPNAC, 7550.

[61] Colvile to de May, 28 May 1822, SPNAC, 7629-31.

[62] De May to Colvile, 8 June 1822, SPNAC, 7652-57.

[63] For Bulger, see *DCB*, 8, pp. 111-13; for Halkett, see *DCB*, 8, pp. 350-52.

[64] *DCB*, 8, p. 112.

[65] Bulger to Colvile, 4 August 1822, SPNAC, 7715-32.

[66] Walter von Hauser to "My Lord and Gentlemen," 8 July 1822, Stanley, ed., *Documents,* pp. 49-50.

[67] Bulger to Colvile, 4 August 1822.

[68] F. Matthey to Colvile, 26 March 1823, SPNAC, 7837-39.

[69] Examination of David Louis DesCombe, 10 February 1823, SPNAC, 7558-61. DesCombe's name does not appear on Walter von Hauser's list.

[70] Examination of John Dubach, 10 February 1823, SPNAC, 7562-64. Jean Dubach is described by von Hauser as "character no good."

[71] Journal of Francis Heron, April 1826, HBCA, B235/a/7.

[72] Chetlain, *The Red River Colony.*

[73] *DCB*, 6, pp. 648-50. For a biography, see Josephy, *The Artist Was a Young Man.*

Early Flooding in Red River, 1776-1861

[1] Ross, *The Red River Settlement: its rise, progress and present state* (London, 1856, reprinted Winnipeg, 1972), p. 107, notes the oral tradition.

[2] There is no mention of flooding in Selkirk's prospectus for Red River entitled *Ossiniboia* (1815), reprinted in Bumsted, ed., *Selkirk Papers,* 2, pp. 8-45, nor in Eric Ross's reconstruction of the geography of the Canadian Northwest in 1811 in his *Beyond the River and the Bay* (Toronto, 1970).

[3] Miles Macdonell to Selkirk, 1 October 1811, SPNAC, A27, 41-53.

[4] Selkirk to Macdonell, 23 December 1811, SPNAC, A27, 54-57.

[5] In June of 1815, the settlement succumbed to a small force of mixed-bloods and fur traders. Most of the settlers decided to move east to Upper Canada on board Nor'wester canoes. One hundred and forty of the approximately 200 people at Red River went east in 1815, most never to return. A handful of stalwarts retreated to Jack River and in collaboration with newly arrived settlers helped to reoccupy the colony in the fall. In the spring of 1816, an armed party of mixed-blood horsemen was met by an armed party of settlers on foot at Seven Oaks.

Shots were fired, and 21 settlers were left dead. Again the colony was temporarily surrendered and abandoned, recaptured early in 1817 after a mid-winter march overland on snowshoes by a band of de Meurons and Indians. For these incidents from the Selkirk perspective, see John Morgan Gray, *Lord Selkirk of Red River* (Toronto, 1964), pp. 98-148, and for the North West Company point of view, see Marjorie Wilkins Campbell, *The North West Company* (Vancouver, Douglas & McIntyre, 1983), pp. 211-218.

[6] For the Swiss regiments, consult Bovay, *Le Canada et les Suisses*, pp. 22-40.

[7] Andrew Colvile to William Johnston, 25 July 1821, SPNAC, 73, p. 19162.

[8] "Diary of Nicholas Garry," *Transactions of the Royal Society of Canada,* section II, 1900, p. 193. For the houses, see Grant MacEwan, *Cornerstone Colony: Selkirk's Contribution to the Canadian West* (Saskatoon, 1977), p. 162.

[9] For Simpson, see John S. Galbraith, *The Little Emperor: Governor Simpson of the Hudson's Bay Company* (Toronto, 1974).

[10] M.A. MacLeod and W.L. Morton, *Cuthbert Grant of Grantown: Warden of the plains of Red River* (Toronto, 1974).

[11] See the essay on Swiss settlers in this volume.

[12] Bovay, *Le Canada et les Suisses*, pp. 40-58.

[13] One of these Swiss settlers was the artist Peter Rindisbacher; see *DCB*, 6, 648-50, and Bovay, *Le Canada et les Suisses*, pp. 59-64.

[14] Quoted in Morton, *Manitoba: A History* (Toronto, 1957), p. 66.

[15] Ross, *The Red River Settlement*.

[16] Bishop Provencher to Bishop Panet, 15 July 1826, Grace L. Nute, ed., *Documents Relating to Northwest Missions, 1815-1827* (St. Paul, 1942), p. 443.

[17] Gunn and Tuttle, *History of Manitoba*, 245-48.

[18] Donald McKenzie to Alexander Colvile, 5 February 1826, SPNAC, 27, 8402-3.

[19] Simpson to Colville, 26 February 1826, SPNAC, 27, 8404-15.

[20] Journal of Francis Heron, HBCA, B235/a/7, entries for April 1826.

[21] Entry for 5 May, 1826, in Francis Heron "Journal of Occurrences, Kept at Fort Garry, In Red River Settlement, from 1st June 1825, until 31st July, 1826," HBCA, B.235/1/7/ folios 32d-46.

[22] John Pritchard to his brother, 2 August 1826, reprinted in S.P. Matheson, "Floods at Red River," *Papers HSSM,* 3rd ser., no. 3 (1947), p. 7.

[23] Gunn and Tuttle, *History of Red River,* p. 248.

[24] The extent of this flood—as well as those of 1852 and 1861—was calculated by Sanford Fleming in 1879 in his *Report on Bridging Red River 1879* (Ottawa, 1879), p. 8. From these calculations later engineers estimated flows.

[25] Heron Diary, 13 May 1826.

[26] John Pritchard to his brother, 2 August 1826, quoted in S. P. Matheson, "Floods at Red River," *Papers HSSM,* 3rd ser., no. 3 (1947), p. 7.

[27] Ibid.

[28] Simpson to Governor and Committee of HBC, 14 June 1826, HBCA, D.4/89, fos. 71-73d.

[29] Simpson to Colvile, 14 June 1820, SPNAC, 27, 8434-39.

[30] *DCB,* 6, p. 649.

[31] Heron Diary, 5 July 1826.

[32] Pritchard to Colvile, 29 August 1826.

[33] Ibid.

[34] See Eric Quayle, *Ballantyne the Brave: A Victorian Writer and His Family* (London, 1967).

[35] *Report of the Royal Commission on Flood Cost Benefit* (Winnipeg, December 1958), p. 15, based on *Report of the Red River Basin Investigation,* 1 (Ottawa, October 1953), p. 25.

[36] More recent flooding suggests the frequency of once every 460 years is a bit optimistic.

[37] *Report of the Royal Commission,* p. 10.

[38] *Report of the Royal Commission,* p. 15.

[39] The damage to 1957 Winnipeg, estimated the Royal Commission of 1956-58, would have been $593 million. See *Report of the Royal Commission,* p. 10.

[40] We have a number of sources for the 1852 flood, among which the fullest and best is Bishop David Anderson's *Notes on the Flood at the Red River in 1852*—really his extended diary of the occurrence—published in London in 1873. Anderson obviously intended the published version of his diary to make a

literary contribution as well as a historical one, and it is carefully calculated for effect.

[41] Weather conditions can be followed in detail in the diary of Dr. William Cowan, at the time army surgeon to the pensioners at Fort Garry. The diary is at the PAM. For a general discussion of this flood, see W. L. Morton's "Introduction" to *London Correspondence Inward from Eden Colvile*, pp. cxi-cxiv.

[42] Anderson, *Notes on the Flood,* pp. 22-23.

[43] Extracts from the letters of Mgr. Provencher, appendix 16 of *Report of the Red River Basin Investigation,* 1.

[44] Estelle Mitchell, *The Grey Nuns of Montreal and the Red River Settlement 1844-1984* (n.p., n.d., but 1987), p. 51.

[45] Eden Colvile to Archd. Barclay, 18 May 1852, in *Eden-Colvile Correspondence,* p. 123.

[46] See "Notes on the rise and fall of the Red River at the Stone Fort Spring 1852," in Rich, ed., *Eden-Colvile Correspondence,* 128-130.

[47] Ibid., p. 125.

[48] Anderson, *Notes on the Flood,* pp. 46-47.

[49] Ibid., p. 25.

[50] Ibid., pp. 98-102.

[51] For the pensioners, see the diary of Dr. William Cowan.

[52] Anderson, *Notes on the Flood,* p. 71.

[53] Colvile to Archd. Barclay, 11 September 1852, in Rich, ed., *Eden-Colvile Correspondence,* p. 167.

[54] Eden Colvile to Archibald Barclay (secretary, HBC, London), 18 May 1852, in Rich, ed., *Eden-Colvile Correspondence,* p. 123.

[55] Ibid.

[56] Eden Colvile to Archd. Barclay, 11 September 1852, in Rich, ed., *Eden Colville Correspondence,* 165-6.

[57] Anderson, *Notes on the Flood,* p. 40.

[58] Colvile to Barclay, 11 September 1852.

[59] James Bird to George Simpson, 6 July 1852, HBCA, d.5/34, folios 49-49d.

[60] Cowan Diary, 23 May 1852.

[61] Colvile to Barclay, 11 September 1852, in Rich, p. 167.

[62] John Balmer Memoirs, PAM, MG 2 B7-4, p. 45.

[63] *Nor'-Wester,* 1 May 1861.

[64] Hind, 1, p. 222. Hind had also insisted that "it appears that there is no possibility of guarding against these inundations, and that part of Red River Settlement above the Watermill Creek, subject to them, will always suffer from the disadvantages inseparable from such devastating occurrences." (p. 396).

[65] As well as the newspaper and Balmer accounts, there are descriptions of the 1861 flood in W. MacTavish to Thomas Fraser, 1 May and 16 May 1861, HBCA A.11/96, fo. 559 and 569d, as well as in Samuel P. Matheson's "Three Red River Floods," HSSM, ser 3, no. 3, 1947.

[66] *St. Cloud Democrat,* 13 June 1861.

[67] The 1958 Royal Commission report estimated the maximum discharge of this flood at 125,000 cubic feet per second, the maximum elevation at the Forks at 760.5 feet, and the elevation above city datum at James Avenue of 32.3 feet. The probable frequency was once every 64 years, and the estimated losses in 1957 Winnipeg of a flood of this magnitude were $266 million.

[68] *Nor'-Wester,* 1 May 1861, 1 June 1861.

[69] *St. Cloud Democrat,* 13 June 1861.

[70] Ibid.

[71] Samuel P. Matheson, *Three Red River Floods.*

[72] *St. Cloud Democrat,* 13 June 1861.

[73] See my "Drought Brings on Famine of '68," *Winnipeg Real Estate News,* 4 July 1997, p. 3.

[74] The best source for early Winnipeg is Alexander Begg and W. R. Nursey, *Ten Years in Winnipeg* (Winnipeg, 1879).

[75] Charles Mair to the *Montreal Gazette,* 31 August 1869, printed 13 October 1869.

[76] Stanford Fleming's elevations would prove extremely useful here.

THE COLONIAL OFFICE, ABORIGINAL POLICY, AND RED RIVER, 1847-1849

[1] For accounts of Red River trade in the early 1840s, see A.S. Morton, *History of the Canadian West*, 806ff., and W.L. Morton, "Introduction" in E.E. Rich, ed., *London Correspondence Inward from Eden Colvile, 1849-1852* (London, 1956), lviii-lxxi.

[2] See Bindon, "Hudson's Bay Company Law," in David Flaherty, ed., *Essays in the History of Canadian Law*, I (Toronto, 1981), pp. 43-87, especially pp. 64-66.

[3] George F. G. Stanley, *Toil & Trouble: Military Expeditions to Red River* (Toronto and Oxford, 1989), pp. 35-40.

[4] A. Christie to Secretary, Hudson's Bay House, 31 December 1844, HBCA 11/95.

[5] E. H. Oliver, ed., *The Canadian North-West; Its Early Development and Legislative Records; Minutes of the Councils of the Red River Colony and the Northern Department of Rupert's Land*, II (Ottawa, 1915), pp. 1303-05.

[6] This document is reprinted in D. Geneva Lent, *West of the Mountains: James Sinclair and the Hudson's Bay Company* (Seattle, 1963), pp. 175-77.

[7] Alexander Christie to James Sinclair et al., 5 September 1845, reprinted in Ibid., pp. 177-79.

[8] Simpson to Lord Metcalfe, 6 November 1845, HBCA, D4./67.

[9] Quoted in Gluek, *Minnesota and the Canadian Northwest*, p. 64.

[10] Morton, Introduction to *Eden Colvile's Letters, 1849-1852*, p. lxx.

[11] The French one is reprinted in *Hudson's Bay Company. (Red River Settlement.) Return to an Address of The Honourable the House of Commons, dated 9 February 1849...*, pp. 4-5, and the instructions in the same, pp. 89-90.

[12] Ibid.

[13] Two very full secondary accounts of the London business exist. As is often the case, the casual reader would be hard-pressed to recognize them as describing the same incidents. The two accounts are in: Galbraith, *Hudson's Bay Company as an Imperial Factor*, pp. 311-30, and Cooper, *Alexander Kennedy Isbister*, pp. 107-42. As well, there are interesting shorter summaries in Rich, *History of the Hudson's Bay Company* vol. 2, pp. 545-47, and Owram, *Promise of Eden*, pp. 26-30. Owram suggests that the focus of the formal complaints against the HBC in the 1840s was "on the effect that the whole system of government had on the native population," but does not fully develop this insight.

[14] As Lord John Russell and William Gladstone demonstrated in 1857 at the hearings of the Select Committee of the House of Commons investigating the Hudson's Bay Company charter, when they cross-examined Sir George Simpson at great length about these matters. Russell and Gladstone extensively quoted from the relevant documents, forcing Simpson to claim in most cases that he did not remember most of the details and incidents involved.

[15] Lent, *James Sinclair.*

[16] Copy of Instructions, 1849 Blue Book, pp. 48-49.

[17] For a biography, see Cooper, *Alexander Kennedy Isbister.*

[18] "Return to an Address of The Honourable the House of Commons, dated 9 February 1849;—for, 'Copies of any Memorials presented to the Colonial Office by Inhabitants of the Red River Settlement, complaining of the Government of the Hudson's Bay Company; of the Instructions given to the Governor-General of Canada for the Investigation of those Complaints; of the Reports of the Officers appointed by Lord Elgin, or by the Colonial Office, for the purpose of such Investigation; and of any Correspondence which has passed between the Colonial Office and the Hudson's Bay Company, and the Inhabitants of the Red River Settlement respectively, upon the subject of the above Memorial" (1849); this document will be hereafter referred to as "1849 Blue Book."

[19] Isbister to Grey, 6 February 1847, 1849 Blue Book, p. 9.

[20] Isbister to Grey, 17 February 1847, 1849 Blue Book, p. 10. It is worth emphasizing that this memorial was not written in Red River, but in London.

[21] Morton, "Introduction." p. lxx n4.

[22] James Michael Reardon, *George Anthony Belcourt, Pioneer Catholic Missionary of the Northwest, 1803-1874* (1955), pp. 81 ff.

[23] "Petition," 1849 Blue Book, pp. 4-5; Isbister to Grey, 28 May 1847, 1849 Blue Book, p. 48. This point needs emphasizing, as there is some confusion over which document represented the principal case made by Isbister and his associates to the Colonial Office. Galbraith, for example, writes as if the Petition was the major document; see *Hudson's Bay Company as an Imperial Factor*, pp. 317-18. Moreover, he conflates the charges of the Memorial and the Petition together. No wonder the Colonial Office was itself somewhat bewildered as to the charges.

[24] Ibid., p. 318.

[25] Cooper, *Alexander Kennedy Isbister*, p. 111.

[26] Galbraith argued that Isbister showed "a marked lack of discrimination between facts and falsehood." *Hudson's Bay Company as an Imperial Factor*, p. 319.

[27] Isbister to Grey, 21 June 1847, 1849 Blue Book, p. 51.

[28] Hawes to Isbister, 5 March 1847, 1849 Blue Book, p. 11.

[29] Isbister to Grey, 5 March 1847, 1849 Blue Book, p.11.

[30] "Letter from Rev. Mr. *Beaver,* referred to by Mr. *Isbister,* and enclosed in that Gentleman's Letter of 5 March 1847," 1849 Blue Book, pp. 12-15.

[31] Enclosure 2, in No. 6, 1849 Blue Book, pp. 15-18.

[32] Pelly to Grey, 24 April 1847, 1849 Blue Book, pp. 20-47.

[33] Galbraith, *Hudson's Bay Company as an Imperial Factor*, p. 16.

[34] Cooper, *Alexander Kennedy Isbister,* p. 117.

[35] Copy of Land Deed, 1849 Blue Book, pp. 45-47.

[36] Certainly this sort of document did not predate 1835, when the Company purchased the settlement. Archer Martin, *The Hudson's Bay Company's Land Tenures and the Occupation of Assiniboia by Lord Selkirk's Settlers, with a List of Grantees under the Earl and Company* (London, 1898).

[37] Certainly the Liberals gave Sir George Simpson quite a rough ride over this deed in his 1857 appearance before the Parliamentary Select Committee.

[38] Isbister to Grey, 26 April 1847, 1849 Blue Book, pp. 47-8.

[39] Hawes to Isbister, 3 May 1847, 1849 Blue Book, p. 48.

[40] Isbister to Grey, 28 May 1847, 1849 Blue Book, p. 48.

[41] Cooper, *Alexander Kennedy Isbister,* 118-123; David McNab, "The Colonial Office and the Prairies in the Mid-Nineteenth Century," *Prairie Forum,* 3 (1978): 21-38.

[42] Quoted in Cooper, *Alexander Kennedy Isbister,* p. 119.

[43] Public Record Office, Colonial Office 42/571.

[44] Cooper, *Alexander Kennedy Isbister,* p. 121.

[45] Merivale, "Fanaticism," *Edinburgh Review,* 59 (April 1834): 30-48.

[46] Hawes to Pelly, 5 June 1847, 1849 Blue Book, p. 50.

[47] Isbister to Grey, 21 June 1847, 1849 Blue Book, pp. 51-52.

[48] Pelly to Grey, 21 June 1847, 1849 Blue Book, p. 52.

[49] Hawes to Pelly, 2 July 1847, 1849 Blue Book, p. 53.

[50] See the list of enclosures in the margin of the printed despatch of Grey to Elgin, June 1847, in 1849 Blue Book, p. 6.

[51] Isbister to Rowand, 3 July 1847, HBCA, A. 10/20.

[52] A. Barclay to Simpson, 11 February 1848, HBCA, D.5/21.

[53] Enclosure of Elgin to Grey, 18 November 1848, HBCA A.13/3.

[54] Simpson to Governor and Committee, 16 November 1848, HBCA A.12/4.

[55] John Stuart McLeod to the secretary of the Aborigines Protection Society, 12 April 1847, and facsimile of document referred to in his letter dated 20 March 1847, 1849 Blue Book, p. 70.

[56] "Observations on the Hudson's Bay Company's Report," 1849 Blue Book, pp. 58-64.

[57] 1849 Blue Book, pp. 78-83.

[58] Ibid., pp. 85-6. The full title of this pamphlet was: *A Few Words on the Hudson's Bay Company: with a statement of the grievances of the Native and half-caste Indians, addressed to the British Government through their delegates now in London* (London, n.d.).

[59] Neither document was reprinted in the Blue Book at this point.

[60] Minute, 9 August 1847, PRO, CO 42/571.

[61] Isbister to Pelly, 12 November 1847, 1849 Blue Book, pp. 105-6.

[62] Pelly to Isbister, 17 November 1847, 1849 Blue Book, p. 106.

[63] Pelly to Isbister, 8 January 1848, 1849 Blue Book, pp. 107-8.

[64] Cooper, *Alexander Kennedy Isbister*, p. 131.

[65] Isbister to Grey, 18 December 1847; Hawes to Isbister, 2 February 1848, 1849 Blue Book, pp. 97-98.

[66] Cooper, *Alexander Kennedy Isbister*, pp. 133-4.

[67] Isbister to Grey, February 1848, 1849 Blue Book, pp. 98-99.

[68] Belcour [sic] to Isbister, 21 December 1847, 1849 Blue Book, pp. 99-100.

[69] Hawes to Isbister, 17 February 1848, 1849 Blue Book, p. 100.

[70] Hawes to Crofton, 8 February 1848, 1849 Blue Book, p. 98.

[71] Quoted in Cooper, *Alexander Kennedy Isbister,* p. 132.

[72] Crofton, "Some Remarks on the Charges (in Abstract) against the Hudson's Bay Company," 12 February 1848, 1849 Blue Book, pp. 101-102.

[73] Report from the Select Committee on the Hudson's Bay Company; together with the Proceedings of the Committee, Minutes of Evidence, Appendix and Index (ordered printed by House of Commons, 1857), Q3418-3427.

[74] Isbister to Hawes, 28 February 1848, Merivale to Isbister, 7 March 1848, 1849 Blue Book, p. 103. It is interesting that when Isbister wrote to Grey, he got a reply from Hawes. When he wrote to Hawes, he got a reply from Merivale.

[75] Elgin to Grey, 6 June 1848, 1849 Blue Book, pp. 8-9.

[76] Quoted in Cooper, *Alexander Kennedy Isbister,* p. 137.

[77] *DCB,* 6, pp. 138-39.

[78] British Library, Add. Mss. 44565 f. 299.

[79] Hawes to Griffiths, 13 January 1849, 1849 Blue Book, p. 109.

[80] 1849 Blue Book, pp. 111-12.

[81] Dawes to Isbister, 23 January 1849, 1849 Blue Book, p. 113.

[82] The files would be resurrected in 1857 at the time of the Parliamentary Select Committee's hearings into the charter of the HBC.

[83] John Macallum to Benjamin Hawes, HBCA, A.10/20.

ANOTHER LOOK AT THE BUFFALO HUNT

[1] The best secondary accounts are: F. G. Roe, "The Red River Hunt," *Transactions of the Royal Society of Canada,* 2nd ser. (1935), 171-218; Marcel Giraud, *The Métis in the Canadian West,* 2 (translated by George Woodcock, Edmonton, 1986), pp. 140-52; Gerhard Enns, *Homeland to Hinterland: The Changing Worlds of the Red River Metis in the Nineteenth Century* (Toronto, University of Toronto Press, 1996), pp. 38-43.

[2] Alexander Ross, *The Red River Settlement,* pp. 241-67; Father Georges Belcourt, "The Buffalo Hunt," in *The Beaver* (December 1944); [Viscount Milton], "Off to the Buffalo Hunt," *Nor'-Wester,* 14 August 1860; "The Buffalo Hunt," *Nor'-Wester,* 28 August 1860.

[3] Ross, *Red River Settlement,* p. 241.

[4] Marcel Giraud, *The Métis in the Canadian West,* 2 vol. (Edmonton, 1986), especially 2, pp. 115–75.

[5] Gunn chapters in *Nor'-Wester,* 1869.

[6] Roe, "Red River Hunt," p. 175ff.

[7] For an account, see MacEwan, *Cornerstone Colony.*

[8] Laurence Barkwell, "Early Law and Social Control among the Metis," in Samuel Corrigan and Laurence J. Barkwell, eds., *The Struggle for Recognition: Canadian Justice and the Metis Nation* (1991), pp. 7–38.

[9] "Off to the Buffalo Hunt," *Nor'-Wester,* 14 August 1840.

[10] Ross, *Red River Settlement,* p. 246; Milton and Cheadle, *North-West Passage,* p. 44.

[11] Hind, *Narrative,* p. 110.

[12] "White Horse Plain Hunters," *Nor'-Wester,* 28 August 1860.

[13] Ross, *Red River Settlement,* p. 248.

[14] Charles Mair to Holmes Mair, 3 November 1868, *Toronto Globe,* 14 December 1868.

[15] Milton, "Off to the Buffalo Hunt."

[16] *Nor'-Wester,* 28 August 1860.

[17] Belcourt, "A Buffalo Hunt."

[18] Ross, *The Red River Settlement,* p. 260.

[19] They are:

1. *Dépouilles,* two layers of flesh along the ribs, extending from shoulder to rump. They are separated by a thin skin or cartilage from another layer of meat which lies below them.

2. *Filets,* sinewy muscles which connect the shoulder blades to the haunches.

3. *Bricoles,* two bands of fat which descend from over the shoulder to the under part of the neck.

4. *Petits filets du cou,* small sinewy muscles found near the extremities of the filets.

5. *Dessous de croupe,* parts immediately above the flanks.

6. *Epaules,* the shoulders.

7. *Dessous d'épaule,* the layers of flesh lying between ribs and shoulders.

8. *Pis,* fatty layer extending under the belly and up the flanks. The udder is included in it.

9. *Ventre,* muscular band of flesh which supports the intestines and extends under the belly from ribs on one side to ribs on opposite side.

10. *Panse,* the stomach, which is considered by the half-breeds to be something of a delicacy.

11. *Grosse bosse,* the hump, which is highest immediately between the shoulder blades. It is composed of a number of broad, thin bones, inclined to the rear and very similar in conformation to the spines on a fish bone. This morsel has a delicious taste.

12. *Gras* or *Suif,* the suet from the interior of the carcass.

13. *Plats-côtes,* or cutlets.

14. *Croupe,* the rump.

15. *Brochet,* meat which covers the stomach.

16. *Langue,* the tongue.

[20] Ross, *Red River Settlement,* p. 258.

[21] The Earl of Southesk, who visited the prairies in 1859-60, wrote that berries in pemmican acted like currant jelly does with venison, "correcting the greasiness of the fat by a slightly acid sweetness." He added, "take scrapings from the driest outside corner of a very stale piece of cold roast beef, add to it lumps of tallowy rancid fat, then garnish all with long human hairs (on which string pieces, like beads, upon a necklace), and short hairs of oxen, or dogs, or both—and you have a fair imitation of common pemmican, though I should rather suppose it to be less nasty." The Earl of Southesk, *Saskatchewan and the Rocky Mountains, A Diary and Narrative of Travel, Sport, and Adventure, during a Journey through the Hudson's Bay Company's Territories, in 1859 and 1860* (Edinburgh, 1875), p 301.

[22] Ibid., p. 253.

[23] Ibid., pp. 263-64.

[24] In *Smithsonian Reports,* 1887, part ii, 367-548.

[25] Ibid., p. 475.

[26] Roe, "Red River Hunt," pp. 209-18.

[27] Ibid., p. 215.

[28] Frank G. Roe, "The Extermination of the Buffalo in Western Canada," *Canadian Historical Review,* 15 (1934); 1-23; *The North American Buffalo,* rev. ed. (Toronto, 1970).

[29] Hind, *Narrative,* 1: 108.

[30] Ross, *Red River Settlement,* pp. 273-74.

[31] Ibid., p. 267.

[32] *Nor'-Wester,* 15 November 1860.

[33] A.A. Den Otter, "An Environmental Perspective on the 1849 Sayer Trial,"unpublished paper presented at the "1849 Conference" at Edinburgh, May, 1999.

[34] *Report from the Select Committee on the Hudson's Bay Company; together with the proceedings of the Committee, Minutes of Evidence, Appendix and Index* (House of Commons, 1857), Q3239.

[35] See the essays on floods and famines in this volume.

[36] The best statement of these arguments is in Ens, "Métis Agriculture in Red River," and in his *Homeland to Hinterland.*

THE QUEEN V. G. O. CORBETT, 1863

The author wishes to thank Arlene Young and Peter Bailey for helpful advice.

[1] J. J. Hargrave reported that the *Montreal Witness* had written, "the report of Mr. Corbett's trial, which filled the *Nor'-Wester* for some weeks, was one of the most disagreeable records which we remember to have seen." See his *Red River* (Fort Garry, 1871), p. 271.

[2] The jury had requested payment in this case at the outset, claiming that their work would be very hard. The judge took the request under advisement and announced at the close of the trial that he thought the jury should be remunerated. Many in Red River insisted the jury were being rewarded for their verdict.

[3] *Nor'-Wester,* 4 November 1862.

[4] The formal indictment does not actually specify the statute, but the presiding judge referred to amendments to 1 Vict. 85, which implies this 1861 legislation.

This statute prohibited the use of poison, noxious substances, or instruments to achieve the abortion. It emphasized that the woman could be charged as well as others, and held it irrelevant if someone other than the woman was charged whether the woman was actually pregnant. That Red River was enforcing the latest British legislation on abortion suggests the extent to which the court system of the settlement had become integrated into the Empire by 1863. As we shall see later in other contexts, Justice Black was clearly making some attempts to regularize proceedings.

[5] See Constance Backhouse, "Involuntary Motherhood: Abortion, Birth Control and the Law in Nineteenth Century Canada," in 3 *Windsor Yearbook of Access to Justice*, (1983): 61-130; G. Parker, "The Legal Regulation of Sexual Activity and the Protection of Females," *Osgoode Hall Law Journal* 21 (1983). For the United States, see James C. Mohr, *Abortion in America: The Origins and Evolution of National Policy, 1800-1900* (New York, 1978). Because very few early abortion cases are well documented, there is little descriptive literature, especially for abortions outside the major urban centres. For one example of an abortion case in a village setting, see Cornelia Hughes Dayton, "Taking the Trade: Abortion and Gender Relations in an Eighteenth-Century New England Village," *William and Mary Quarterly*, 3rd ser., 48: 1 (January 1991), 19-49.

[6] The case thus has little to do with most of the literature on nineteenth-century abortion, such as Mohr's book cited above or Leslie J. Reagan, *When Abortion Was a Crime: Women, Medicine, and Law in the United States, 1867-1973* (Berkeley, 1997).

[7] The best discussion of the Quarterly Court is in R. St. G. Stubbs, *Four Recorders of Rupert's Land* (Winnipeg, 1967). But see also Richard Allan Willie, *"These Legal Gentlemen": Lawyers in Manitoba, 1839-1900* ([Winnipeg], 1994), especially pp. 1-44, and Dale and Lee Gibson, *Substantial Justice: Law and Lawyers in Manitoba, 1670-1870* (Winnipeg, 1970), pp. 1-64.

[8] Council minutes, 13 June 1852, reprinted in E. H. Oliver, ed., *The Canadian North-West—Its Early Development and Legislative Records* vol. 1 (Ottawa, 1914): pp. 386-87.

[9] William A. Cohen, *Sex Scandal: The Private Parts of Victorian Fiction* (Durham and London, 1996), p. 10. See also R. B. Martin, *Enter Rumour: Four Early Victorian Scandals* (London, 1962), and H. Montgomery Hyde, *A Tangled Web: Sex Scandals in British Politics and Society* (London, 1986).

[10] Red River had experienced its first sex scandal in 1850, when the mixed-blood wife of a Hudson's Bay Company chief factor (who had experienced a stroke) became involved with an English officer who often ate at the HBC mess table. The officer went to court "to clear the reputation of a lady," and the court case of *Foss* v. *Pelly* resulted in a finding for Foss with an assessment of high damages against the defendants. See Sylvia Van Kirk, "The Reputation of a Lady": 4-11. But *Foss* v. *Pelly* was not reported in a local newspaper, since none was

founded in the settlement until 1859, and it did not achieve the same degree of public notoriety as did the Corbett case.

[11] For the insurgency, see my *Red River Rebellion*.

[12] John Gillis, "Servants, Sexual Relations, and the Risk of Illegitimacy in London, 1801-1900," *Feminist Studies*, 5 (1979): 142-173; Anna Clark, *Women's Silence Men's Violence: Sexual Assault in England, 1770-1845* (London and New York, 1987), passim; Laura Fasick, *Vessels of Meaning: Women's Bodies, Gender Norms, and Class Bias from Richardson to Lawrence* (DeKalb, IL, 1997), pp. 141-66. For women and the law in nineteenth-century British North America, see Constance Backhouse, *Petticoats and Prejudice: Women and the Law in Nineteenth Century Canada* (Toronto, 1991).

[13] Clark, *Women's Silence*, p. 104.

[14] Anna Clark, "The Politics of Seduction in English Popular Culture, 1748-1848," in Jean Radford, ed., *The Progress of Romance: The Politics of Popular Fiction* (London, 1986), pp. 46-70; Susan Staves, "British seduced maidens," *Eighteenth Century Studies*, 14:2 (1979/80): 42-55.

[15] Winifred Hughes, *The Maniac in the Cellar: Sensation Novels of the 1860s* (Princeton, 1980). The underlying theatricality of the police court system in Ontario in this period has been remarked upon by Paul Craven in "Law and Ideology: The Toronto Police Court 1850-1880," in David Flaherty, ed., *Essays in the History of Canadian Law*, 2 (Toronto, 1983).

[16] Anthea Trodd, *Domestic Crime in the Victorian Novel* (New York, 1989), p. 10. See also Joseph Litvak, *Caught in the Act: Theatricality in the Nineteenth-Century English Novel* (Berkeley, 1994), and Elaine Hadley, *Melodramatic Tactics: Theatricalized Dissent in the English Marketplace, 1800-1885* (Stanford, 1995).

[17] Corbett's career in Red River is considered in four published works by Frits Pannekoek: "The Anglican Church and the Disintegration of Red River Society, 1818-1870," in Carl Berger and Ramsey Cook, eds., *The West and the Nation: Essays in Honour of W. L. Morton* (Toronto, McClelland and Stewart, 1976); "The Rev. Griffiths Owen Corbett and the Red River Civil War of 1869-70," *Canadian Historical Review*, 57 (1976); 133-49; "Some Comments on the Social Origins of the Riel Protest of 1869-70," HSSM, ser. 3, nos. 34-5 (1977-8, 1978-9): 39-48; *A Snug Little Flock*. See also *DCB*, 13, 215-217.

[18] *Report of the Select Committee on the Hudson's Bay Company; together with the proceedings of the committee, Minutes of Evidence, Appendix and Index* (London, 1857), pp. 156-80. Subsequent scholarship would acknowledge that critics like Corbett had a point, and were unfairly treated by the committee. See Owram, *Canadian Expansionist Movement*, p. 60; Cooper, *Alexander Kennedy Isbister*, pp. 239-74.

[19] See "A Few Reasons for a Crown Colony," printed as a handbill in 1859, reputedly on Corbett's own printing press.

[20] Gerhard Ens, *Homeland to Hinterland,* p. 126.

[21] Letter of W. Bremner and John Swain to the *Nor'-Wester,* dated White Horse Plains, 25 November and printed in the issue of 12 December. The writers, who included eleven Métis with French names, headed by Patrick Breland, insisted that they were Catholics who found Corbett's "bigotted" religious views offensive.

[22] For Hunter, see *DCB,* 11, pp. 436-37, and J. A. Mackay, "James Hunter" in W.B. Heeney, ed., *Leaders of the Canadian Church* 2nd ser., (Toronto, 1920), pp. 79-85. He had a distinguished career as a translator of Cree into English. The "outraged father" was a standard feature of both real life and fictional seduction cases in Britain and Canada at this period, because the girl's honour and labour were his property. See Constance Backhouse, "The Tort of Seduction: Fathers and Daughters in Nineteenth Century Canada," *Dalhousie Law Journal,* 10 (1986): 45-80. Some evidence was given at the trial that Simon Thomas wanted to be financially compensated for what had happened to his daughter.

[23] The trial report in the *Nor'-Wester* quotes Hunter as saying: "Witness said do you know anything about that [to John Taylor]—meaning the charge against Corbett. He said he did. The conversation was all in whispers. Witness asked, Is he innocent? and he said No. Witness asked, Is he guilty? and he said Yes. Has he confessed he is guilty? and he said Yes. Witness put up his hand and said, Hush. Witness requested Taylor to come into his witness's house after the conversation; was anxious to know the exact words Corbett used to him when Corbett came over to him at Headingly, before Taylor came down. He told me Corbett had gone to see him. Taylor told me that after Corbett received the Bishop's letter he came over to his place and saw him outside winnowing wheat and mentioned receiving this letter from the Bishop, and that he read the letter to him (Taylor) and said, 'No doubt I am to blame, but go and see the girl and see if she can put it on anyone else, and tell her to keep quiet and come back as quickly as possible.'"

[24] J. J. Hargrave, *Red River,* p. 267.

[25] Samuel Taylor Journal, 1 December 1862, PAM MG2 C13.

[26] See Eric Trudgill, *Madonnas and Magdalens: The Origins and Development of Victorian Sexual Attitudes* (New York, 1976), esp. pp. 290ff. W. R. Greg in *The Westminster* in 1850 saw the typical prostitute as a creature of an unfortunate love affair living "in remorse, despair, privation, brutality and disease until an early death took her trembling to damnation." Quoted in Trudgill, p. 287.

[27] For the ideal, see Deborah Gorham, *The Victorian Girl and the Feminine Ideal* (Bloomington, 1982); Patricia Thomson, *The Victorian Heroine: A Changing Ideal 1837-1873* (London, 1956).

[28] The bail business is discussed in detail in the *Nor'-Wester,* 24 December 1862.

[29] Ibid., p. 263.

[30] *Nor'-Wester,* 12 December 1862.

[31] Samuel Taylor Journal, 6 December 1862.

[32] G. O Corbett to the *Nor'-Wester,* 4 December 1862.

[33] *Nor'-Wester,* 12 December 1862.

[34] Ibid., pp. 260-69.

[35] As well as the works by Pannekoek already listed, see Gibson and Gibson, *Substantial Justice*, pp. 52-54; St. George Stubbs, *Four Recorders of Rupert's Land*, pp. 147-55; Willie, *"These Legal Gentlemen,"* pp. 35-37; and Erica Smith, "'Gentlemen, This is no Ordinary Trial': Sexual Narratives in the Trial of the Reverend Corbett, Red River, 1863," in Jennifer Brown and Elizabeth Vibert, eds., *Reading Beyond Words: Contexts for Native History* (Peterborough, ON, 1996), pp. 364-80.

[36] See Stubbs, *Four Recorders.*

[37] Ibid., p. 271.

[38] The full court report obviously was an important literary form in the nineteenth century in Canada, and deserves further study. The published court transcription in *The Queen* v. *Corbett* was only one of several important ones in western Canada over the next twenty years. The trial of Ambroise Lépine for the murder of Thomas Scott in 1873-74 produced more transcriptions. There are two reports of this trial: one in a publication entitled *Preliminary Investigation and Trial of Ambroise D. Lépine for the Murder of Thomas Scott, Being a full report of the proceedings in this case before the Magistrates' Court and the several Courts of Queen's Bench in the Province of Manitoba* (Montreal, 1874), which was based on the court reports of various reporters for eastern Canadian newspapers; and one in Winnipeg's *Free Press,* which was based on the work of local reporters. The treason trial of Louis Riel in 1885 also produced a full trial transcript, which has recently been reprinted as *The Queen v Louis Riel,* with an introduction by Desmond Morton (Toronto, 1974). For a discussion of legal discourse as narration, see Bernard S. Jackson, "Narrative Theories and Legal Discourse," in Christopher Nash, ed., *Narrative in Culture: The Uses of Storytelling in the Sciences, Philosophy, and Literature* (London and New York, 1990), pp. 23-50, and his *Law, Fact and Narrative Coherence* (Merseyside, Deborah Charles Publications, 1988). For genre, consult Joseph P. Strelka, ed., *Theories of Literary Genre* (University Park, PA, and London, 1978); Heather Dubrow, *Genre* (London and New York, Methuen, 1982); and Adena Rosmarin, *The Power of Genre* (Minneapolis, 1985). For narrative, see Wallace Martin, *Recent Theories of Narrative* (Ithaca and London, 1986).

[39] For one account of Ross's stage management, see Smith, "'Gentlemen, This is no Ordinary Trial.'"

[40] Quarterly Court Minutes, 1863, PAM MG 2 B4-1, 243-273.

[41] *Nor'-Wester*, fifth day.

[42] Quarterly Court Minutes, 1863.

[43] Smith, "'Gentlemen, This is no Ordinary Trial.'"

[44] For other cases, see footnote 5 above.

[45] See footnote 34.

[46] Gibson and Gibson, *Substantial Justice*, p. 54.

[47] Our best source for Mapleton is the Samuel Taylor Journal, referred to above.

[48] There were many references to "Maria Doggy" and the "Doggy" family in the evidence.

[49] Smith, "'Gentlemen, This is no Ordinary Trial,'" p. 380.

[50] Clark, *Women's Silence Men's Violence,* pp. 81-83.

[51] Smith, "'Gentlemen, This is no Ordinary Trial,'" p. 380.

[52] Judith R. Walkowtiz, *City of Dreadful Delight: Narratives of Sexual Danger in Late-Victorian London* (Chicago, 1992), esp. pp. 85-92.

[53] Margaret Lane, "Introduction" to *Ruth* (London, 1967), p. xi.

[54] Elizabeth Barrett Browning, *Aurora Leigh and Other Poems,* introduced by Cora Kaplan (London, 1978), 37-390, especially pp. 140-194.

[55] Cora Kaplan, introduction to *Aurora Leigh,* p. 5.

[56] *Aurora Leigh,* p. 140 (lines 810-812).

[57] Ibid., lines 999-1000.

[58] Ibid., sixth book, lines 768-770.

[59] Karen Dubinksy, *Improper Advances: Rape and Heterosexual Conflict in Ontario, 1880-1929* (Chicago and London, 1993).

[60] Clark, *Women's Silence;* Carolyn Conley, "Rape and Justice in Victorian England," *Victorian Studies* 29 (1986): 523-4; Dubinsky, *Improper Advances;* Carolyn Strange, "Patriarchy Modified: The Criminal Prosecution of Rape in York County, Ontario, 1880-1930," in Jim Phillips et al, eds., *Essays in the History of Canadian Law,* vol. 5,

Crime and Criminal Justice (Toronto, 1994), pp. 207-51; Mary Odem, *Delinquent Daughters: Protecting and Policing Adolescent Female Sexuality in the United States, 1885-1920* (Chapel Hill, 1995).

[61] The best study of Ross remains that of Leonard Lawrence Remis, "James Ross: 1835-1871: The Life and Times of an English-speaking Halfbreed in the Old Red River Settlement" (M.A. diss., University of Manitoba, 1981). For Hunt, see obituary in the *Winnipeg Free Press,* 22 November 1903.

[62] Hargrave, *Red River,* pp. 271-2.

[63] Ibid., p. 270.

[64] John M. Riddle, *Eve's Herbs: A History of Contraception and Abortion in the West* (Cambridge, MA, 1997); Backhouse, "Involuntary Motherhood," pp. 84-6; Angus McLaren and Arlene Tigar McLaren, *The Bedroom and the State: The Changing Practices and Politics of Contraception and Abortion in Canada, 1880-1980* (Toronto, 1986).

[65] Backhouse, "Involuntary Motherhood," p. 82.

[66] Trial day 1, *Nor'-Wester,* 3 March 1863.

[67] Black to the *Nor'-Wester,* 11 September 1862.

[68] *Nor'-Wester,* 24 April 1869.

[69] Lane, introduction to *Ruth* p. vi; Thomson, *Victorian Heroine,* p.122.

[70] *Nor'-Wester,* 30 March 1863.

[71] *Nor'-Wester,* 24 April 1869.

[72] *Nor'-Wester,* 12 May 1863.

[73] See Dale Gibson, *Attorney for the Frontier: Enos Stutsman* (Winnipeg, 1983), 77-96.

[74] *DCB,* 13 (Toronto, 1994), pp. 216-17.

[75] A lengthy account of Mrs. Corbett's life—which does not mention her husband—appeared in the *Winnipeg Free Press,* 18 October 1910.

THE RED RIVER FAMINE OF 1868

[1] For an example, see the *Nor'-Wester,* 14 January 1860.

[2] For early fires, see PAM Ross Papers, 113 (1854); PAM Riel Papers, 1 (1860 St. Boniface Cathedral fire); PAM RRS/Taylor Journal 1849-63, 58, 61 (1860, 1861 fires).

[3] For accounts of hailstorms in 1859, 1861, 1862, 1864, and 1866, see PAM RRS/ Taylor Journal 1849-63, pp. 46, 64, 72, and RRS/Taylor Journal 1863-7, pp. 10, 33, 35, 36.

[4] "History of the Red River Settlement," thirteenth paper, *Nor'-Wester,* 15 August 1861.

[5] *Nor'-Wester,* 24 April 1869.

[6] Josephine Singa, "Biological control of grasshoppers (Orthoptera:Acridae) in Manitoba with emphasis on predators and parasitants of the eggs," (M.Sc. diss., University of Manitoba, 1994); H.W. Moore, "An Intensive Study of the Grasshoppers of Economic Importance at Arnaud, Manitoba, 1935," (M.Sc. diss., University of Manitoba, 1936); Norman Criddle, "Some Phases of the Present Locust Outbreak in Manitoba," *Annual Report: Entomological Society of Ontario,* 51(1923): 19-23; Norman Criddle, "Notes on the Habits of Injurious Grasshoppers in Manitoba," *Canadian Entomologist,* 65 (1933): 97-103.

[7] Jonathan Carver, *Travels through the Interior Parts of North America in the years 1766 and 1767* (London, 1768).

[8] Quoted in J.A. Munro, "Grasshopper Outbreaks in North Dakota 1808-1948," *North Dakota History,* 16 (1949), 143.

[9] Frederick Matthey to Lord Selkirk, 30 August 1818, SPNAC.

[10] "Diary of Nicholas Garry," *Transactions Royal Society of Canada,* section II (1900): 138-9.

[11] P.W. Riegert, "A Century of Locusts and Mortages," *Prairie Forum,* 2 (1977), 121-128.

[12] Samuel Taylor Journal, PAM, I, p. 83.

[13] Riegert, "A Century," p. 122.

[14] *Nor'-Wester,* 4 August 1868.

[15] Ibid., 24 April 1869.

[16] Hargrave, *Red River*, p. 446. One American observer in 1868 reported that near Devils Lake the grasshopper bodies "formed rows from four to six feet long and two to three feet wide." Quoted in Munro, "Grasshopper Outbreakes," 146.

[17] *Nor'-Wester*, 4 July 1868.

[18] Hargrave, *Red River*, pp. 440–41.

[19] A similar storm struck Winnipeg in June of 1919, just as the Winnipeg General Strike was ending.

[20] Roe, "Its Extermination of the Buffalo in Western Canada," *The North American Buffalo: A Critical Study of the Species in Its Wild State* 2nd ed. (Toronto, 1970), esp. pp. 467–88.

[21] *Nor'-Wester*, 11 August 1868.

[22] Assiniboia Council Minutes, August 1868.

[23] Hargrave, *Red River*, p. 447.

[24] *Times*, 20 September 1868, reprinted in the *Nor'-Wester*, 24 October 1868.

[25] *Nor'-Wester*, 22 September 1868.

[26] Ibid., 29 September 1868.

[27] Ibid., 10 October 1868.

[28] G. M. Grant, quoted in Robert Machray, *Life of Robert Machray* (Toronto, 1909), p. 157.

[29] *Essex Record*, 5 September 1868.

[30] *Canadian Free Press*, 4 September 1868.

[31] *Nor'-Wester*, 10 October 1868.

[32] Ibid.

[33] Ibid.

[34] Ibid.

[35] Ibid. Snow (1824–1888) had been born in Lower Canada and educated in Potsdam, New York. His career in Red River was quite controversial. He was assaulted by some of his workmen, convicted of selling liquor to the Indians, and charged with speculating in land.

[36] *Nor'-Wester*, 17 October 1868.

[37] Executive Relief Committee, Minute Book, PAM MG 2B6-1.

[38] Ibid.

[39] Ibid., 28 October 1868.

[40] Ibid.

[41] *Nor'-Wester,* 12 December 1868.

[42] Hargrave, *Red River,* p. 449.

[43] Ibid., p. 450.

[44] *Nor'-Wester,* 21 November 1868. An earlier issue of the *Nor'-Wester,* on 17 October 1868, had reported from the *Saint Paul Press* that food prices in the settlement had been kept down to prevent a "mob."

[45] *Nor'-Wester,* 14 November 1868.

[46] Ibid., 21 November 1868.

[47] Ibid.

[48] Ibid.

[49] Ibid.

[50] Ibid.

[51] *Nouveau Monde,* 1 February 1869. A translation appears in Morton, ed., *Alexander Begg's Journal,*

[52] *Nor'-Wester,* 24 April 1869.

[53] Ibid.

[54] Riegert, "A Century."

JOHN CHRISTIAN SCHULTZ AND THE FOUNDING OF MANITOBA

[1] The literature on Riel is enormous. See, for example, G.F.G. Stanley, *Louis Riel* (Toronto, 1963), and Maggie Siggins, *Riel: A Life of Revolution* (Toronto, 1994).

[2] For a biography of McTavish, see Fred Elmer Bartlett, "William Mactavish: The Last Governor of Assiniboia" (M.A. diss., University of Manitoba, 1964); for Boulton,

consult his *Reminiscences of the North-West Rebellion* (1885), and Keith Wilson, *Charles Arkoll Boulton* (Winnipeg, 1984).

[3] Leonard Lawrence Remis, "James Ross: 1835-1871:The Life and Times of an English-speaking Halfbreed in the Old Red River Settlement" (M.A. diss., University of Manitoba, 1981).

[4] See N. Jaye Goossen, "A 'Wearer of Moccasins':The Honourable James McKay of Deer Lodge," *The Beaver* (Autumn 1978): 44-53.

[5] Schultz has always polarized opinion, but his life has not yet produced a full-length biography. The mistitled unpublished doctoral dissertation by N.A. Ronaghan, " The Archibald Administration in Manitoba, 1870-1872," University of Manitoba, 1987, is really as much about Schultz as Archibald; Ronaghan is quite hostile. A more balanced account is in volume 12 of the *DCB*, written by Lovell C. Clark. For a particularly critical view, published on the Internet, see John Joseph Bauché, "Louis Riel." Bauché says, "There are few villains in Canada's frontier history as vivid and menacing as Dr. John Schultz," adding he was "an aggressive, obnoxious bigot." Almost equally hostile is Alexander Begg's 1871 caricature of Schultz as "Mr. Cool" in his novel *Dot-it-Down*. Cool makes continually disparaging remarks about the "half breeds" of the settlement.

[6] See, for example, A.H. Trémaudan's history of the Métis, translated by Elizabeth Maguet in 1982 as *Hold High Your Heads* (Winnipeg, 1982), which argues that Schultz, "Raging in his heart at having to yield to the efficient organization of the Métis, and taking advantage of the fact that Scott, the executed man, had belonged to the Orange Lodge, . . . lost no time in painting the situation of Canadians in the West in darkest colours." (p. 93).

[7] Ronaghan, 1, 1-3.

[8] Quarterly Court Minutes, 20 November 1861.

[9] Quarterly Court Minutes, January 1863. Ronaghan, who claims that Schultz can be recorded as treating only two cases in Red River—in one of which the patient died—ignores the court testimony.

[10] *Nor'-Wester*, 25 August 1866.

[11] "Diary of A.W. Graham," in Elgin Historical and Scientific Institute, *Reminiscences of Early Settlers and Other Records* (St. Thomas, ON, 1911).

[12] Archives de l'archevêche de Saint-Boniface, reg. des mariages, 11 sept. 1867; *Nor'-Wester*, 21 September 1867; Hargrave, *Red River*, pp. 322-24.

[13] Ibid., p. 323.

[14] *New Nation*, 3 September 1870.

[15] David Gagan, "The Relevance of 'Canada First,'" *Journal of Canadian Studies,* 5 (1970): 36-40; Norman Shrive, *Charles Mair: Literary Nationalist* (Toronto, 1965).

[16] Charles Mair to Holmes Mair, 19 November 1868, reprinted in the *Toronto Globe,* 4 January 1869.

[17] Hargrave, *Red River,* pp. 423-25.

[18] *Nor'-Wester,* 21 January 1868.

[19] Hargrave, *Red River,* pp. 427-38.

[20] Ibid., pp. 437-38.

[21] For a discussion of the historiography of the Rebellion, see my *Red River Rebellion,* pp. 245-54.

[22] John Dennis told the parliamentary committee in 1874 that Schultz had said "that a short time previous to my [Dennis's] arrival in this country that he and Mr. Snow had staked out and bought from the Indians, lands at St. Anne's Point de Chene, a mile square, which the French half-breeds laid claim to in some way." Schultz allegedly asked Dennis whether these land transfers would be recognized by the Canadian government and Dennis said no. Canada, Parliament, House of Commons, *Report of the Select Committee on the Causes of the Difficulties in the North-West Territory in 1869-70* (Ottawa, 1874), pp. 186-87. It must be remembered that Dennis blamed Schultz for the Canadian debacle in December 1870 and took every opportunity to blacken his name.

[23] Hargrave, *Red River,* p. 458. Apart from the Dennis testimony in 1874, there is little evidence that Schultz had any direct connection with the exploitative activities of John Snow, the chief Canadian agent on the roadbuilding.

[24] Testimony of Ritchot, in Canada, Parliament, House of Commons, *Report of the Select Committee on the Causes of the Difficulties in the North-West Territory in 1869-70* (Ottawa, 1874), p. 68.

[25] Gerhard J. Ens, "Prologue to the Red River Resistance: Pre-liminal Politics and the Triumph of Riel," *Journal of the Canadian Historical Association,* new ser., 5 (1994): 111-124, especially 114-5.

[26] Ibid., : 68 ff.

[27] J. Murray Beck, *Joseph Howe:* vol. 2, *The Briton Becomes Canadian, 1848-1873* (Montreal and Kingston, 1983), p. 258.

[28] Ibid.

[29] Alexander Begg, *The Creation of Manitoba: A History of the Red River Troubles* (Toronto, 1871), p. 34.

[30] Bown to Macdonald, 18 November 1869, National Archives of Canada, Macdonald Papers, vol. 101.

[31] *Begg's Journal,* 21 November 1869, p. 175.

[32] Ibid., pp. 173-74.

[33] Ibid., pp. 177-78. Begg claims that the petition was written by Schultz, but this cannot be confirmed, since no copy of it survives.

[34] Notes by J.W., between 4th and 22nd November 1869, in Canada, Parliament, *Correspondence and Papers Connected with the Recent Occurrences in the North West Territories* (Ottawa, 1870), 59-63.

[35] Begg records on 23 November that Schultz had sent word to Hugh O'Lone "that he (the Dr.) was not responsible for Dr. Bown's doings but O'Lone could not see it in the same light as birds of a feather generally flock together." *Begg's Journal,* p. 183.

[36] *Begg's Journal,* p.184.

[37] See, for example, "Red River" to the *Montreal Herald,* 4 December 1869; *Begg's Journal,* pp. 187-88.

[38] Riel to Schultz, 27 November 1869, in Raymond Huel, ed., *The Collected Writings of Louis Riel/Les Ecrits Complets de Louis Riel: volume 1: 29 December/décembre 1861-7 December/décembre 1875* (Edmonton, 1985), pp. 33-34.

[39] For Dennis's activities, see Canada, Parliament, *Correspondence Relative to the Recent Disturbances in the Red River Settlement* (Ottawa, 1870), pp. 94 ff.

[40] Schultz to John Dennis, 4 December 1869, in Canada, Parliament, *Correspondence Relative to the Recent Disturbances in the Red River Settlement* (Ottawa, 1870), p. 93.

[41] This list is reprinted in F. H. Schofield, *The History of Manitoba,* 1 (Winnipeg, 1913), p. 243.

[42] Graham Diary, 5 December 1869.

[43] Ibid.

[44] *Correspondence Relative to the Recent Disturbances,* p. 86.

[45] Charles Boulton, *Reminiscences of the North-West Rebellions* (Toronto, 1886).

[46] Quoted in Beck, *Hoseph Howe,* vol. 2, p. 262.

[47] John Harrison O'Donnell, *Manitoba As I Saw It: From 1869 to Date: With Flashlights on the First Riel Rebellion* (Toronto, 1909), p. 35.

[48] Graham Diary, 24 January 1870. Schultz was still dining on his escape when he met with Lord and Lady Aberdeen in 1893. Lady Aberdeen reported in her journal that Schultz addressed the H.H. Club after dinner "regarding his experiences in prison, his escape & his snow-shoe journey of 700 miles with a price on his head during the Riel rebellion." Lady Aberdeen added, "This was all told with such a quiet dignity & simplicity & with such foregetfulness of self, suppressing the account of his own hardships, being marched off from his wife at midnight on Christmas Eve, being imprisoned for two months in a solitary cell in a Manitoba winter without any fire with the thermometer 40 degrees below zero & such like." John T. Saywell, ed., *The Canadian Journal of Lady Aberdeen 1893-1898* (Toronto, 1960), p. 33.

[49] R. G. MacBeth, *The Making of the Canadian West*, p. 61. In this work, MacBeth's son wrote, "In after years when I heard Sir John Schultz say that he 'had still the shattered remnants of a good constitution,' I used to account for the 'shattering' by thinking of the desperate leap from the prison, the running with maimed limb and scanty clothing six miles in an arctic atmosphere, and then the fearful journey on foot across the rocky shores and wind-swept bays of Lake Superior to the cities of the East."

[50] Boulton, *Reminiscences*, p. 107.

[51] *St. Paul Daily Pioneer*, 2 April 1870. The men involved were John Tait, A.H. Murray, Thomas Sinclair, Edward Hay, John Hodgson, William Leask, George Calder, Andrew Mowatt, Donald Gunn, Jr., Adam McDonald, Joseph Monkman, Henry Prince, Alex Ross, and Dr. Beddome.

[52] Reprinted in the *Toronto Globe*.

[53] Morton, ed., *Begg's Journal*, p. 310.

[54] See "Why Shoot Thomas Scott?" elsewhere in this volume.

[55] *Toronto Globe*, 8 April 1870.

[56] Canada, Parliament, Senate, *Report of the Select Committee of the Senate on the Subject of Rupert's Land, Red River, and the Northwest Territory* (Ottawa, 1870).

[57] Northcote Diary, in Morton, ed., *Birth of a Province*, p. 79.

[58] Ibid., p. 126. Northcote wrote of the Senate appointment, "Such a step would be very mischievous. Schultz and his like are just the men to stir up an Indian war. His compensation may be accounted for by his having a good many influential creditors in Canada, who don't see any way of getting their debts paid except by getting him a grant from the public purse. His rumoured appointment, if true, is a sop to Ontario, intended to counteract the reception of Ritchot and Scott, and the provisions in the Manitoban Act which are thought too favourable to the French."

[59] Ritchot Journal, 11 May 1870, in Morton, ed., *Birth of a Province*, pp. 150-51.

[60] Schultz to Cartier, 7 June 1870, NAC Macdonald Papers, vol. 103.

[61] Ronaghan, "Archibald Administration," p. 396.

[62] Schultz's critics, including Allan Ronaghan, see this attack on Spence as part of the "Reign of Terror" in Manitoba against the former members of the provisional government, instead of as a personal matter between Schultz and Spence.

REPORTING THE RESISTANCE OF 1869-1870

[1] See Bumsted and Owen, "Victorian Family in Canada": 12-18.

[2] *Nor'-Wester,* 14 March 1860.

[3] The first historical account of the Institute, and of other early intellectual endeavours, was by Mrs. George Bryce in "Early Red River Culture," *Proceedings of the Historical and Scientific Society of Manitoba,* no. 57 (1901).

[4] Leslie Castling, "Red River Library."

[5] Aileen Garland. "The Nor'Wester [sic] and The Man Who Established It," HSSM papers 3, no. 16 (1958).

[6] Ross's work appeared in London in 1856 as *The Red River Settlement.* Gunn's would be published in book form in 1880, its later sections co-edited by Charles R. Tuttle.

[7] Bruce Braden Peel, *Early Printing in the Red River Settlement 1859-1870 and Its Effect on the Riel Rebellion* (Winnipeg, 1974), pp. 19-35.

[8] Other French papers that occasionally covered Red River included: *Le Minerve, Le Journal de Québec, Le Canadien* (Quebec), *Le Pays* (Montreal), *La Gazette de Sorel, Le Courrier de Canada* (Quebec) *L'opinion publique* (Montreal), and *La Gazette des familles canadiennes* (Quebec).

[9] Owram, *Canadian Expansionist Movement.*

[10] See the article on the famine in this volume.

[11] For Mair, consult Norman Shrive, *Charles Mair: Literary Nationalist* (Toronto, 1965).

[12] George Denison, *The Struggle for Imperial Unity: Recollections and Experiences* (Toronto, 1909).

[13] Mair's papers, which include considerable autobiographical material written in later years, are at Queen's University. As well as the biography by Shrive, consult Fred Cogswell, *Charles Mair and His Works* (1980).

[14] Printed from 11 October, 1869 to 25 February 1870.

[15] Hargrave's early upbringing may be followed in the letters of his mother, edited by M.A. MacLeod as *Letters of Letitia Hargrave* (Toronto, 1947). I am indebted to an unpublished manuscript by Leslie Castling for many insights into Hargrave and his work.

[16] W. L. Morton, ed., *Begg's Red River Journal*, p. 415n.

[17] *Canadian Monthly*, 1 (May 1872): 479-80.

[18] For further discussion of these points, see Patricia Spacks, *Gossip* (New York, 1985).

[19] William Ross to James Ross, 9 February 1856, PAM, Ross Family Papers, MG2 C14, p. 162.

[20] Printed 11 October 1869. W.L. Morton in his edition of the Alexander Begg diary wrote that Hargrave's letters began in the *Herald* on 21 October 1869, a date repeated in the *DBC*, vol. 11, p. 409. See Morton, ed., *Begg's Red River Journal*, p. 415n. This date, which saw the publication of the letter originally dated 25 September 1869, misses the letter of 18 September published in the newspaper on 11 October.

[21] Letter of 18 December, 1869, printed *Montreal Herald and Daily Commercial Gazette*, 7 January 1870.

[22] Printed in *Montreal Herald and Daily Commercial Gazette*, 17 February 1870.

[23] Printed 25 February 1870.

[24] Isaac Cowie, *Company of Adventurers*, p. 153.

[25] *Manitoba Free Press*, 10 March 1894.

[26] For the "moribund" characterization, see Pannekoek, *A Snug Little Flock*, p. 215.

[27] I use the term "participant historian" and develop its meaning in William Toye, ed., *The Oxford Companion to Canadian Literature* (Toronto, 1984), pp. 351-52.

[28] Morton, ed., *Begg's Journal*, p. xiv.

[29] Ibid., 10 December 1869.

[30] "Justitia" letter, 17 December 1869, printed 6 January 1870.

[31] Begg, *Creation of Manitoba,* pp. 182–83.

[32] According to Hargrave, in his letter dated 11 December, "Yesterday a large body of the French collected in Fort Garry, and went through the ceremony of "Raising the National Flag" on the Fort flagstaff. Speeches were made by Riel and others, and the brass band of the scholars at the Roman Catholic school at St. Boniface played a series of airs, after each of which a volley of musketry was fired, the Company's Field Pieces, which were stationed at intervals outside the Fort gates, being also discharged at various periods of the performance. The device on the banner consists of three *fleur de lys* on a white ground with a shamrock underneath. The insurgents subsequently marched to the American consulate in Winnipeg, which they saluted with music, cheers, and volleys of musketry. This is said to have been done as a compliment to the only foreign power having a resident representative there." Hargrave's more careful description of the flag, with three *fleur de lys* over a single shamrock, makes it appear somewhat less menacing than Begg's account of the two emblems "combined."

[33] Begg, *Creation of Manitoba,* p. 304.

[34] It seems possible that Riel went to Saskatchewan in 1884 to recover the sense of accomplishment that he had experienced in the early days of 1869-70.

[35] *News-Letter,* 4 October 1870.

[36] Begg, *Seventeen Years in the Canadian North-West* (London, 1884), p. 4.

[37] George T. Denison, *The Struggle for Imperial Unity* (Toronto, 1909), pp. 14-21.

Why Shoot Thomas Scott? A Study in Historical Evidence

[1] One publisher of a study of Scott's execution hyped it as "the story of an obscure young Irish-Canadian whose execution by a firing squad was probably the most fateful event of Canada's first century." See Robert Walter Weir Robertson, *The Execution of Thomas Scott* (Toronto, 1968).

[2] Among the chief authorities are: Alexander Begg, *The Creation of Manitoba* (Toronto, 1871); [Joseph Edmund Collins,] *The Story of Louis Riel the Rebel Chief* (Toronto, 1885); Charles Arkoll Boulton, *Reminiscences of the North-West Rebellions, with a Record of the Raising of her Majesty's 100th regiment in Canada* (Toronto, 1886), especially pp. 87-138; W.F. Bryant, *The Blood of Abel* (Hastings, NB, 1887), especially pp. 50-53; George Young, *Manitoba Memories: Leaves from My Life in the Prairie Province, 1868-1884* (Toronto, 1897), pp. 100-147; A.G. Morice, "À propos de la mort de Scott," *Les Cloches de Saint Boniface,* 13 (1914): 49-51; Georges

Dugas, "Encore la mort de Scott," *Les Cloches de Saint-Boniface*, 13 (1914): 148-50; Auguste de Trémaudan, "The Execution of Thomas Scott," *The Canadian Historical Review*, 6:3 (1925): 222-36; Edwin E Kreutzweiser, *The Red River Insurrection: Its Causes and Events* (Gardenvale, QC, n.d.), pp. 126-36; A.G. Morice, *A Critical History of the Red River Insurrection* (1935), passim; George F.G. Stanley, *The Birth of Western Canada: A History of the Riel Rebellions* (Toronto, 1936), especially pp. 99-106; William McCartney Davidson, *Louis Riel 1844-1885* (Calgary, 1955), especially pp. 66-69; Joseph Howard, *Strange Empire: Louis Riel and the Métis People* (New York, 1952), especially pp. 182-96; Lamb, *Thunder in the North* (1957); E.B. Osler, *The Man Who Had to Hang: Louis Riel* (Toronto, 1961), especially pp. 93-111; Stanley, *Louis Riel* (Toronto, 1963), especially pp. 100-117; Robert Walter Weir Robertson, *The Execution of Thomas Scott* (Toronto, 1968); Hartwell Bowsfield, *Louis Riel: The Rebel and the Hero* (Toronto, 1971), especially pp. 49-51; Peter Charlebois, *The Life of Louis Riel in Pictures* (Toronto, 1978), especially pp. 65-71; J.E. Rea, "Thomas Scott," *DCB*, 9 (Toronto, 1976), pp. 707-09; Thomas Flanagan, *Louis 'David' Riel: 'Prophet of the New World,'* rev. ed., (Toronto, 1994), pp. 33-36; Lewis H. Thomas, "Louis Riel," *DCB* (Toronto, 1982), pp. 736-56; Bernard Saint-Aubin, *Louis David Riel: Un destin tragique* (Montreal, 1985), especially pp. 112-22; Maggie Siggins, *Riel: A Life of Revolution* (Toronto, 1994), especially pp. 123-64.

[3] George Stanley, *Louis Riel* (Toronto, 1963), p. 115.

[4] Rea, *DCB*, 9, 707.

[5] For another version of the life of Thomas Scott, see my "Thomas Scott and the Daughter of Time," *Prairie Forum*, 23:2 (Fall, 1998), 145-170.

[6] None of those Métis involved in the Scott trial and execution—except for Joseph Nolin—ever testified under oath as to their recollections. Lépine was convicted of Scott's murder, but he did not take the stand on his own behalf. In later years, some of the participants spoke of the case, and their reminiscences were used by historians and biographers.

[7] There are two published reports of this trial, *Regina v. Lépine*. One is in a publication entitled *Preliminary Investigation and Trial of Ambroise D. Lépine for the Murder of Thomas Scott, Being a full report of the proceedings in this case before the Magistrates' Court and the several Courts of Queen's Bench in the Province of Manitoba* (Montreal, 1874). This report was based on the court reports of various reporters for eastern Canadian newspapers. The other report appeared in Winnipeg's *Free Press*, and was based on the work of local reporters. The two sets of reports have much in common, partly because the various participants distributed their set speeches in advance to the press, but also because the reporters pooled their resources. But the two reports are not identical, and there is significant new material in the *Free Press* accounts. In addition to the printed reports, the trial notes of Chief Justice Edmund Burke Wood also survive. These, in the Provincial Archives of Manitoba (PAM), provide over 160 pages of judge's scribble, often virtually illegible, on the testimony. Most of those writing about Scott and Riel are

singularly unacquainted with the trial material, a rich source of information on what is, after all, the central point of the connection between the two men.

[8] Donald Smith to Joseph Howe, 28 April 1870, published in the *Toronto Globe,* 29 April 1870. Despite its date, it seems likely that this account was written somewhat earlier.

[9] W.L. Morton, ed., *Begg's Red River Journal,* pp. 327-88; *The New Nation,* 4 March 1870 (but really published 8 March 1870); Letter from Fort Garry to the *Courrier de St. Hyacinthe,* translated and reprinted in the *Globe,* 7 April 1870; Bishop A.-A.Taché to Joseph Howe, 11 March 1870, reprinted in Morton, *Begg's Journal,* pp. 497-501; Reports of Allan and Coombes, the *Globe,* 15 April 1870.

[10] Those eyewitnesses who testified at the Lépine trial were: George Young, John McLean, and a number of fellow prisoners (William Chambers, Alexander McPherson, Alexander Murray, William Farmer, D.U. Campbell, and George Newcombe). Other Anglophone eyewitness evidence from Scott's fellow prisoners was provided in Charles Boulton's memoirs (1886) and George Young's memoirs (1897); various manuscript accounts of Charles Mair in the Mair Papers, Queen's University; P.G. Laurie (Storer Papers, Saskatchewan Archives); John H. O'Donnell, *Manitoba as I Saw It From 1869 to Date* (Toronto, 1909), esp. 30 ff; A.W. Graham ("Diary of A.W. Graham," *Proceedings of the Elgin Historical and Scientific Institute,* 1912); Henry Woodington, "Journal of Henry Woodington, 22 September 1869 to 17 February 1870," PAM, reprinted in part in *Niagara Historical Society,* 25 (1912); George Winship and James Ashdown Comments thereon (1914, PAM, MG 3 B15); Peter McArthur ("Recollections of Peter McArthur 1934-5," PAM NG11A1); George Sanderson (Irene Spry, ed., "The Memoirs of George William Sanderson," *Canadian Ethnic Studies* 17 [1985]: 115-134). Métis testimony was produced by A. H. de Trémaudan in a document originally printed as "The Execution of Thomas Scott," *Canadian Historical Review* 6 (1925): 222-36.

[11] Riel accounts begin with: "Memoire ayant trait aux difficultès de la Rivière-Rouge," in George Stanley, ed., *The Collected Writings of Louis Riel/Les Ecrits Complets de Louis Riel Volume 1 29 December/décembre 1861 – 7 December/décembre 1875* (Edmonton: University of Alberta Press, 1985), hereafter cited as CW, pp.197-201. This was the item printed and annotated by Trémaudan in the *CHR* in 1925. Subsequent accounts appear in a letter from Riel and Lépine to Lieutenant-Governor Morris, dated 3 January 1873, and reprinted with annotations by Trémaudan as "Letter of Louis Riel and Ambroise Lépine to Lieutenant-governor Morris, January 3, 1873," *The Canadian Historical Review,* reprinted in *CW,* pp. 243-57; in "L'Amnistie. Mémoire sur les causes des troubles du Nord-Ouest et sur les negotiations qui ont amené leur eglement amiable," which was published by *Le Nouveau Monde* of Montreal in 1874 and drew an attack from Dr. James Spencer Lynch, which led to an answer from Riel printed in *CW,* I, pp. 323-49; Riel to Donald Smith, 12 Feb. 1874, in Beckles Willson, *The Life of Lord Strathcona and Mount Royal* (Boston, 1915), p. 359; "Mémoire ayant trait aux difficultès de la Rivière-Rouge," 1874/5, in *CW,* 1, pp. 416-20; "Mémoire ayant trait aux difficultès de la Rivière-Rouge," 1874/5, in *CW,* 1, pp. 421-22; and "Lettre ayant trait à

l'amnistie," March 20, 1875, in *CW*, 1, pp. 431-44. The interview with the *Winnipeg Daily Sun* of June, 1883, is reprinted in *CW*, 2, pp. 413-23.

[12] Ronaghan, "Archibald Administration," pp. 211-12.

[13] Several witnesses at the Lépine trial mention Scott's discomforts.

[14] Maggie Siggins insists, with regard to the diarrhea, that "to verbally abuse someone with racial attacks seems an odd way to seek help." Siggins, *Riel*, p. 160n.

[15] One of the occupational hazards of being a Riel biographer, it would seem, is the temptation to invent dialogue, especially for the confrontation between Riel and Thomas Scott. One particularly blatant invention is in a biography of Riel written for younger readers by Rosemary Neering. See her *Louis Riel* (Markham, ON, 1999), pp. 27-28, where snippets of documentable dialogue are combined with racial epithets for which there is no contemporary evidence. When we first meet Scott in this book, he is "calmly spitting out the window at the guard's feet," which would certainly account for a guard's anger—were there any evidence for the gesture.

[16] *CW*, 2, p. 416.

[17] Young, *Manitoba Memories*, p. 133.

[18] Smith to Joseph Howe, 28 April 1870.

[19] PAM, MG 2 B4-1, District of Assiniboia Minutes of Quarterly Court, Sheriff's Court Book.

[20] Morton, ed., *Begg's Journal*, p. 173.

[21] Stanley, *Louis Riel*, p. 111; Siggins, *Riel*, p.160.

[22] Stanley, *Louis Riel*, p. 388, note 52. See testimony of Alexander Murray, *Winnipeg Free Press*, 16 October 1870.

[23] These charges first appeared in 1874 in Riel's response to James Spencer Lynch, reprinted in *CW*, 1, pp. 323-49.

[24] *CW*, 2, pp. 413-23.

[25] Stanley, *Louis Riel*, p. 111.

[26] Donald Smith to Joseph Howe, 28 April 1870.

[27] *CW*, 1, pp. 246-47.

[28] Donald Smith to Joseph Howe, 28 April 1870.

[29] *CW*, 1, p. 200.

[30] *CW, I,* p. 246.

[31] Stanley, *Louis Riel,* p. 116.

[32] Flanagan, *Louis 'David' Riel* (1994 edition), p. 33.

[33] *Globe,* 4 April 1870.

[34] *Globe,* 15 April 1870.

[35] Opposite the title page is an illustration of an Aboriginal-white military encounter, obviously set on the East Coast somewhere.

[36] *Story of Louis Riel,* p. 117.

[37] Charlebois, *Life of Louis Riel,* p. 66.

[38] Kreutzweiser, *Red River Insurrection,* pp. 132-33.

[39] Stanley, *Louis Riel,* p. 115.

[40] In general, see Lawrence J. Barkwell, "Early Law and Social Control among the Metis."

[41] A.G. Morice, *Critical History,* pp. 168, 206, 281n, 283.

[42] Charlebois, *Life of Louis Riel,* pp. 66-67.

[43] Siggins, *Riel,* p. 159.